INSTITUTE OF JEWISH STUDIES
UNIVERSITY COLLEGE LONDON

SCRIPTA JUDAICA

EDITED BY A. ALTMANN AND J. G. WEISS

III

EXCLUSIVENESS AND TOLERANCE

Oxford University Press, Amen House, London E.C.4
GLASGOW NEW YORK TORONTO MELBOURNE WELLINGTON
BOMBAY CALCUTTA MADRAS KARACHI KUALA LUMPUR
CAPE TOWN IBADAN NAIROBI ACCRA

SCRIPTA JUDAICA · III

EXCLUSIVENESS AND TOLERANCE

Studies in Jewish-Gentile Relations in Medieval and Modern Times

BY

JACOB KATZ

OXFORD UNIVERSITY PRESS

1961

PRINTED IN GREAT BRITAIN
AT THE UNIVERSITY PRESS, OXFORD
BY VIVIAN RIDLER
PRINTER TO THE UNIVERSITY

TO MY WIFE

PREFACE

THE material for this book has been collected over a period of many years. The decision to write it in its present form, and to publish it first in English, was made during my stay in Manchester at the Institute of Jewish Studies where I served as guest lecturer during the academic year 1956–7. The general conception of the work, as well as the working out of details, profited from my close contact with Professor A. Altmann, the then Director of the Institute.

After the transfer of the Institute to University College London, Mr. J. G. Weiss, M.A., the new Director of the Institute, bestowed upon the book the benefit of his unremitting scrutiny.

I am indebted to the many people who assisted me in stylizing and editing the work, the more so since my own knowledge of English would not have permitted me to accomplish the task unaided. My thanks go to all those who gave me advice and help but who are too numerous to mention by name. My special thanks go to Mr. D. Cohen, Mrs. G. Frankel, and Miss A. Mittwoch of London; Dr. S. Applebaum, Mrs. E. Erlich, and Mrs. Batia Rabin of Jerusalem; and to my colleague Professor Chaim Rabin of the Hebrew University for translating some of the Hebrew texts.

The preparation of this book was greatly helped by the support of the cultural funds of the Conference of Jewish Material Claims Against Germany.

J. KATZ

The Hebrew University of Jerusalem
July 1959

CONTENTS

ABBREVIATIONS

B.H. *Beth Ha-Beḥirah* (R. Menaḥem Ha-Me'iri's Commentary on the Talmud).

B.T. Babylonian Talmud.

Ḥ.M. *Ḥoshen Mishpaṭ* (4th section of Jacob b. Asher's *Ṭurim* and Joseph Caro's *Shulḥan 'Arukh*).

JJLG *Jahrbuch der jüdisch-literarischen Gesellschaft in Frankfurt am Main.*

JQR *Jewish Quarterly Review.*

MGWJ *Monatsschrift für die Geschichte und Wissenschaft des Judenthums.*

O.Ḥ. *'Oraḥ Ḥayyim* (1st section of Jacob b. Asher's *Ṭurim* and Joseph Caro's *Shulḥan 'Arukh*).

REJ *Revue des Études Juives.*

Y.D. *Yoreh De'ah* (2nd section of Jacob b. Asher's *Ṭurim* and Joseph Caro's *Shulḥan 'Arukh*).

INTRODUCTION

THIS book sets out to throw light on the changes of attitude on the part of the Jews towards their non-Jewish environment during the Middle Ages and down to the Era of Enlightenment. Our investigation is further circumscribed by its geographical range. With one exception, that of Rabbi Menaḥem Ha-Me'iri, who forms the subject of Chapter X, all the material has been drawn from the province of Ashkenazi Jewry in the wider sense, i.e. from the Jewries of northern France and Germany in the Middle Ages and from the life of their descendants in Germany and eastern Europe (Poland and Lithuania) between the sixteenth and eighteenth centuries.

In spite, however, of the limitations set to the period under review, our analysis should enable us to comprehend the problem of Jewish-Gentile relations in its entirety. The relationship of the Jew with the Gentile in the Middle Ages, and indeed throughout the post-biblical period, rested on a fully evolved tradition. In so far as this special problem is concerned, the history of the Jews at any later period, prior to emancipation, or in any country of the Diaspora, may be regarded as a variation on the same theme.[1] At any given time Jewish-Gentile relations may appear to have differed according to the country concerned, but the differences were in reality no more than mutations of the same pattern. Hence although we confine ourselves to certain historical and geographical limits, in describing the problem we may nevertheless hope to gain an insight into the problem as a whole.

It would be well to commence our investigation by summarizing the tradition concerning Jewish-Gentile relations as handed down to Ashkenazi Jewry from earlier periods; and an account of this tradition will therefore be given, point by point, as we encounter the various problems. Neither the content of this tradition, nor the literary form in which it was transmitted, is simple. As regards

[1] The methodological problems arising from the nature of Jewish history in the Diaspora are dealt with in my article 'The Concept of Social History and its Possible Application in Jewish Historical Research', *Scripta Hierosolymitana*, iii, 1956, pp. 292–312.

the latter, there is a difference between the biblical, aggadic, and halakhic literatures. Each of them contained elements capable of influencing both the mental and the practical attitude of Jews towards Gentiles. The Bible and the 'Aggadah provided the historical and also the legendary records which accounted for the distinctiveness of Jewry from other nations. From these sources, too, was derived the conception of the religious status and destiny of Israel in the present and in the future. The halakhic literature, on the other hand, was apt to be consulted in every instance where contact with Gentiles had any bearing on ritual, or on juridical or moral conduct.

An appreciation of the various branches of tradition as potential sources of influence on the attitude of Jews towards Gentiles does not imply that we are free to use the literary records of that tradition uncritically as a basis for our historical inquiry. To sum up all that has been said in the Bible, the 'Aggadah, and the Halakhah concerning the relationship between Jews and Gentiles, and to claim the result as the pattern which Ashkenazi Jewry followed, would be entirely misleading. Such a summing up would, in actual fact, fail to display any consistent pattern, for the tradition which was handed down to Ashkenazi Jewry was already full of inconsistencies. Even if no other factor had played a part in the attitude adopted by the Jews towards contemporary Gentiles, the inconsistency of tradition alone would have compelled them to apply some form of selectivity before they could rely on it.

It is therefore our task to ascertain, by critical media, what methods of selection the Ashkenazi Jews actually did employ. In other words, we must discover which parts of the tradition relating to Jewish-Gentile relations retained their historical force, and which parts were neutralized and treated as a dead letter.

The answer to the above question is relatively simple in the case of halakhic literature. As the Halakhah was the binding religious law regulating communal as well as private life, contemporary halakhists considered it one of their main responsibilities to determine the valid form of the Halakhah for any and every case. Apparent contradictions of detail had to be reconciled, and other difficulties overcome, before this objective could be attained. This led to a sifting and continuous reinterpreting of the Halakhah by a method of which we shall learn more later. Here it is sufficient to note that, since this process of reinterpretation was applied throughout our period also to the tradition of Jewish-Gentile relations, it ought to be possible to discover what the attitude towards Gentiles was at any given moment, at least so far as the norms of the Halakhah were concerned.

It is much more difficult to obtain the same result with regard to the biblical and aggadic literature, or develop any systematic theory of evaluation which Ashkenazi Jewry did not develop. In principle, anything handed down from ancient times was held to be true and significant. Certainly, no sentence or dictum even of the 'Aggadah would have been discarded as representing merely the opinion of its author in talmudic times. It is true that such an attitude was adopted by Spanish Jewish authorities in order to refute the accusations of Christian opponents and as part of a genuine criticism of certain details of the tradition.[1] Among Ashkenazi Jews, however, such an approach would have been considered as bordering on heresy.

Thus Ashkenazi Jewry can be said to have accepted every detail of the tradition bearing upon Jewish-Gentile relations. Possible incompatibilities in detail were not necessarily discussed or even noticed. Since no direct practical conclusions were to be drawn from such statements, no practical need for harmonization arose. Such questions as what had been the original point of divergency between Jews and Gentiles, by what propensities they differed from each other, and what would be their ultimate fate at the end of days could be left undecided. Nevertheless there is no doubt that even in the sphere of such theoretical thinking some selectivity was practised. One sentence exercised special appeal and was therefore often repeated; another was perhaps tacitly disregarded. Some explicit, though casual, attempts were made to reconcile contradictory statements. Where we do encounter such attempts, it is not difficult to discover the author's real opinion.

[1] See *Enṣiqlopediah Talmudith*, i, p. 662. All the sources limiting the religious authority of the 'Aggadah date either from gaonic times or from Spain; cf. I. Heinemann, *Darekhey Ha-'Aggadah*, Jerusalem, 1950, p. 187; F. Y. Baer, *Toledoth Ha-Yehudim bi-Sefarad Ha-Noṣerith*, Tel Aviv, 1945, p. 106.

Even where we are unable to rely upon more or less explicit assertions of this sort, we shall not necessarily be left without indications as to the prevailing influence governing the sentiments of any particular period. For these generations were themselves not unproductive in the field of literature. They produced religious poetry, as well as biblical and talmudic exegesis, and recorded in permanent form sermons and comments upon moral and religious topics. Even where they had nothing substantial to add to the tradition, the repeated quotation of an ancient source or its variant is sufficient indication as to the individual author's trend of thought.

In order to ensure a productive approach to the sources, we must differentiate between the various spheres to which their contents apply. For the term 'attitude towards Gentiles' refers to a very complex phenomenon which possesses all the aspects implied by contact between members of different social units. 'Attitude' implies, first of all, some ideological appreciation of the nature and essence of the society with which the group in question is confronted. Such appreciation is likely to be based upon a comparison between its own character and that of its opponents. In this case such a summing-up was closely connected with the difference in religion which was regarded as the point of divergence between the two communities. Any dissimilarities in propensity or moral conduct—genuine or imagined—which Jews observed among Gentiles were either attributed to, or at least assumed to be connected with, the difference in religion. A more or less abstract, stereotyped notion of the Gentile is part and parcel of the Jewish conception of the Gentile world—much as an even more rigid stereotype of the Jew was perpetuated in the mind of the Gentile.[1]

One of our main tasks, therefore, will be to reconstruct the picture which Jews held to be an accurate representation of the religion, nature, and morality of the Gentile world.

[1] See J. Parkes, *The Conflict of the Church and the Synagogue*, 1934, p. 158; C. Roth, 'The Medieval Conception of the Jew: A New Interpretation', *Essays and Studies in Memory of Linda R. Miller*, 1938, pp. 171–90; J. Trachtenberg, *The Devil and the Jew: The Medieval Conception of the Jew and its Relation to Modern Antisemitism*, 1943; G. Kisch, *The Jews in Medieval Germany*, 1949, pp. 323–41.

The word 'attitude', however, has also a practical bearing. The existence of the Jews was dependent upon economic relations with Gentiles: but were not these relations impeded by the mutually exclusive religious affiliations of the parties? The same question is even more relevant with regard to social intercourse. We shall have to consider separately the Jewish attitude towards political and juridical institutions, i.e. the rulers and the courts of law of the Gentile State. Finally, there is the field of juridical and moral controls regulating the relationship between individual members of the two sections of society. Without such controls, no relationship could have been maintained at all.

It is necessary to commence by indicating these problems; we shall have to analyse them, and to demonstrate the means by which the answers to them have been sought. In describing different types of attitude we shall encounter additional distinctive individual attempts at definite solutions. The last part of our study will show how far the entire problem was altered when historical development led to the transition from the Middle Ages to the Age of Enlightenment.

PART I

THE PROBLEM AND ITS TERMS OF REFERENCE

I

THE POSITION OF THE JEWS

THE relationship between Jews and Gentiles is at all times a reciprocal one. The behaviour of the Jews towards their neighbours is conditioned by the behaviour of the latter towards them, and vice versa. A real insight into this relationship can therefore be gained only by concentrating our attention simultaneously on both sides of the barrier. Every attitude of the Jew towards the non-Jew has its counterpart in a similar attitude of the Gentile towards the Jew. Similarity does not mean, however, that exactly the same pattern of behaviour is to be observed both on the Jewish and on the Christian side, for the position of each is different. The Christian is a member of the majority group, the group which possesses political power. The Christians regard themselves as the indigenous population of their country. The Jews, on the other hand, are a 'national' as well as a religious minority. In this connexion the decisive factor is not so much that the Jews are of a different racial origin, but rather that they are connected, in their own consciousness as well as in that of others, with a particular and distinct part of the common Jewish-Christian tradition. They are regarded as the descendants of biblical Israel. While this fact is common ground to both Jews and Christians, the evaluation of it by each is wholly conflicting. For the Jews it implies that they alone are in possession of the whole revealed religious truth. They are a party to the biblical Covenant with God, while the Gentiles fall into the category of 'The Sons of Noah', who are bound by the Covenant between God and Noah, which was enjoined upon all humanity. As we shall see later, the Jewish evaluation of contemporary Christendom turned mainly on the question whether Christians satisfied the terms of the Noachide Covenant, which included belief in the unity of God. There was, however, no doubt that Gentiles, Christians not excluded, stood outside the bounds of the biblical Covenant in the full sense of the term.

For the Christians, on the other hand, the descent of the Jews from biblical Israel signified nothing more than a physical fact. Their evaluation of its spiritual import was a negative one. For according to the Christian conception, the biblical Covenant with Israel ceased with the appearance of Jesus and was perpetuated in those who accepted the Messiahship of Jesus. Furthermore the Jews, who rejected that Messiahship, had drawn upon themselves the curse pronounced upon those who broke the Covenant.[1]

The antagonism between Jews and Christians in the Middle Ages is therefore not simply the disparity of two groups divided by religion. The antagonism—and we would do well to bear this in mind throughout our investigation—is that of conflicting exponents of the same tradition.

However, we are not yet concerned with practical conclusions to be drawn from conceptual differences in the respective theologies. We have mentioned them only in order to point out the singularity of the Jewish position in predominantly Christian countries. The 'racial' or 'national' difference between Jews and Gentiles is here substantiated by the theological conceptions which underlay them. Neither Jewish residence, both settled and temporary, in Christian countries, nor even the very existence of the Jew was taken for granted, and they had to be justified in terms of some ideology that counterbalanced the theological conception. Such an ideology underlay the ecclesiastical (and more especially the Papal) decrees which approved the Jews' residence in Christian countries and protected them from forced conversion and maltreatment. An explicit doctrine to this effect, supported by theological ratiocination, had already been evolved by the early Christian Church Fathers and was fully developed in the theories of Bernard of Clairvaux and Thomas Aquinas.[2] Such ecclesiastical and theological toleration could, however, hardly rank as an effective guarantee of security.

[1] J. Parkes, *Conflict*, pp. 49–60. The material reflecting the use of the theory is ably set out in A. Lukyn Williams, *Adversus Judaeos*, Cambridge, 1935.

[2] See J. Aronius, *Regesten zur Geschichte der Juden im fränkischen und deutschen Reiche bis zum Jahre 1273*, pp. 111–13, 324–7. A detailed analysis of Thomas Aquinas's attitude is given by G. Caro, *Sozial- und Wirtschaftsgeschichte der Juden*, i, 1908, pp. 308–13.

Consequently, the Jews had to seek the protection of the holders of political power. In the latest phase of the period under consideration, i.e. from the thirteenth century onwards, the form that this protection assumed was the explicit definition of the Jews as being the 'king's serfs', *servi camerae*.[1] The king, or, more correctly, the sovereign of the given country or locality, became the protector and simultaneously the 'owner' of the Jews. It depended upon him whether, and under what conditions, Jews might be allowed to reside or settle in the territory under his rule. The dependence of the Jews for their existence on the goodwill of the ruler was, however, already an accepted fact in the period preceding the development of its legal definition. As early as the Carolingian era Jews settled and traded in France on the basis of a royal charter. Similarly, the great communities in the Rhenish cities, Spiers, Worms, and Mayence, were established through the granting of such charters by the local bishop or by the Emperor, according to the political status of the locality. Even where the terms of the charters were most generous, not only with regard to economic facilities, religious liberty, and judicial autonomy, but also regarding the political status of the Jews, the charters as such had not lost the character of conditional grants. The Jews of France and Germany from the ninth until the eleventh century were allowed to trade and to transact business almost without restriction. They played a conspicuous part in foreign trade, especially with the countries of the Near East and the Slavonic north-east of Europe. Their share in local trade, as well as in the provision of credit, was considerable. Their religious liberty was guaranteed, the only restriction being the prohibition of proselytization and the owning of Christian slaves (which was tantamount to converting them into Jews by virtue of circumcision). On the other hand, they were protected by the authority of the law from forced conversion by the Church or the laity.[2] Where the Jews constituted themselves into a regular community, the community had at least judicial authority over

[1] The evolution of the concept of chamber serfdom has been much discussed. See Aronius, *Regesten*, pp. 139–42; Kisch, *Germany*, pp. 143–53.

[2] The position of the Jews in the Middle Ages has been frequently described; see Caro, *Wirtschaftsgeschichte*, i, pp. 128–58; Parkes, *The Jew in the Mediaeval Community*, London, 1938, pp. 44–53.

its members. This legal authority was based on Jewish talmudic law, but its effectiveness was conditioned by the consent of the sovereign or even by his actual co-operation. The Jewish community disposed only of moral, or at best passive, means of coercion—as, for instance, exclusion of recalcitrant members from participation in Jewish public worship, on which spiritual welfare depended. In extreme cases, where such coercive measures were of no avail, the communities had to resort to the direct aid of the State's secular arm.[1]

A feature of the high political standing of the Jews in the early part of our period was the permission to bear arms, granted to the Jews in France and Germany well into the thirteenth century. This fact is perhaps to be viewed less as providing a means of self-protection than as a sign of political status. As a result of this permission, the Jews ranked with the knights and the feudatories who belonged to the upper strata of medieval society.[2]

This situation, though well authenticated, has no essential bearing upon the position in which the Jews found themselves in Christian countries. Historians have repeatedly tried to account for the terrible fate which befell the Jewish communities in the centuries after the Crusades, when persecution, wholesale massacre, and expulsion made Jewish life insecure, degrading, and by normal human standards hardly worth living. Usually, the Crusades have been taken as a turning-point in Jewish history; it was then that the outbreak of popular violence demonstrated the vulnerability of the Jewish position. According to this theory, it was as a result of this experience that the Jews sought the protection of the rulers. The same experience taught the rulers to regard the Jews as a defenceless class, which had no choice but to accept whatever limitations and conditions they might impose upon it in exchange for a guarantee of Jewish life and property.[3] A deeper analysis of the facts, however, will cause us to qualify this theory. Jewish existence had been dependent upon royal

[1] L. Finkelstein, *Jewish Self-Government in the Middle Ages*, 1924, pp. 1–19.

[2] Kisch, *Germany*, pp. 119–28.

[3] H. Graetz, *Geschichte der Juden*, 3rd edn., vi, pp. 83, 95; Parkes, *Community*, pp. 83–89; Kisch, *Germany*, p. 108; less definitive, Caro, *Wirtschaftsgeschichte*, i, pp. 230–1.

protection in earlier periods also, thanks not so much to occasional outbreaks of violence, which had already been occurring, as to the absence of any other legal basis for their residence and activity in the countries concerned. The terms of the royal charters granted to the Jews by Charlemagne and his successors were certainly more generous than those of the sovereigns and municipalities of the thirteenth century.[1] The Jews of that time were better off economically and had a higher social status. Their precarious political standing, however, although not explicitly formulated as it was later to be, with the emergence of the term *servi camerae*, was fundamentally the same. As their right of residence was not rooted in the conception of public law, it had to be acquired through a special grant vouchsafed by the wielder of political power.

The alien character of the Jew in Christian countries was not merely a negative phenomenon created by the fact that the Jew was not indigenous. The definition of the Jew by Christian tradition as the 'breaker of the Covenant' carried with it a notion of positive degradation. This contempt, furthermore, was not necessarily actuated by the Christian's attitude towards all Jews. At times the antagonistic notions concerning Jews abated and normal human relations sprang up between neighbours, partners, and participants in some common undertaking. Yet behind such 'natural' relationships there always lurked the ideology of separateness based on the religious conceptions of both the Jewish and the Christian groups. It is the aim of this book to show how these conceptions influenced the relationship in so far as they were held by Jews; but our perspective will be neither sane nor realistic unless we bear in mind that the religious dissociation was a mutual one. Historiography has, until now, dealt more with the Christian dissociation from the Jews than with the reverse, more especially where our period is concerned. The attitude of Christian medieval society, secular as well as religious, towards the Jews has been repeatedly described.[2] Our analysis of the Jewish attitude should serve to

[1] The *privilegia* granted to the Jews by Charlemagne and Louis the Pious are reprinted in Aronius, *Regesten*, pp. 26–33. Further analysis in Parkes, *Community*, pp. 155–66; Caro, *Wirtschaftsgeschichte*, pp. 128–58.

[2] The fullest treatment is that of Parkes, *Community*, especially chaps. 2 and 3; see also S. Grayzel, *The Church and the Jews in the XIIIth Century*, especially

complement such descriptions. But in order to make clear the complementary character of our account, it is necessary to summarize the Christian position.

The reasons for allowing the Jews to settle in Christian countries have been stated above. As we have seen, powerful motives were at work to secure for the Jews the necessary protection to guarantee their existence. This security was, however, impaired as a result of religious motives, which were of great weight in medieval society. These made themselves felt through two different channels. The Church, by virtue of its allotted task, was in duty bound to see that the demands of religion were fulfilled. The representatives of the Church were therefore the natural guardians of society in this respect, and they stepped forward whenever accepted ideals appeared to be weakening. Since Christian tradition regarded social segregation from non-Christians, and especially from Jews, as a religious duty, it was incumbent upon the guardians of religion to secure its observance. Among the Papal statutes which guaranteed the Jews existence in the Christian countries, we find decrees and enactments full of warnings and admonitions to abstain from social intercourse with Jews.[1]

It is not difficult to trace definite lines of development in the Christian attitude towards Jews even within the period under review. In the early phase of this period, from the ninth to the eleventh century, indications of the desire for separateness are less frequent and the measures taken to supplement it less harsh. Formal enactments of the Church in this direction became the order of the day only with the fourth Lateran Council, in the year 1215. The compulsory wearing of the Jewish badge, intended not only to remove Jews from social contact with Christians, but also to

chaps. 1, 5, 7. The Jewish attitude is most extensively treated by M. Guttman, *Das Judentum und seine Umwelt*, Berlin, 1927. Other treatments will be mentioned below.

[1] See the letters of Agobard and Amulo, bishops of Lyons, in Aronius, *Regesten*, pp. 33–40, 46–48; Parkes, *Community*, pp. 49–53; Williams, *Adversus Judaeos*, pp. 348–65; [A.] Bressolles, *Saint Agobard, évêque de Lyon*, 1949, pp. 103–19. Contrary to the views of earlier authors, who considered Agobard's and Amulo's protests against fraternization with Jews as an outburst of antisemitism, a more judicious appreciation is gaining ground. Parkes, Williams, and especially Bressolles maintain with good reason that the bishops' protests were within the rights and even the duties imposed on them by ecclesiastical tradition.

brand them as a distinct social group—and one of inferior rank at that—was then for the first time introduced.[1] Warnings not to mix freely with Jews, and to desist from common meals and social intercourse, had, however, been uttered also in the earlier period by religious authorities of both high and low standing. These admonitions could be supported by quotations from the early Church Fathers, as well as by decisions of Synods, the validity of which could not be questioned.[2] Even Christian hagiography could serve as a source of authority, for one of the Christian saints was praised for having avoided all intercourse with pagans and Jews, and for refraining from even greeting them in passing.[3]

Historians who have dealt with this chapter of Jewish-Christian relations have often asserted that the frequent repetition of these ecclesiastical warnings indicates that such precepts were not much heeded by the Christian public.[4] In view of their nature and the method of public admonition, it is doubtful whether such a conclusion is permissible, or of much significance. Prescriptions to refrain from social intercourse with individuals with whom economic relationships were continuous could scarcely ever be wholly effective. Neighbourly and even friendly relations between individual Jews and Christians always occurred, despite oppressive rules and the ideologies held by both sides. Such occasional infringements were sufficient to call forth public admonitions from those whose duty it was to secure the implementation of the accepted religious standards. The period between the ninth and eleventh centuries seems to have been comparatively lenient in applying the rules of segregation. Free social intercourse between Jews and Christians was fairly common at that time. We are not, however, entitled to describe the period as altogether free from religious interference in this field. If the religious prescriptions on both sides were not strictly enforced or even publicly asserted, neither were they officially disavowed or authoritatively abrogated. They could at any time be put into force by some zealous partisan

[1] See Grayzel, *Church*, pp. 41–75.

[2] Bressolles, *Agobard*, p. 113, lists the sources used by Agobard in substantiating his protest.

[3] Aronius, *Regesten*, pp. 4, 39.

[4] See for instance Graetz, *Geschichte*, v, pp. 44–45.

of religion. As we know, this sometimes happened on the Jewish as well as on the Christian side. Relationships between Jews and Gentiles could therefore not escape the religious cleavage under which society laboured at that time.

Yet it would not be correct to attribute the social distance between Jews and Christians to their respective religious institutions, the Church and the Rabbinate. The Rabbinate had never achieved institutional hierarchy and authority to the same degree as had the Catholic Church. During the period of the Ashkenazi Middle Ages its institutional character was especially weak.[1] Differentiation between the Rabbis, i.e. the learned talmudists, and the laity certainly existed. We may therefore regard the Church and the Rabbinate as the agencies responsible for implementing the rules of separation. It may even be assumed that without the activity of these institutions the rules of segregation might have fallen into disuse. But if we follow up this conjecture, we shall soon realize the absurdity of splitting a society into its component parts and laying the blame for any one of its features on any particular component; for a picture of medieval society which does not include the Church or the Rabbis is pure fantasy. Institutional religion based on a well-defined tradition is a fundamental aspect of the Middle Ages. The existence of the Church and the Rabbis is, in fact, merely the institutional expression of the central part which religion played in the life of society.

This statement relates closely to our particular problem. Taking into consideration the all-pervasive character of both the Christian and the Jewish religions in the Middle Ages, we are forced to the conclusion that the social segregation of the adherents of the two religions was unavoidable. Jews and Christians were able to meet in a friendly spirit on those occasions which brought them together; they may have tried to deal with each other according to some ethical standard. They could, however, scarcely penetrate

[1] Concerning the different stages in the development of the Rabbinate, see J. Katz, *Tradition and Crisis: Jewish Society at the End of the Middle Ages* (Hebrew), Jerusalem, 1958, pp. 196–9. Zeitlin's theory about the supposed 'foundation' of the Rabbinate by Rashi (S. Zeitlin, 'Rashi and the Rabbinate: The Struggle between Secular and Religious Forces for Leadership', *JQR*, xxxi, 1940–1, pp. 1–58) may be disregarded.

into each other's social sphere, for the life of each community was permeated by its own religious symbols and emblems. Intimate occasions, such as family celebrations, communal gatherings, and even festive entertainments, were dominated by, or at least associated with, religious ceremonies. Those who were not adherents of whichever religion was concerned felt themselves to be—as indeed they were—excluded from such gatherings.

It would be wrong to see in this blending of religious symbols with social life solely an outward obstacle, for in religiously directed epochs religious symbols play a positive role in the structure of society. In the Middle Ages Christians as well as Jews could be most easily united by the appeal of religious ideas within institutions of a sacred character. Since the religious ideas and symbols of both communities were mutually exclusive—that which one section held in awe being very often an abomination to the other—the members of both sections lacked corresponding reactions. The Christian and Jewish communities were virtually two distinct societies. The fact that they nevertheless existed in the same economic and political framework was the source of their manifold problems and shortcomings.

One may object to the use of the word 'shortcomings' as expressing a moral judgement. For if our introductory analysis is valid, both sections, Jews as well as Christians, acted in harmony with their own nature in adopting an attitude of segregation. What more can be demanded from any society at any time? In judging our own nation or religion in past epochs, even more than when judging those of others, we should refrain from applying scales of values alien to them. It would, however, be a grave exaggeration to say that either Christian or Jewish society was entirely devoid of those humanitarian aspects in the light of which a tendency towards segregation would become morally delinquent.[1] It is true that, when they ignored the call of humanity, they did so in

[1] Instances on the Jewish side will be found below. On the Christian side see R. Anchel, 'La Tolérance au moyen-âge', *Les Juifs de France*, 1946, pp. 93–124. Bressolles, *Agobard*, p. 118, points out that Agobard himself retained the notion of *humanitas* and moderation, and not only of prudence, as his guide in his attitude towards the Jews, although without drawing any practical conclusions from it.

compliance with the demands of duties which were, in their estimation, of a higher value. These were the duties of religion in its medieval form. It was in this field of religious devotion that both the Christians and the Jews of the Middle Ages excelled. We are, however, entitled to know what the price of their devotion amounted to in terms of the neglect of other values. When such a balance is drawn up in respect of other people's religion, this is done out of motives of self-defence. It is the test of the historian to be able to apply the same method to his own religious group.

II

DOCTRINAL DIFFERENCE

AS indicated in the previous chapter, it is necessary to examine the Jewish attitude towards Christianity on several levels. First there is the theoretical conception held by the Jewish community concerning its own origin, its religious constitution, its creeds, and its hope for the future. All these are conceived not only in terms of self-evaluation, but also in clear-cut contradistinction to tenets and beliefs held by others; in the Middle Ages it is Christian society and the Christian Church with which the Ashkenazi Jewish community is confronted, and self-conscious distinctiveness is consequently orientated with reference to these.

It was at this theoretical level, and more especially concerning the historical account of the Jewish community's distinctiveness, that the Middle Ages could rely almost exclusively upon biblical and talmudic tradition. The biblical account of Israel's election was an accepted fact which accounted also for the contemporary separatism of the Jewish community. The fact of being chosen by God for His service meant that Israel had been singled out from the ranks of the other nations and had been assigned a position *sui generis*. Israel's election was predicated by the whole tradition; it is explicitly stated in some of the principal prayers in the liturgy,[1] and the concept is one of those widely held by and familiar to every practising Jew. We shall see later what this consciousness of election amounted to in terms of religious responsibility and readiness to endure the lot of the martyr and the outcast. Here we are concerned with its effect on the feeling of standing apart and its conceptual elaboration.

More theoretically minded generations inquired into the philosophical significance of Israel's election by God, and evolved a

[1] The 'Blessing of the *Torah*', to be repeated every day, and the *Qiddush* of the festivals are the most conspicuous versions of this trend. On the idea of election in talmudic literature, see S. Schechter, *Some Aspects of Rabbinic Theology*, New York edn., 1936, pp. 57–64.

theory of innate predisposition, which designated the Jewish nation as the future bearer of the Divine Revelation;[1] Ashkenazi Jewry, less sophisticated, seems to have accepted the tradition at its face value. Following the talmudic version of the idea of election, it attributed Israel's preference to his willingness to bear the yoke of the *Torah* in contrast to the other nations who recoiled from the religious responsibility involved. Rashi (R. Solomon Yiṣḥaqi, 1040–1105), whom we have every reason to accept as the most representative and influential figure of his period, repeated three times in his commentary on the Bible the legend according to which the Holy One, Blessed be He, approached the Edomites and other nations and offered them the *Torah*. Only after the other nations had rejected the *Torah* did Israel become the sole repository of the Holy Law.[2]

In quoting the above *'aggadah*, or in alluding to it, Rashi and the poets[3] made no special mention of the Christians. The concept of *'ummoth ha-'olam*, the Nations of the World, however, included the Christians as a matter of course. The dichotomy between Jews and Gentiles which governed the thought of post-biblical and talmudic times continued to be used by Jewish authors, although they were naturally aware of the differentiation which the acceptance of Christianity introduced into the ranks of the Gentile world. We shall see later on[4] that for certain practical purposes this differentiation was explicitly acknowledged. However, as we shall show, this was the case in the face of some particular stress only, when some detail of the tradition concerning Gentile-Jewish relations could not be implemented. Thus the contradiction between the actual practice of the community and the prescriptions of the Halakhah had to be resolved. This was done by taking cognizance of the difference between the nations of biblical and talmudic times on the one hand and contemporary Christians

[1] The most outstanding exponent of this theory is Judah ha-Levi in his *Kuzari*. See J. Guttmann, *Die Philosophie des Judentums*, 1933, pp. 144–6.

[2] On Deut. ii. 26, xxxiii. 2; Song of Sol. ii. 3; the talmudic source of the legend is *Sifrey*, Deut. xxxiii. 2, and B.T., *'A.Z.*, 2b.

[3] Such an allusion exists, for instance, in the poem of R. Ephraim ben Isaac of Regensburg for the liturgy of Pentecost: *Studies of the Research Institute for Hebrew Poetry in Jerusalem* (Hebrew), iv, pp. 139 f., l. 29.

[4] See *infra*, Chaps. III–IV.

on the other. Such differentiation was, however, limited to the particular problem concerned; tradition in its entirety remained unaffected by such qualifications of its particulars. That is why the biblical and talmudic tradition could still serve to orientate the medieval Jewish community in its relationship to the non-Jewish world. Unless the contrary is stated, the term 'Nations of the World' (we shall encounter other names later on) includes members of Christendom.

By interpreting the repeated quotation of a passage as an indication that it formed an integral element of contemporary thought, we may be able to reconstruct the Jewish conception of the Gentile world and of the differences which separated Jews from Gentiles. The above-mentioned traditional notion regarding the Gentiles' rejection of the *Torah* occupies a central position in this conception. Its sequel is the belief that it resulted in the establishment of a differing status for Israel and the Nations respectively. Israel became the nation nearest to God.[1] Israel differs from the other nations in his submission to the 613 Commandments of the *Torah*.[2] Israel alone devotes himself to the study of the *Torah*,[3] an occupation which, in halakhic Judaism, is reckoned the highest religious virtue. On Israel alone God bestows His *Shekhinah* (Divine Presence). Prophecy is granted to individuals among the Nations, as well as Israel, in order to counter the possible complaint that they have been left without spiritual guidance. Their prophecy, however, does not attain to the same high order which was vouchsafed to the prophets of Israel.[4]

The elements of this conception of spiritual supremacy originated in talmudic times, when Jewish self-consciousness became more pronounced on account of the clash with the pagan world. Medieval exponents of Judaism used these statements as a means of defining the Jewish position *vis-à-vis* Christianity; they made particular use of those aggadic expositions which were originally formulated to refute Christian doctrines.[5] Rashi and the poets

[1] Rashi, Exod. xix. 5.

[2] Rashi, Ruth i. 16.

[3] Rashi, Lev. xix. 33.

[4] Rashi, Exod. xxxiii. 16–17; Num. xxii. 5–8.

[5] The origin of the above-mentioned thesis of the superiority of the Jewish prophets has been sought by some scholars in polemics directed against the

referred to the aggadic statement that Israel's exile had not deprived him of his status; the Divine Presence dwells with Israel even in exile, and, when he is redeemed, the *Shekhinah* will be redeemed with him.[1] The affirmation of this belief is the direct answer to the Church's assertion that, with the advent of Jesus, Israel's election had become obsolete.

Although in their polemics in the Middle Ages Jews and Christians alike resorted to terms and concepts derived from ancient times, we must realize that in so doing they found an adequate expression for their own feelings and ways of thinking. The Jewish-Christian controversy in the Middle Ages is a direct continuation of the ancient polemic. The continuity of thought and feeling in Jewish society is demonstrated by the actual history of some of the principal terms which were used to designate Christianity. The biblical name of Edom was, in talmudic times, applied to Rome. In medieval poetry, however, it is synonymous with Christianity.[2] And this is but one instance only of those in which biblical expressions are applied to Christianity by the use of terms which had retained certain associations.[3] This was due, of course, to the medieval propensity to typological thinking. At the same time it is also an indication of the essential continuity running from biblical times to the period of the authors who used this term in their literary works.

It is only modern historical reconstruction which thinks of the Middle Ages as separated from antiquity by the watershed of historical events, the greatest of which was the supersession of the Roman Empire by new states. The medieval world regarded itself as a continuation of the Life of ancient times—the Jew, perhaps, feeling this even more than the non-Jew. We shall see later on that, as far as the validity of the law was concerned, one concept of time, that of *ha-zeman ha-zeh* ('this time'), comprehended

figure of Jesus. What is certain is that it was already used for this purpose in midrashic times. See E. E. Urbach, 'Derashoth Ḥazal ʿal nevi'ey 'ummoth ha-ʿolam we-ʿal parashath Bileʿam', *Tarbiz*, xxv, 1956, pp. 272–89.

[1] Rashi, Deut. xxx. 3. The reflection of this motif in the Christian-Jewish polemics is extensively treated by J. Bergmann, *Jüdische Apologetik im neutestamentlichen Zeitalter*, Berlin, 1908, pp. 131–45.

[2] See Levy's and Jastrow's Dictionaries *s.v.*; L. Zunz, *Die synagogale Poesie des Mittelalters*, p. 453.

[3] See Zunz, op. cit., pp. 462–70.

the period between the destruction of the Temple and its hoped-for rebuilding in the messianic age. Similarly, in terms of the biblical division of world history into periods, contemporary times implied the period of the fourth Kingdom foretold by Daniel, which was reckoned to have begun with the emergence of the Roman Empire. The fall of the Empire, that is of the Christian (and, for that matter, the Moslem) states, was to usher in the messianic age.[1]

Although the details of the vision of the future remained blurred and inconsistent, it contained the hope of heavenly judgement, i.e. the granting of reward to the righteous and the punishment of the wicked. This idea of eschatological retribution meant, for the medieval Jew, compensation for Israel's suffering in Exile.[2] Since the Christian peoples and their rulers were instrumental in causing the afflictions of *Galuth* (Exile), the anticipated retribution was destined to affect them in person. Though this expectation was out of harmony with the belief that Exile was a divinely ordained punishment for the sins of Israel, the Jews had a ready answer in the passage of the prophet Zechariah (i. 15): 'for I was but a little displeased, and they helped forward the affliction'.[3] In other words, the nations were afflicting Israel beyond the divinely ordained measure.

In quoting passages from the Talmud and the Midrash, Rashi and his contemporaries expressed their own ideas, for the questions requiring answer were to them real questions. They may have been actually posed in controversies with disputants,[4] and, even if they were not, they were known to be the stock Christian

[1] Rashi makes use of this midrashic apology on Gen. xv. 10–14. An allusion to it is found in R. Gershom's poem 'Zekhor Berith Avraham', A. M. Habermann, *Rabbenu Gershom Me'or ha-Golah, Seliḥoth u-Phizmonim*, Jerusalem, 1944, p. 31.

[2] A concise expression of this attitude is to be found in the dictum: 'The scourge with which Israel is smitten will in the end be smitten itself.' Rashi, Isa. xvii. 12. The midrashic source of this saying is in *Mekhilta*, *Beshallaḥ*, on Exod. xiv. 25, ed. Weiss, § 5, pp. 39 f.

[3] Rashi, Ps. lxix. 27. Cf. also Rashi on Zech. in loc.

[4] On disputations in the Middle Ages, see *infra*, Chap. IX. On Rashi's anti-Christian polemic, see F. I. Baer, 'Rashi weha-Meṣi'uth ha-historith shel zemanno', *Tarbiz*, xx, 1950, pp. 320–32, and the recent article (in Hebrew) by J. Rosenthal, 'Anti-Christian Polemic in Rashi on the Bible', in *Rashi, His Teachings and Personality*, New York, 1958, ed. S. Federbush, Hebrew part, pp. 45–54.

arguments against the Jews. Since Jews understood their own situation to be one of permanent defence against the temptations of the majority religion, a readiness to meet polemical questions became an intellectual necessity.

The intellectual armoury of the medieval Jew was not limited to the answers derived from midrashic sources, that is, from the period of the first clash of the Synagogue with the Church. The exponents of Judaism, especially in the generations after Rashi, continued to add to the corpus of *apologia* and polemic. The polemics of Rashbam, R. Joseph Qara, and R. Joseph Bekhor Shor belong rather to the sphere of medieval dialectic than to that of aggadic illustration. The development of Christian dialectics, which were also directed against Jewish disputants, may have been responsible for producing a Jewish counter-dialectic. In any case in the commentaries of the above-mentioned authors replies to Christian arguments on points of biblical exegesis are to be found which do not follow traditional lines. Their disputations concerned Christian criticisms of certain precepts of the *Torah*, and the Jewish authors endeavoured to make the latter appear in an intelligible and rational light.[1]

Thus Jewish polemic appears to have possessed an apologetic function. The defenders of the Jewish faith, however, were not content with repelling Christian attacks; at times they counter-attacked, and some of their remarks were directed against the central dogmas of Christianity. Jesus' Messiahship is either directly contested, or refuted by inference through the statement that the true Messiah is still to come in the future.[2] Similarly, the dogma of the Trinity is repudiated indirectly by the emphatic affirmation of God's unity,[3] while explicit polemics were also directed against it.

[1] Rashbam's attempt to attribute the dietary laws to hygienic considerations is perhaps the best example of this. He states explicitly that this explanation is intended as a refutation of Christian arguments against the reasonableness of these precepts. See Rashbam's commentary to Lev. xi. 3. Other instances are quoted in D. Rosin, *R. Samuel b. Meir als Schrifterklärer*, 1880, pp. 84–86. Cf. also S. A. Poznański's *Perush le-sefer Yeḥezq'el u-therey 'asar*, Introduction, pp. 34–35, 41–49.

[2] See Rashbam on Gen. xlix. 10, Rosin's edn.; Bekhor Shor's commentary on Gen. xlix. 10, ed. Jellinek, 1856, 2nd edn. by Gad, Jerusalem, 1956. Other passages are listed in Rosin and Poznański, locc. citt.

[3] See Zunz, *Literaturgeschichte der synagogalen Poesie*, pp. 629–30.

R. Joseph Bekhor Shor interpreted the *Shema'*, i.e. the Jewish declaration of faith, as containing a categorical denial of this central Christian dogma. This instance is a most remarkable indication of how far a controversial attitude penetrated to the very roots of Jewish religious life.

The threefold mention of God in the verse (Deut. vi. 4) *Hear, O Israel: The Lord our God, the Lord is one* was adduced by Christian interpreters as a proof of the Trinity. R. Joseph Bekhor Shor derided this interpretation, and declared that, on the contrary, the verse contains a specific denial of this Christian dogma.[1] As the point concerns the formula of the *Shema'* which was repeated by every Jew twice a day, the controversy transcended the sphere of purely academic exegesis. R. Joseph's explanation was utilized not only in polemics with Christians,[2] but also as a commentary to the prayers.[3] Thus this essay in polemic actually became associated with the central formula in the daily declaration of faith. I consider this to be the most impressive proof of Jewish sensitivity to Christian propaganda.

The necessity of warning people against the temptations of Christianity was of paramount importance to those who felt themselves to be responsible for the fate of the Jewish community. It will suffice to quote here one of the introductory passages of the great work of R. Moses of Coucy, *Sefer Miṣwoth Gadol*, known briefly as the *Semag*.[4] This book is well known to be a compendium of halakhic expositions, more particularly of the Ashkenazi schools, down to the thirteenth century. At the same time, however, the author's aim was clearly also educational and moralistic. He defines his task in these words:

'When the Lord of all things wanted to give the *Torah*, He made the heaven and the heaven of heavens to rest upon Mount Sinai with mighty thunderings and lightnings and He called to Moses, His chosen one, and said to him: *Behold, I come to you in a thick cloud so that the people shall*

[1] Bekhor Shor's commentary on Deuteronomy was published by A. Zweig, in *MGWJ*, xxi, 1913. The passage occurs on p. 727.

[2] See Z. Kahn, 'Étude sur le livre de Joseph le zélateur', *REJ*, i, 1880, p. 20.

[3] *'Or Zarua'*, i, p. 7.

[4] On him see Graetz, *Geschichte*, vii, pp. 57–58; E. E. Urbach, *Ba'aley Ha-Tosafoth*, Jerusalem, 1955, pp. 384–8. References here are to the Venice edn., 1547.

hear when I speak to you and shall also believe in you for ever (Exod. xix. 9). And what need was there for this, since it is early stated that on the occasion of the crossing of the Red Sea . . . *they believed in the Lord, and His servant Moses* (Exod. xiv. 31)? In spite of this, thus spoke the Holy One, Blessed be He, to Moses: "It is my desire that Israel believe of you that you are a prophet on account of the miracles and signs which you have performed; but as to the *Torah* which I desire to give, I do not wish them to believe you on account of any miracle or sign, but because they have heard with their own ears that I speak to you." The reason why the Holy One, Blessed be He, did so was in order that, when Israel should be in exile and a Gentile (i.e. a Christian) or Ishmaelite (i.e. a Moslem) should tell them to forsake their *Torah* and to serve other gods and should produce for them a sign or a miracle, Israel should be able to answer him: "Even if you multiply miracles and signs like Moses the son of Amram, we will believe you concerning the supplanting of our *Torah* by another only if we hear, with our own ears, that the Lord speaks with you. For even Moses His chosen one, the faithful one in His house, did not ask us to believe him concerning the *Torah*, except after we had heard that He spoke with him. After the death of Moses, prophets arose in Israel and spoke in riddles and allegories and hidden things. Because of this, the Nations said that the prophets prophesied concerning a new *Torah* of their own. For this reason the Holy One, Blessed be He, sent Malachi, the last of all prophets, who uttered two things at the end of his words to conclude all the prophecies: *Behold, I will send you Elijah the prophet before the coming of the great and dreadful day of the Lord* (Mal. iii. 23); that is to say, I am the last of all the prophets, and from myself until the coming of Elijah no prophet will arise. And behold, I say unto you in the name of the Holy One, Blessed be He: *Remember ye the Torah of Moses my servant which I commanded unto him in Horeb for all Israel, the statutes and judgments* (Mal. iii. 22); that is to say, it shall not enter your hearts that the prophets who arose before me prophesied concerning changes in the *Torah* of Moses, for they all came to strengthen the *Torah* of Moses." With this argument I would preface my exposition when addressing the exiles of Jerusalem dwelling in Spain and other lands of exile among Edom, so as to make their hearts firm in the service of God; then I would expound to them matters of Halakhah.'[1]

The method used is homiletical, the object being to convince

[1] *Semag*, p. 95b. In the year 1236 the author undertook a journey of preaching through Spain and France. See Graetz and Urbach, locc. citt., and *infra*, Chap. VIII.

the hearers and readers that Judaism had preserved its religious significance, and the community its religious destiny.

Jewish polemics against Christianity played no mean part in stimulating thought and literary productivity. They certainly added to the acuteness of Jewish self-consciousness, and to the conciseness of definitions of what exactly Judaism stood for. But we must not overrate the contribution which they made towards the retention of the bulk of Ashkenazi Jewry within the fold of Judaism.

The demonstration of Jewish tenets by exegetical methods and, in part, also by aggadic exposition operated on a rationalistic level. The effect of such reasoning depended, however, on an emotional attachment to the community, its way of life, and its tradition. And even on the conceptual level this was based on symbols which operated more immediately than did the dialectics involved. We have already encountered some of these basic concepts in aggadic quotations from Rashi, e.g. on the conjunction of God's destiny with that of Israel.[1] The Jewish Middle Ages conceived of the relationship between God and Israel as a most intimate mutual dependence approximating to a mystic union. The terms *Keneseth Yisra'el* ('the Congregation of Israel') and *Ha-Qadosh Barukh Hu* ('the Holy One, Blessed be He') are a dual concept and the dialogue between them is that of passionate lovers; this is demonstrated by the interpretation, in this spirit, of the Song of Solomon.[2] This same theme of mutual dependence and union is repeatedly expressed in the religious poetry of the Middle Ages[3]—a sure sign that the conception owed its perpetuation, not merely to the

[1] See *supra*, p. 16, n. 1.

[2] Rashi follows, at least as far as the interpretation of the content is concerned, the allegorical interpretation of the Midrash. See S. Salfeld, *Das Hohelied Salomos bei den jüdischen Erklärern des Mittelalters*, Berlin, 1879, pp. 39–41. The same may be said of most of the commentaries of that time; see Salfeld, op. cit., pp. 46, 49, 52.

[3] See for instance the poem "Eloah Niqra' by R. Gershom in Habermann's *Rabbenu Gershom Me'or ha-Golah, Seliḥoth u-Phizmonim*, Jerusalem, 1944, pp. 12–14, a few lines of which are quoted below. The Christian appeal to accept Christianity is refuted by an allusion to B.T., *Berakhoth*, 6a, where the uniqueness of both God and Israel is attributed to their respective dependence on each other. The declaration of faithfulness to God is one of the main motifs of medieval Jewish poetry. See Zunz, *Die synagogale Poesie des Mittelalters*, p. 15.

strength of tradition, but also to the fact that it was a living force. By this conception Israel's election ceases to be a problem, for the mutual dependence of God and Israel appears as a pre-ordained fact. It leads instinctively to the conviction that the fidelity of Israel, despite his sufferings, constitutes his faithfulness to his own essential nature.

Similarly, the adherence of the individual Jew to his community was assured—at least so long as no process of alienation, or experience of conversion, severed him from his social origin. Against the danger of such an occurrence, an early initiation into the conceptual framework of Jewish tenets and destiny was directed as a precaution. These concepts were embodied in and permeated all the primary sources on which Jewish education was founded.[1] They were not only formulated in words, but also expressed in ceremonial performed both by the individual and by the congregation. Both Jewish festivals and everyday religious ceremonies fulfilled this function of focussing attention on historical events as related in Holy Writ. They also preserved hopes for the national future, and to an even greater extent served to represent the basic religious tenets concerning the relationship between God and *Keneseth Yisra'el*[2]—every Jewish community being itself a kind of embodiment of this almost mystical conception. To such a degree was the individual imbued with the 'spirit' of Judaism, that intellectual reflection upon its tenets could have meant very little.

Just as positive attachment to the Jewish world of faith exercised its binding influence, so the visible representation of Christianity served as a tremendous deterrent. The acceptance of an alien religion always involves the overcoming of inhibitions naturally caused by the visible symbols of a religion in which one has not been reared from early childhood. Such aversion can be overcome only by the act of conversion. The symbols of Christianity, which Judaism regarded as a competitive religion, could be relied upon to repel every unconverted Jew. During the period in

[1] Rashi's commentary on the *Torah* became the basic instrument of instruction; see M. Güdemann, *Geschichte des Erziehungswesens und der Kultur der Juden in Frankreich und Deutschland*, 1880, pp. 15–16.

[2] Perusal of the Jewish prayer-book is sufficient to make the reader aware of the educational impact of the daily service.

question this shrinking from the visible tokens of Christianity was a common occurrence; for these are the centuries in which the western Catholic Church was clothing its tenets in their most conspicuous visible representation. Every Jew who lived in a Christian country between the eleventh and sixteenth centuries encountered some embodiment of the Christian religion at every turn. Even had their religion not emphatically prohibited visible representation of the Godhead, such representations would still have repelled the Jews, who had not shared the intellectual and emotional experiences which made these representations meaningful to Christian worshippers. Throughout the literature of the time we find the rejection of Christianity expressed in the form of the repudiation of one of its visible symbols, more particularly that of the crucified Christ. A few lines from Rabbenu Gershom's (tenth century) poem should suffice to illustrate this feature:

> They decree upon us not to call to the Lord
> . . . .
> to accept the despised idol as god,
> to bow to the image, to worship before it.[1]

The rejection of the Christian appeal is thus directed against the image of the human being who was elevated to the status of God. As the Jew could not accept the divinity of Jesus, it was a mockery to be asked to pay reverence to his visible representation. To the Jew, it was tantamount to idolatry. The underlying feeling of the unconverted Jew whenever he is approached with the invitation to accept Christianity is the feeling of being confronted with a choice between a pure faith and idol worship.

Such was the Jew's attitude towards Christianity, at least when its evaluation concerned the choice between that religion and his own religious heritage.

[1] Habermann, op. cit., p. 12. For the translation my thanks are due to Prof. Ch. Rabin.

III

ECONOMIC INTERCOURSE AND THE RELIGIOUS FACTOR

RASHI, in his description of the Jewish religious position, resorted to a dichotomy, placing Jewry on one side and all the other nations of the world on the other. Since for the Talmud and midrashic literature Christianity was reckoned but one of the many heretical sects to be combated, Rashi followed their lead and did not make explicit references to it. Christianity was included in the notion of *'ummoth ha-'olam* the 'Nations of the World', i.e. the Gentiles.

This borrowing of talmudic phraseology is not merely the result of Rashi's linguistic conservatism. On the doctrinal level, Rashi and the whole of Ashkenazi Jewry which he represented saw no reason to differentiate between Christians and those nations of whom the biblical, and more especially the talmudic, sources had spoken. Israel alone was regarded as the true servant of God. The other nations, Christians not excluded, were *'ovedey 'avodah zarah*, that is adherents of 'alien worship' or idolaters.

But if this generalization was accepted without difficulty on the doctrinal level, there were other levels of thinking at which it could not pass entirely uncontested. As is well known, the talmudic tradition included a whole body of precepts and prohibitions which were intended to regulate the contact of Jews with Gentiles. The aim of these regulations was to keep Jews away from idolaters, at least in so far as intimate relationships, and especially participation in or support of idol worship, were concerned.[1] With some variation, these regulations were adhered to by the Jewish community in talmudic times.[2] Many of these prescriptions were also accepted

[1] See Mishnah, *'A.Z.*, English translation by H. Danby, *The Mishnah*, Oxford, 1933, pp. 437–45. The tractate *'A.Z.* was earlier published, with notes, by W. A. L. Elmslie, Cambridge, 1911.

[2] This is evident from many passages in the Talmud with which I cannot deal here. See I. Baer, 'Israel, the Christian Church and the Roman Empire from the days of Septimius Severus to the "Edict of toleration of 313 C.E." ' (Hebrew, English summary), *Zion*, xxi, 1956, pp. 1–49.

by the early Christian Fathers for the regulation of the conduct of their adherents in their relationships with non-converted Gentiles.[1] But for the Christians such prescriptions could have been only in the nature of guidance or advice which became rapidly antiquated with changing conditions. Not so for the Jews. As the regulations concerning idolaters were embodied in the Talmud, they continued to be valid and binding according to the Jewish conception. If Christians had been regarded as idolaters it would have been incumbent upon the Jews to comply with every detail of the law.[2] We shall presently see why this was impossible in practice. A glaring contradiction had arisen between the law, which was still of full theoretical validity, and reality. This contradiction could easily be resolved if Christians were exempted from the category of idolaters and given a special status. This was, in fact, accomplished by the leading halakhists. How this exemption was reconciled with the doctrinal conception of a strict dichotomy between Israel and the Gentiles is not easy to explain. We shall be able to make this clear only after a detailed examination of the nature of the problem encountered by medieval Jewry and the system of juristic thought —the Halakhah—on the basis of which the solution was proposed.

The main characteristic of talmudic law is that it is based fundamentally on biblical revelation.[3] It is defined as the 'Oral Tradition' in contrast to the written Law of the Bible. This definition, however, concerns the outward appearance of the two sources only, and not their real nature. Since both sources are attributed to

[1] Elmslie quotes many parallels to Mishnah, *'A.Z.*, from Tertullian, op. cit., pp. 91–93. Other sources in J. Bergmann, *Jüdische Apologetik im neutestamentlichen Zeitalter*, 1908, pp. 15–24. See also Baer, op. cit., pp. 8–11.

[2] Christians were explicitly included in the prohibition against 'Dealing with them in days of their festivals' according to the original reading in B.T., *'A.Z.*, 7b. See R. N. Rabbinowicz, *Diqduqey Soferim*, x, p. 15. Cf. the German translation, L. Goldschmidt, *Der Babylonische Talmud*, ix, p. 449; the English translation, I. Epstein (editor), *The Babylonian Talmud, Neziḳin*, vii, p. 24, n. 9, ignores the original version.

[3] The theory of the law is concisely set out by Maimonides in the introduction to his *Mishneh Torah*, English translation by M. Hyamson, New York, 1937. The factors limiting the possibility of abrogation are stated by Maimonides in *Hilkhoth Mamrim*, chaps. 1–2. The problem is thoroughly dealt with by Z. H. Chajes, *Mishpaṭ ha-hora'ah*, Zolkiew, 1840. At that time the reform movement in Judaism was rendering the problem acute, and Chajes was stating the traditional view.

Divine Revelation, they are equally valid and binding. Talmudic law could no more be abrogated than could biblical law. It is true that some precepts and rulings of the Talmud were designated as rabbinic enactments, and these could not, on principle, have the same claim to eternal validity as biblical law. But the abrogation of even these parts of talmudic law was hedged round by conditions which made it virtually impossible. The only way of developing the law was by interpretation, the rules and methods of which are themselves a part of talmudic tradition. The great events and far-reaching changes which had occurred in the history of the nations, as well as in that of Israel since talmudic times, were not in themselves any reason for abolishing any part of the talmudic law. The period of the Talmud and that of the Middle Ages were both regarded as belonging to the same era—that of *ha-zeman ha-zeh* ('this time'),[1] which was bounded by the destruction of the Temple at its beginning and the coming of the Messiah at its end. The medieval Jew had therefore to find guidance for his practical religious problems in the talmudic sources. This, however, was not easy to achieve—least of all where his relationship to the non-Jewish world was concerned.

For, in contrast to the ideological conception of unbroken continuity, there was in fact a hiatus between the talmudic era and the Middle Ages. In the former, Jews lived in their own country or in that of their first Exile, Babylonia, in compact masses. The laws and enactments which were designed to keep Jewish society apart from that of idolaters clearly envisaged a situation of constant contact between Jews and Gentiles living within one single economic unit. But the Jewish section of society was in fact so compact and varied in its composition that restrictions of contact with the non-Jewish section did not entrench unduly upon the economic existence of the Jews.[2] The limitations included in these

[1] M. Jastrow's definition in his *Dictionary of the Targumim*, &c., i, p. 404, 'after the dissolution of the Jewish common-wealth' is vague. Cf. the commentary on the Mishnah by R. Obadiah of Bertinoro, *Ma'aser Sheni*, 5. 7; cf. *Tosafoth*, *Giṭṭin*, 36a.

[2] What economic consequences the laws of segregation entailed in the time of the Mishnah is beyond the scope of the present inquiry. The question was raised by G. Allon, *Toledoth ha-Yehudim be-'Ereṣ Yisra'el bi-thequfath ha-Mishnah weha-Talmud*, i, pp. 43–44, but not sufficiently treated there.

laws are of several kinds. From a sociological point of view they can be classed under the following headings:

1. The prohibition of intermarriage, and of any sexual relationship.[1]

2. The prohibition to eat together. This was partly the outcome of the dietary laws which, whatever their original reasons, acted as deterrents to social intercourse. In addition, some prohibitions were purposely enacted in order to keep Jews from fraternizing with Gentiles. Tradition, at least, attributed the enactment of many laws to this motive. The most conspicuous of these prohibitions is that of the partaking of wine touched by a Gentile and any kind of cooked food which was prepared by him.[2] Social intercourse between Jews and Gentiles was entirely frowned upon. To accept an invitation from a Gentile was forbidden to a Jew, even when special arrangements were made to satisfy his ritual requirements.[3]

3. There is a special and emphatic prohibition preventing the Jew from having any contact with Gentiles while they are taking part in, or preparing themselves for, any form of idol worship. The Jew was forbidden to do any work which could be considered as accessory to idol worship.[4] Neither was the Jew permitted to derive any benefit from it. This prohibition had many practical implications. The best known is that mentioned in the Mishnah—*'Avodah Zarah* 1. 1—according to which 'For three days before the festivals of the Gentiles it is forbidden to do business with them—to lend to them or to borrow from them, to lend them money or to borrow money from them, to repay them or to be repaid by them.' The Jew was to avoid market-places, arenas, &c, which were even remotely connected with the mere token worship of idols such as habitually took place at the opening of the market or at the beginning of a performance.[5]

Thus the business relations of Jews and Gentiles were temporally restricted. The type of goods and merchandise in which dealings with Gentiles were permitted was also severely limited

[1] B.T., *Qiddushin*, 66b, 68b; Maimonides *Hilkhoth 'Issurey Bi'ah*, 12. 1–5.
[2] B.T., *'A.Z.*, 29b, 34b, 38a; Maim., *Hilkhoth Ma'akhaloth 'Asuroth*, 17. 9–21.
[3] B.T., *'A.Z.*, 8a; Maim., *Hilkhoth Ma'akhaloth 'Asuroth*, 17. 15.
[4] See for instance B.T., *'A.Z.*, 16a.
[5] B.T., *'A.Z.*, 13a, 18b.

Transactions at any time in utensils and materials which were likely to be used in the performance of idol worship were forbidden.[1] The same applied to labour. Jewish workmen could not take part in erecting buildings which were dedicated to, or at least used for the purpose of, idol worship.[2] Conversely, the Jew was not himself allowed to employ a Gentile worker to handle certain goods, especially victuals, which had a ritual use. No Gentile could slaughter animals for a Jew[3] or do the cooking for him.[4] As mentioned above, the wine of the Jew could not be touched by a Gentile.

The strict observance of these precepts presupposes the existence of a large Jewish population enjoying the opportunity of meeting non-Jews in various fields of activity but able to dispense with contact with them or at least able to tolerate restrictions on free intercourse with them. Such conditions prevailed at the period reflected by the basic laws of the Mishnah. Later, between the second and fifth centuries, conditions changed, so that the practice of the law was rendered more difficult. At any rate we find in the final redaction of the Mishnah and especially of the Talmud indications of the wish to diminish these restrictions.[5] This phase of development in the relationship between Jews and Gentiles is not our direct concern here. It interests us only in so far as changing conditions found expression in Halakhah, inasmuch as this duly became part of the tradition on which Ashkenazi Jewry relied for orientation in its own problems.

Nevertheless, even after the more lenient tendency of later talmudic sources has been allowed for, Ashkenazi Jewry found itself confronted with a glaring contradiction between accepted usage and the theoretically valid talmudic law. In a manner which

[1] B.T., *'A.Z.*, 13b; Maim., *Hilkhoth 'Avodath Kokhavim*, 9. 6–7.

[2] B.T., *'A.Z.*, 16a, 19b; Maim., *Hilkhoth 'Avodath Kokhavim*, 9. 11.

[3] Mishnah, *Ḥullin*, 1. 1.

[4] See *supra*, p. 27, n. 2.

[5] The period for business dealings outside Palestine was restricted to one day weekly by Samuel (third century, Babylonia), B.T., *'A.Z.*, 7b. Rabbi Yoḥanan (third century, Palestine) taught that Gentiles outside Palestine did not count as idolaters at all, B.T., *Ḥullin*, 13b. On this see *infra* in this chapter. See the recent article of E. E. Urbach, 'Hilkhoth 'Avodah Zarah, &c.', *'Ereṣ Yisra'el*, v, 1958, pp. 189–205.

is characteristic of the earliest stage in the growth of every Jewish centre of settlement,[1] Ashkenazi Jewry developed its customs by adjusting itself to prevailing conditions without having full regard for the niceties of the demands of Halakhah. A comparison between prevailing customs on the one hand, and the precepts of Jewish law on the other, could have been drawn only after the settlement had succeeded in producing competent halakhists who tried to control public as well as private life. In Germany and northern France this happened towards the end of the tenth century. From that time on halakhists began to scrutinize the accepted local customs and usages, comparing them with what they found stated in the Jewish legal sources. This process of collation continued during the whole era of the tosaphists (twelfth to thirteenth centuries). The work of the tosaphists can be summed up as an attempt to reconcile the various halakhic sources amongst themselves and also with contemporary accepted usage.[2]

The tosaphists found scarcely any field in which theory and practice were so much at variance with each other as that of the relationship between Jews and Gentiles. Most of the above-mentioned regulations, whose purpose was to keep the Jew from contact with non-Jews during their religious worship, and those excluding trade in certain wares with Gentiles were being tacitly disregarded. Jews did business with non-Jews on the latter's holy days and dealt in any commodity which had market value.[3] So far as economic dealings were concerned, the talmudic prescriptions had fallen almost entirely into abeyance.

The reasons for this are quite obvious. As we have seen, early in talmudic times compliance with talmudic precepts was facilitated by the fact that Jewish society was an almost self-supporting body. The position of Ashkenazi Jewry, however, was quite different. The Jewish settlers in France, Germany, and, for that matter, in almost every other country of Europe were tiny groups who

[1] See S. W. Baron, *A Social and Religious History of the Jews*, New York, 1937, ii, pp. 117–22.

[2] Cf. E. E. Urbach, *Ba'aley Ha-Tosafoth*, especially the last chapter, pp. 523–74. Cf. also my remarks on this work in *Qiryath Sefer*, Jerusalem, 1957, pp. 9 ff.

[3] We shall meet instances of this throughout our investigation. Here I note only some of the most conspicuous; see *Tosafoth*, *'A.Z.*, 2a, 13a, 15a.

succeeded in acquiring some position in society at large through discharging specialized functions—chiefly as merchants, money-lenders, and the like. In exchange for fulfilling these functions they were dependent on the other sections of society to provide their most basic needs. The Jew bought his food as well as his clothing from non-Jews and had to rely upon them for various kinds of services. Under such circumstances voluntary abstinence from business dealings with Gentiles for certain periods, or restrictions involving certain types of merchandise, would have had disastrous consequences for his economic existence.

The halakhists were not blind to this great difference between the conditions of one period and another. The great tosaphist, Rabbi Isaac, as we shall see, refers to it twice.[1] The stating of the facts, however, did not imply a legal justification for the change of any part of the religious law. Justification had to be found in conformity with the rules of halakhic interpretation. Changed conditions could serve as such a justification if it could be assumed that the law had foreseen a situation arising in which Jews would become a minority amongst non-Jews, and had exempted such a case in advance. This was the argument put forward by the above-mentioned halakhist—who thus enabled himself to discard the law which had originally forbidden the lending of money on interest even to a Gentile. The same argument was used to invalidate another precept, the prohibition of selling cattle to Gentiles. The Mishnah (*'Avodah Zarah*, I. 6) forbids this, for a reason that was already obscure to the talmudic sages in Babylonia in the third century.[2] In the Middle Ages, however, the prohibition was universally waived. The contradiction between law and practice was pointed out by the tosaphists, and in order to solve the difficulty Rabbi Isaac resorted to the distinction between the two periods. The argument runs that the taking of interest from a Gentile as well as the selling of cattle was forbidden by the law only under conditions where abstention from such a practice did not entail an economic loss and was not detrimental to making a

[1] *Tosafoth, Bava Meṣi'a,* 70b; *'A.Z.*, 15a.

[2] Cf. B.T., *'A.Z.*, 15a. *The Zadokite Documents* (ed. Ch. Rabin), xii. 9, gives the reason 'in order that they may not sacrifice them'.

livelihood. In the case where Jews lived amongst Gentiles as a minority, the prohibitions were automatically invalidated.[1]

This insight into the difference between the two periods, and particularly the solution of the legal problem arising from it, was one man's achievement. Yet even the tosaphist R. Isaac, who put the theory forward, did not do so in order to lay down a principle which might serve as a comprehensive directive in the regulation of the entire practical problem. The argument was used merely as an answer to a question which pointed out the contradiction between the law and accepted practice in these two instances: Jews did lend money to Gentiles and did sell them cattle, thereby neglecting the letter of the law. By distinguishing between conditions where Jews lived in compact masses and those where Jews lived as a minority, the reconciliation between practice and law was achieved. But the reasoning by which this reconciliation was effected did not acquire the nature of a principle. Any corollary whereby the same principle might have been held to render other laws patient of abolition would not have been acceptable.

In this example we have one of the main characteristics of halakhic thinking, which we shall have to bear in mind if we wish to handle our problem successfully. The Halakhah is, in origin, a body of case law which does not lay down principles, but rather discusses concrete instances and the decisions pertaining to them. With the passage of time, many of the decisions given were, indeed, explained as being based on principles which were in fact logically implicit in them. Nevertheless, even after the principles were formulated, they could not be used as a fountainhead of legal ruling. The many other decisions and principles on which they were supposedly based prevented the expansion of their logical consequences. One of the main tasks of the halakhic interpreter, therefore, was to reconcile the conclusions which were to be drawn from decisions regarding individual cases and from the principles inferred from them. But whether such a reconciliation of the details was achieved or not, no principle could, *a priori*, possess universal validity. Thus the above-mentioned distinction between the two sets of conditions—economically self-supporting Jewish society on

[1] *Tosafoth* quoted *supra*, p. 30, n. 1.

the one hand, and Jews as a minority on the other hand—resulted in the formulation of no general principle. To try to extend this distinction beyond its original application, and thereby to propose the abolition of some law which was still practised, would have been to transgress the accepted methods of interpretation; and any such attempt would have met with strong opposition.

This inquiry into the method of halakhic thinking may help us to grasp the exact meaning of certain passages which we find in the halakhists and which are related to our more restricted problem, that of the Jewish attitude towards Christianity.

As we have seen above, changes in conditions in the Middle Ages rendered many talmudic laws obsolete. This situation could be justified by pointing to other changes which had also occurred between the two periods. The Mishnah and the Talmud, when speaking of other nations, generally referred to the idolaters of whom the Gentile environment was chiefly composed. But this situation altered radically during the Middle Ages. Ashkenazi Jewry, in the period in question, was confronted by nations who accepted Christianity as their faith. Could this not be an argument justifying the disappearance of laws which were originally promulgated in order to separate Jewish believers from the environment of idolaters? Such a distinction was indeed indicated by some of the halakhists. The exact meaning of such passages requires careful scrutiny before we can arrive at any far-reaching conclusions as to the real opinion of the halakhists concerning the nature of the Christian religion.

On three occasions we find the halakhists distinguishing between the Gentiles of the two periods, namely, the talmudic period and the Middle Ages. The first occasion is connected with the problem of business dealings with Gentiles on their festival days. The precept which had forbidden such dealings was never observed in the Ashkenazi countries. That this practice was at variance with the valid law had already been noticed at the time of Rabbenu Gershom, i.e. in the tenth century.[1] The problem was brought to

[1] The exact dates of R. Gershom's life are doubtful. His birth is placed 950–60, his death 1028–40. Cf. A. Aptowitzer, *Mavo' le-Sefer Ravyah*, Jerusalem, 1938, p. 331; S. Eidelberg, *Teshuvoth R. Gershom Me'or ha-Golah*, New York, 1955, pp. 12–13.

Rabbenu Gershom's attention when a local halakhic authority attempted to impose the original talmudic law on his community.[1] According to the latter, no business dealings could be transacted on the day of the Gentile festival itself. Rabbenu Gershom repudiated this decision on the following grounds. Since, according to the talmudic definition, many days must be counted as Gentile festivals and the Jews' livelihood depended on their business dealings with Gentiles, they could not, in any case, comply with such a prohibition. Thus the following talmudic ruling had to be applied: 'Let Israel go their way: it is better that they should err in ignorance than presumptuously' (B.T., *Beṣah*, 30a). This is Rabbenu Gershom's first argument for setting aside the over-zealous opinion of his junior colleague. Then he adds another reason why it is incumbent on the halakhic authorities to allow the accepted practice to stand. As the case is to be regarded as a *she'ath hadeḥaq* (case of urgent necessity) one can rely upon the opinion of a talmudic authority, Rabbi Yoḥanan, who taught that 'the Gentiles outside the land (of Israel) are not idolaters; they are but continuing the customs of their ancestors' (B.T., *Ḥullin*, 13b). On what assumptions Rabbi Yoḥanan made his statement is not quite clear. Rabbenu Gershom, at any rate, interpreted him in a purely technical sense: the idolatrous practices of the Gentiles outside the land of Israel were not to be regarded as such. Consequently, the prohibitions of the Mishnah against dealing with idolaters during their festivals did not apply to his contemporaries, the Christians dwelling outside the land of Israel.

The application of the above pronouncement to this particular point did not imply that Christians were not idolaters for all religious purposes; the contrary is proved not only by what we have learned, for instance, from Rabbenu Gershom's religious poems quoted in the previous chapter, but also from the phrasing of his opinion in this individual case. For here he clearly assumes that the Gentiles in question, i.e. the Christians, do worship idols, but that their action does not count as such in its strict halakhic sense.[2] It was by a juridical formula that he made his case, and not

[1] Eidelberg, op. cit., pp. 75–77.

[2] This is clearly indicated in the concluding sentence of R. Gershom: 'Since

by a genuine distinction based on historical or theological considerations. The same applies to all the other authorities who have cited this decision without mentioning its originator.[1] It is certain that it was never intended to be the basis for a halakhic principle, and certainly not for a theological judgement.

Very similar is the case regarding which Rashi and other halakhists stated that the Gentiles of their time were not 'versed in the worship of idols'. This opinion is put forward in order to exempt the wine of contemporary Gentiles from being regarded as 'libation wine' and so prohibited to the Jew not merely for drinking purposes, but also as a source of any advantage whatsoever.[2] It is obvious that the statement was intended to serve this special purpose only. It possibly involves a recognition that in Christian practice there is no libation. But even so, it states a change in religious custom only, and has no significance as a classification excluding Christianity from the category of idol worship.

The last and perhaps the most important instance is that in which a similar sentence is used concerning a Jew's acceptance of a Gentile's oath. According to the talmudic precept (B.T., *Sanhedrin*, 63b) a Jew ought to avoid entering into partnership with a Gentile lest litigation arise between them, in the course of which the Gentile might take an oath in the name of an idol. In such a case the Jew would have transgressed the biblical commandment in Exod. xxiii. 13: *and make no mention of the name of other gods, neither let it be heard out of thy mouth*, the second clause being interpreted to mean 'nor cause to be heard'.

This precept implied that a Jew should not accept an oath from a Gentile, whatever might have been the cause of such an obligation. In consequence the Jew would have to forgo the advantage of being able to impose an oath on his Gentile opponent. This consequence was in fact pointed out by Rashi who, in an actual case

"the Gentiles outside the land of Israel do not worship idols", even though they *do* worship them it does not count as idolatry.' This sounds like a contradiction in terms. The sentence, however, makes good sense as a differentiation on the lines here indicated.

[1] See *Tosafoth*, *'A.Z.*, 2a.

[2] I. Elfenbein, *Teshuvoth Rashi*, New York, 1943, 327. Elfenbein analyses Rashi's *Responsa* in an article in *Rashi, His Teachings and Personality*, ed. S. Federbush, New York, 1958, pp. 63–98.

of litigation against a Gentile, relinquished his claim rather than make his opponent take a Christian oath.[1] Rashi's grandson, Rashbam, accepted this consequence as a binding rule. But this was certainly in contradiction to the general practice. In view of the manifold business relationships with non-Jews such conduct could have been adhered to only at the cost of great economic loss. It is understandable, therefore, that other halakhists sought a justification for disregarding this precept. Rabbenu Tam, Rashbam's younger brother, on the grounds of an ingenious analogy, found that in case of economic loss this prohibition was to be disregarded. In addition to this justification, another reason is reported in some sources in the name of Rabbenu Tam; it seems, however, to have originated from his nephew, the above-mentioned R. Isaac.[2] The passage runs as follows:

> According to Rabbi Isaac this [the taking of a Gentile's oath] is permitted—in our days—on other grounds, namely that since they [the Gentiles] swear by their scriptures, sacred to them, known as *Evangelium*, which they do not regard as a deity, and although they mention the name of Heaven, meaning thereby Jesus of Nazareth, they do not, at all events, mention a strange deity, and moreover they mean thereby the Maker of Heaven and Earth too; and despite the fact that they associate the name of Heaven with an alien deity, we do not find that it is forbidden to cause others [i.e. Gentiles] to make such an association (*leshattef*). Likewise, no transgression of the prohibition *Thou shalt not place a stumbling-block before the blind* (Lev. xix. 14) is involved, since such *shittuf* (association) is not forbidden to the Sons of Noah.[3]

Here we seem to have the nucleus of a theory of religious

[1] Elfenbein, op. cit., 180; Urbach, *Ba'aley Ha-Tosafoth*, p. 200, n. 37, made a case for attributing this story not to Rashi but to Rabbi Isaac the tosaphist. His arguments are, however, not conclusive. Moreover, he overlooked the passage quoted below (see next note) which shows that R. Isaac accepted the view of Rabbenu Tam and not that of Rashbam.

[2] S. Albeck, 'Yaḥaso shel R. Tam le-va'ayoth zemanno', *Zion*, xviii, 1954, p. 109 (Hebrew), convincingly proved R. Isaac's authorship, since it is in line with his tendency to differentiate between talmudic times and his own. See next note.

[3] The text is taken from Rabbenu Yeruḥam's *Sēfer, 'Adam we-Ḥawwah*, 17, 5. Other versions in *Tosafoth*, *Bekhoroth*, 2b, *Sanhedrin*, 63b. D. Hoffmann accepted Rabbenu Yeruḥam's text as the most intelligible, *Der Schulhan Aruch und die Rabbinen*, &c., pp. 11–12. Cf. Albeck, loc. cit. A more thorough analysis of this passage will be given in Chap. XIII.

tolerance. The assertion that the Gentiles are not bound to uphold the strict unity of the Godhead opens up the possibility of condoning the Christian adherence to the doctrine of the Trinity so far as the Gentiles, though not the Jews, are concerned. Such a logical implication of the passage was indeed accepted by later writers, whose minds were moving in the direction of religious tolerance.[1] They were glad to find the kernel of their thought in an early authority. But the author of this passage himself certainly did not draw all the conclusions implied.

The limited implications of the above-mentioned passages can be ascertained not only from their context, but also by indirect inference. For, as we shall see later, had these passages contained a firm principle, they could have been applied to many other cases—as was in fact done by Menaḥem Ha-Me'iri in the fourteenth century.[2] Ha-Me'iri did indeed exclude Christians from the term 'idolaters', but he did so, as we shall see later, on philosophical and theological grounds. Holding firmly to this principle, he was able to use it as a general justification for not observing all the precepts concerning Jewish-Gentile relations which were obsolete in his time. The tosaphists, who accepted these decisions out of purely halakhic considerations, restricted them to these special cases. Thus they adhered to the accepted halakhic method, limiting the validity of any conclusion to the special case out of which it was evolved.

[1] Cf. Chap. XIV. [2] Cf. Chap. X.

IV

SOCIAL AND RELIGIOUS SEGREGATION

THE reluctance of the halakhists to exclude Christian worship absolutely from the category of idolatry is quite understandable. The gulf which separated the two religions (both in dogma and spiritual outlook) was only one reason for this. Doctrinal differences became the more acute because of the social situation of Jewry in Christian countries. We have had occasion above to define this situation as the position of a minority dependent upon the broader society of which it formed part. This prompted the halakhists, as we have seen, to forgo any attempt to reintroduce the original talmudic laws of segregation in so far as economic activity was concerned. But the same situation induced them to retain the precepts which were designed to prevent the Jewish community from coming into intimate contact with non-Jews in the social and religious spheres. For the Jewish community was now in far greater danger of being absorbed by its social environment than it had been at the time when these precepts originated. The Christian Church was more zealous in its efforts to entice Jews to join its community than any pre-Christian sect or denomination with which Jews had come into contact in previous epochs had been. It possessed better means of persuasion and inducement, since it based its beliefs on the same tradition as Judaism itself, namely the teachings contained in the Old Testament. Lastly, the dependence of the Jewish community on the economic resources and services of its Gentile environment was likely to bring Jews into constant contact with Christians, in a way which exposed them to the influence of the Christian religion.

We shall better be able to appreciate the problem with which Jewish society was confronted if we first survey the more distinct features of their situation. As mentioned above, Jewish communities consisted at this time of tiny groups of ten people, or in most places even fewer; in a few places only did they amount to hundreds.

Even more decisive than the restricted numbers of the communities was the lack of variety in occupation and economic position. Reliance on a livelihood derived from the investment of capital in trade or in some other financial undertaking became, in this period, more and more the distinctive characteristic of Jewish economic existence.

The social implication of this was a double one. Firstly, the business dealings of the Jews brought them into close contact with Gentiles of varying status. The picture of the Jew waiting at home for the Gentile to come to borrow money or to pay a debt is a realistic one, at least for the period commencing with the Crusades.[1] But it reflects one aspect only of the situation. In this period many Jews had also to call at the house of the Gentile to offer their services as traders or money-lenders.[2] On some occasions the Jew followed the Gentile into the law courts as a result of their dealings.[3] For a Jew to be obliged to stay overnight in the house of a Gentile or to eat a meal there was not, perhaps, an everyday occurrence; on the other hand, it was not entirely out of the ordinary.[4] In this way business connexions facilitated social contact.

Social intercourse with Gentiles was indirectly forced upon the Jew to an even greater extent by his inability to supply his needs from Jewish sources alone. The Jewish household was dependent upon the Gentile for its meat and milk, grain, wine, and beer, and other foods.[5] Nor could the Jew dispense with the Gentile's services either inside or outside his household. Gentiles were employed as domestic servants as well as for special projects or on

[1] Such a situation is reflected in some of our sources, e.g. Eliezer b. Nathan (Raben), Prague edn., p. 148. The much quoted generalization of *Leqeṭ Yosher*, Berlin, 1903, i, pp. 118–19, applies to the author's time, i.e. the fifteenth century.

[2] G. Caro, *Wirtschaftsgeschichte*, i, pp. 426, 434–5; M. Hoffmann, *Der Geldhandel der deutschen Juden während des Mittelalters*, pp. 7 ff.; H. J. Zimmels, *Beiträge zur Geschichte der Juden in Deutschland insbesondere auf Grund der Gutachten des R. Meir Rothenburg*, pp. 46 ff.

[3] G. Kisch, *Germany*, pp. 173–4, 245–7.

[4] The lodging of Jews in the house of a *ma'arufya* (i.e. someone with whom he stands in permanent business relationships; cf. next chapter) is mentioned in *Ravyah*, 404 (ed. V. Aptowitzer, i, p. 462). Taking a meal is mentioned in *Tosafoth*, *'A.Z.*, 31b; *'Or Zarua'*, *'A.Z.*, 163.

[5] This is evident from the preoccupation with the ritual problems deriving from this fact, as we shall see later.

particular errands.[1] No Jew was able to harvest his grapes, whether the vineyard was his own or its crop purchased from a Gentile.[2] Jews employed Gentiles as their agents in transferring money, as well as wares and commodities.[3] How pervasive this dependence of the Jewish household on Gentile help was can be gathered from a story derived from a certain French community in the twelfth century: The eve of Passover coincided with the Christian Easter, so that no Gentile help was available and the Jews were therefore unable to bake their *maṣṣoth* in the afternoon ready for the evening, as was their habit in other years.[4]

One would assume that such conditions would be likely to render ineffective any ritual precepts, the intention of which was to keep Jewish and Gentile society apart. The impact of the situation is clearly seen in the way in which the halakhists dealt with the problems so created. The outcome, however, was more in the nature of a change in the function of the ritual than its neglect or abandonment.

Originally, Jewish ritual had fulfilled the function of securing the social segregation of the Jewish community from its Gentile environment. Under 'normal' conditions (where the constitution of a separate Jewish society was feasible), the effect of such ritual was to strengthen the tendency among Jews to rely as much as possible on each other. If the meat, wine, milk, and cheese of the Gentiles were forbidden, the Jew was thrown back, willy-nilly, on his own brethren for the production of these commodities.[5] As under changed conditions this was impossible, the outcome had necessarily to be different. Had the Jews not possessed a

[1] The charters granted to the Jews furnished this permission: cf. J. Parkes, *Community*, pp. 159, 161–3. The repeated ban by the Church on the employment of non-Jewish servants by Jews is rightly interpreted as a sign that the prohibition was not heeded; cf. S. W. Baron, *A Social and Religious History of the Jews*, 1937, ii, p. 41. Internal sources confirm this impression. The problems arising out of Gentiles' presence in the Jewish household are manifold: cf. I. A. Agus, *Teshuvoth Ba'aley Ha-Tosafoth*, 26; *Ravyah*, 841; *Tosafoth*, *Kerithoth*, 9a; *Semag*, p. 167a bottom; *Tosafoth*, *'A.Z.*, 12a, 61a, &c.

[2] See *infra*, pp. 40–41, for a discussion of the problem relating to wine touched by a Gentile.

[3] *Semag*, p. 167a; *Tosafoth*, *'A.Z.*, 61a.

[4] *Ravyah*, 452; Aptowitzer's surmise (*Mavo' le-sefer Ravyah*, p. 439) that the Jews were themselves forbidden to do work on Sundays is unfounded.

[5] Such must have been the result of these precepts in talmudic times.

deep-rooted conviction of the truth of their religion, and had they not actively sought to maintain their separate identity, the tendencies inherent in medieval conditions would inevitably have ended by breaking down the social barrier erected by Jewish ritual. As it was, Jewish ritual merely underwent certain alterations. We may describe the nature of the change by saying that, from a system of prescriptions which ensured the social cohesion of those who felt bound by them, it became a method of personal conduct enabling the individual to preserve his inward sense of aloofness from those with whom he came into everyday social contact.

This change is clearly reflected in the modifications of the laws concerning segregation. The Mishnah (*'A.Z.*, 2. 6) simply states, for instance, that the bread of Gentiles was forbidden to the Jew. In talmudic times the prohibition was not universally observed. It was, however, only under medieval conditions, when Jews could not rely upon production by Jewish bakers, that the eating of Gentile bread was permitted by the authorities.[1] The observance of the former prohibition became a sign of special strictness of ritual conduct, such as was confined to the exceptional few.[2] There was a much more stringent ban on Gentile wine. Being the article of sacred use in libation as well as the medium of close social intercourse and fraternization, it stood under a complete interdict.[3] The talmudic prohibition included the deriving of any benefit from a Gentile's wine. This ban excluded wine as a possible article of merchandise for Jews and, as we have mentioned in the previous chapter, this would have entailed intolerable economic hardship. The prohibition on drinking, however, was felt to be an indispensable means of social segregation. So it remained forbidden for the Jew to drink a Gentile's wine. As Jews were neither capable of growing their own vines nor of preparing wine without Gentile help, the solution was sought in a division of labour. Gentiles did the preparatory stages of the work. It had to be

[1] Rabbenu Gershom is the only one who adheres to the original prohibition. S. Eidelberg, *R. Gershom*, p. 20. Cf. Eliezer of Mainz (see p. 38, n. 1), 303; *Tosafoth*, *'A.Z.*, 35b; *'Or Zarua'*, *'A.Z.*, 187–8; *Rosh*, *'A.Z.*, 2. 27; *Tosafoth*, *Beṣah*, 16b.

[2] See *infra*, Chap. VIII.

[3] Both reasons are stated in B.T., *'A.Z.*, 29b, 36b.

determined casuistically from which stage in the production the grape juice was considered to be proper wine. From that moment on no one but a Jew was allowed to prepare wine for Jewish use. It is true that such distinctions had already appeared in talmudic discussions. But only in the Middle Ages did the division of the actual work become a usual feature of wine-production.[1]

The weight of the tradition which connected wine, particularly, with sacred worship as one of its media intensified the ritualistic attitude towards it. Logically, one might suppose that other alcoholic drinks such as beer and mead ought to have been placed in the same category as wine. The Talmud did, indeed, mention that they were prohibited, but indicated certain modifications which would make their use permissible under certain conditions.[2] Not being for sacred use, these liquids escaped the emphatic prohibition which applied to everything connected with idol worship. As beer was the common beverage in the Middle Ages, this was an additional reason for accepting a less ritualistic attitude concerning it. Nevertheless it was on casuistic grounds only that these liquids were excluded from the prohibition. The effect of the exclusion was far-reaching. In fact it was only drinking with Gentiles by way of entertainment that remained forbidden.[3] As, however, some limitations continued to be valid, the observance of these necessarily remained a part of the code of personal conduct in an environment which was deemed to offer attractions liable to seduce the Jew from his religious affiliation.

Similar consequences were entailed by the fact that Jews found themselves compelled, more and more, to rely upon the personal services of free Christian servants who lived with them in the same household. This situation developed only later: until the eleventh century, and occasionally even later, Jews bought slaves whom they then circumcised and so converted into 'half' Jews.[4] In the event of

[1] Cf. B.T., *'A.Z.*, 55a ff.; Eliezer of Mainz (see p. 38, n. 1), 309; *Tosafoth*, *'A.Z.*, 55b, 60a.

[2] B.T., *'A.Z.*, 31b.

[3] *Tosafoth*, *'A.Z.*, 31b; *'Or Zarua'*, *'A.Z.*, 163; *Rosh*, *'A.Z.*, 2. 15.

[4] As late as the end of the eleventh century Jews were explicitly allowed to purchase pagan (but not Christian) slaves; see Parkes, *Community*, Appendix, p. 392, para. 8, 10 in Henry IV's charter. The Hebrew sources relating to the problem are listed in S. Assaf, "'Avadim u-seḥar 'avadim 'eṣel ha-Yehudim bimey

manumission the slave became, with certain very slight reservations, a full Jew, and even while he was a slave he was for ritual purposes regarded as a Jew.[1] He could handle the wine of his owner and do his cooking. Not so the Christian servant, to whom the restrictions of the segregative laws applied.

The halakhists dealt extensively with the situation and the problems arising out of it. Some of them understood quite clearly the incongruity between circumstances as they were and the law which had to be applied to them. For the Gentile, far from being kept at arm's length, was in fact incorporated into the Jewish household.[2] On the other hand, it was also observed that, since the servant was of a lower social status, contact with him would not have the same dangerously attractive influence as would social intercourse between Jews and Gentiles of equal standing.[3] On these grounds it was suggested that servants in Jewish households be exempted from certain ritualistic restrictions. This lenient tendency, however, did not prevail. In the first generations after the problem had become acute there was hesitation on the matter. Some halakhists allowed a Gentile servant to do the entire housework including cooking—thereby disregarding the prohibition of *bishshul nokhri* (cooking done by a Gentile). However, we also have a report of one great authority, Rabbi Eliezer of Metz, who, because of doubt with regard to the *ḥallah* (which must be made from dough prepared by a Jew), would not allow his Gentile servant to do the kneading; this was therefore done by the Rabbi's wife.[4] Such restrictions would, of course, have made it futile to employ domestic help. So in the course of time a middle way was found. The servants were allowed to do all the domestic work, but the Jew or his wife maintained the fiction of participating in every household task done by the servant.[5] Once again we have here a

ha-Beynayim', *Be'oholey Ya'aqov*, pp. 236–7. The article appeared previously in *Zion*, iv, 1939, pp. 91–125.

[1] Maim., *Hilkhoth Sheḥiṭah*, 4. 4; cf. *Kesef Mishneh*, ibid.

[2] *Tosafoth*, *'A.Z.*, 38a; *'Or Zarua'*, *'A.Z.*, 163; *Mordekhai*, *'A.Z.*, 830.

[3] It is quoted as a suggestion of an anonymous halakhist by Eliezer of Mainz (see p. 38, n. 1), according to R. Joel Sirkis, *Bayith Ḥadash*, *Yoreh De'ah*, 113; cf. *She'eloth u-Theshuvoth Rashba* (attributed to Ramban), 149.

[4] *'Or Zarua'*, 1. 760.

[5] Eidelberg, *R. Gershom*, 20; Eliezer of Mainz, 303. The actual part of the

method of maintaining personal detachment from Gentile society even while actually living together in the same household with a representative of it.

We would be wrong to assume that this was the result of nothing but a petrified ritualistic attitude. The ritual situation is an accurate expression of the prevalent socio-religious one. A Christian servant was treated humanely in a Jewish household, according to the accepted standards of that time, but such humane conduct was necessarily limited by the nature of the Jewish family. The life of the Jewish family was based on its religious rites and ceremonies, and into these a Christian servant could not have been integrated. The situation is well characterized by the custom of distributing presents on the day of *Purim* to non-Jewish servants also. This practice was objected to by Rashi because it included Gentiles in an act which should have been reserved as a Jewish religious ceremony.[1] The ritual of segregation, even if only a relic, expressed the real nature of this situation.

Since no neutral social sphere was developed in the Middle Ages, social segregation between Jews and Gentiles was merely the logical consequence of their religious separation. To shun the other's religious rites was not merely prudent; avoidance of contact with the visible expressions of the Christian faith became almost an instinct with the Jew, who felt himself endangered spiritually, and perhaps even physically, whenever he encountered a Christian gathering performing its religious rites. We shall find many examples of this in the attitude of the *Ḥasid* (see Chapter VIII). At the reflective level, this trend was both controlled and encouraged by the halakhic tradition. As we have seen above, economic necessity was the reason for dispensing with many prescriptions whose intention was to prevent the Jew from coming into contact with 'alien worship'; and this dispensation was endorsed by the halakhists, although by such endorsement the Halakhah was but bowing to the force of reality, and no principle was established on the grounds of which a general dispensation could have been

Gentile's work in the Jewish household is reflected in *Tosafoth*, *'A.Z.*, 12a; *'Or Zarua'*, *'A.Z.*, 124. For the final regulation regarding the employment of Gentile servants see *Shulḥan 'Arukh*, *Yoreh De'ah*, 113.

[1] I. Elfenbein, *Teshuvoth Rashi*, 131.

given. The abrogation of certain details of the law was either an explicit concession to economic necessity or was made as a result of casuistic considerations. These very often entailed a distinction between the 'idols', i.e. the images venerated in Christian worship and their associated ritual objects on the one hand, and the economic value which they represented on the other. If the Christian priest himself quenched the lights which were burning in front of the holy image, or damaged the chalice used in worship, and then sold them to a Jew, did he not himself remove from them their sacral and, in Jewish eyes, obnoxious character?[1] Is not the garment of a priest given in pawn to a Jew to be regarded as the former's private property, even if it is used for the performance of religious ceremonies?[2] From such considerations emerged the obvious tendency to detract from the sacral quality of such objects and reduce them to their economic value. The method of dialectics in vogue in contemporary Jewish as well as Gentile society helped to achieve this objective.

Whether concessions were made by means of such dialectics, or merely in compliance with economic needs, they always retained the nature of a compromise. That 'alien worship' included Christian worship was inherent in the argument, and was sometimes explicitly stated; as, for instance, in the first source, where the problem of lending money on a priest's garments was discussed, by R. Gershom *Me'or Ha-Golah*.[3] The inquirer proposed a solution based on a consideration of the priestly garments as not belonging to the category of 'objects used in alien worship', but simply as the private property of the priest. R. Gershom rejects this view, using, characteristically, the analogy of the garments of the priests of the Temple at Jerusalem, which were regarded as sacred. In the same way, *mutatis mutandis*, the garments of the Christian priest must be regarded as pertaining to the ritual. It is because of the economic need that R. Gershom justifies the granting of permission to lend money on a priest's garments. Those who used dialectical distinctions in order to find a justification betrayed the

[1] *Tosafoth*, *'A.Z.*, 14b, 50a.

[2] *Tosafoth*, *'A.Z.*, 50b. This lenient view was not, however, universally accepted. R. Eliezer of Metz protested against permission being given on such grounds, *Sefer Yere'im*, p. 37a; cf. 36a.

[3] Eidelberg, *R. Gershom*, p. 21.

inconsistent character of their decisions by the qualifications which they attached to them. Some dealings were allowed, but others remained within the scope of the original law. In principle, then, Christian worship was still regarded as 'alien worship' even though the number of exceptions prevented the law of segregation from exercising any practical effect.

At any rate, permission was granted only where economic necessity demanded it, or where the process of neutralization could be facilitated by regarding the sacred objects as mere commodities. The images of Christian worship themselves were never exempted from the prohibition.[1] Reservations were also made where Christian worship was encountered *per se*, especially where no economic interests were involved. R. Eliezer of Metz besought his fellow Jews not to follow a Christian procession in the street for, even if unintentionally, they would thereby be joining in the accepted way of Christian worship. He adds that one could, by dialectical distinction, preclude this from being regarded as real worship, but that 'one should not rely on distinctions'.[2]

After analysis of the above facts, we may make some remarks on the interrelations between the social and religious forces which moulded the destiny of the Jewish community in this period. Economic necessity weighed heavily, and compelled the adjustment of tradition to prevailing circumstances. At the same time no less strong an influence was exercised by tradition, which operated as a corrective to this tendency. Such force was derived from the conservatism inherent in every tradition. This conservatism manifested itself in the retention by the Jewish communities of their historical identity, in spite of changes of environment and conditions and in the face of fierce religious opposition by Christianity. The fact that Rashi identified his community with the Israel of which biblical and talmudic tradition had spoken allowed him to interpret the events of his own time by using terms and concepts drawn from that tradition. The same motive prompted the halakhists to justify the legality of the adjustments in terms of

[1] This is implicit in the instances of the exemptions we have noted. Sometimes it is stated explicitly, e.g. Eliezer of Mainz, 289.

[2] *Sefer Yere'im*, p. 128a–b.

the ancient tradition. In spite of the apparent deviation from older practices, Jewish life was made to appear as a continuation of that of earlier times.

We may now formulate a view as to the real function of the Halakhah in the period in question. Its function was that of holding the balance between the two driving forces, namely the necessary adjustment to new conditions and the preservation of Jewish identity. That the Halakhah followed in the wake of social change has been observed very often by historians.[1] Again and again we have had occasion to refer to instances of this. But the other function, that of safeguarding Jewish identity by means of rationalization, is no less conspicuous a task. It was the achievement of the Halakhah that it prevented the community and the individual from being engulfed by the social and religious life of the Christian environment, by setting a limit to what might be conceded to the force of circumstances. The Halakhah was not responsible for creating the wish for social and religious disengagement. This arose spontaneously, from the community's adherence to its own image of its past as pictured by tradition. The barrier which served as the means of separation was but the logical consequence of the religious or mystical thinking of the Jewish community which accepted this position. The Halakhah was called upon to elaborate the details of the socio-religious separation. It did so by relying upon its own historical sources, and by taking into consideration the prevailing conditions. Its task was, in any case, to regulate and control; not to create, in the sense of producing new religious values or suggesting original social settings.

That the Halakhah was not the originator either of the adjustment or of the state of separateness is corroborated by its method of justification and control which we have repeatedly encountered during our analysis. Before concluding this chapter we may refer to one instance where this characteristic stands out with special clarity.

We possess a fragment of correspondence between two great halakhists of the twelfth century, Rabbenu Tam and his nephew, Rabbi Isaac. The correspondence concerns the problem of wine

[1] Lately much stressed by E. E. Urbach in his *Ba'aley Ha-Tosafoth*, pp. 50, 79, 203, 290, 430; cf. my remarks in *Qiryath Sefer*, 1955, pp. 9 ff.

prepared or touched by a Gentile. As we have seen above, economic conditions made the granting of permission for trading in such wine highly desirable. Rabbenu Tam gave permission and in his ingenious way found a justification for it in the sources. He put forward the suggestion which we have already noticed, namely that the Gentiles of his day did not fall within the category of idolaters in whose wine, during talmudic times, it was forbidden to trade. His correspondent was quite willing to acquiesce in this, but raised the objection that on this supposition one should be consistent and allow the wine of contemporary Gentiles for drinking, which appeared to him as inconceivable. Rabbenu Tam was so impressed with this argument that he withdrew his original ruling and resolved to find another justification for permitting wine as merchandise which would not entail the consequence of its being permitted for drinking also.[1]

One may well query the logic of this controversy. If Rabbenu Tam's original supposition is correct, why do these two halakhists recoil from the consequences of their own thought? The talmudic sources do not make any distinction between the Gentile's wine as an object of trade and as a commodity for personal consumption. If, therefore, the halakhists decided that contemporary Gentiles were not included in the prohibition, they would have been entitled to waive the prohibition for both purposes. That they did not do so was because, even though the two kinds of use were found to be logically on the same level of prohibition, in reality there were opposing interests connected with them. The use of wine for business was an economic necessity, and to grant permission for this purpose did not imply any social contact with non-Jews. The drinking of the wine, however, was regarded as leading to social and even sexual intercourse, as expressed in the concise definition of the Talmud: 'Their wine was forbidden on account of their daughters.'[2] The former concession, therefore, could be accepted, but the latter had to be rejected uncompromisingly. The weightiest factors bearing on the decision were thus the two tendencies, economic and religious, and the arguments of the Halakhah were merely a rationalization.

[1] *Tosafoth*, *'A.Z.*, 57b. [2] B.T., *'A.Z.*, 36b.

V

JURIDICAL AND MORAL CONTROLS

THERE remain some additional aspects of the relationship between Jewish and non-Jewish society. Jews were, of course, cognizant of the political and juridical institutions of the Gentile society within whose framework they had to conduct their lives. They had also to evolve a standard of moral behaviour in their dealings with both individuals and institutions outside their own social unit.

The usual legal basis on which Jews were admitted, and on which they were tolerated, in the Western countries was a *privilegium*,[1] i.e. a particular concession granted by the prevailing political authority in their locality. There is no indication that Jews claimed the right of residence on any other grounds, e.g. that of autochthony or inheritance. Even before the rise of the concept of *servi camerae*, which from the first half of the thirteenth century onwards made the Jews also the legal property of their rulers,[2] the dependence of the Jewish community on those who held political power was fully acknowledged on the Jewish side. Being free from political ambitions, Jews sought only the protection of the rulers; protection of life and property (and very often economic prosperity) was dependent on the goodwill of those with political power. Jews had every reason to favour public order, since any disturbance of it was likely to prove to their detriment.

The subjection of the various Jewish communities to the sovereigns of their respective countries could easily be justified by the Jews in terms of talmudic law and religious tradition. *Dina de-malekhutha dina* ('the law of the State is law'), the famous dictum of Samuel, one of the leading talmudic figures of Babylonian Jewry (third century),[3] was repeatedly quoted during the Middle

[1] For the definition of the term cf. G. Kisch, *Germany*, p. 135.

[2] For the much discussed problem of the development of *servi camerae* see Kisch, op. cit., pp. 143 ff.

[3] D. Hoffmann, *Mar Samuel, Rector der jüdischen Akademie zu Nahardea in Babylonien*, 1873, pp. 41–42.

Ages, in order to define the border-line between Jewish and non-Jewish law, where both of them had a valid claim. Because of the practical interest attaching to the definition of this dictum, it underwent various interpretations which seem to reflect some of the current political theories in the Middle Ages. According to one school of thought, originating from Rabbi Samuel ben Meir (Rashbam), the validity of laws and royal decrees derive from their being tacitly accepted by the subject.[1] This concept is in accordance with the general trend in medieval society to consider the ruler not as an original law-giver but merely as the guardian of the accepted legal system.[2] A younger contemporary of Rashbam, Rabbi Eliezer of Metz, connected the maxim of *dina de-malekhutha dina* with feudal law, according to which the ruler was the original possessor of all landed property in his country. If that were so, he was entitled to stipulate on what condition people might inhabit his country. On the same theory, the condition was the rendering of certain payments and services in return for permission to live on his land.[3]

Both these theories were intended to limit the power of the ruler to legislate. Such limitation was indeed taken for granted, and had in fact already been stated by Rashbam's brother, Rabbenu Tam. Laws and decrees of the ruler were valid only if they were based on the traditional law of the country or, according to another version, if they were imposed equally on all the inhabitants.[4] Arbitrary demands imposed upon certain individuals or sections of the population were of no validity.

It is outside the scope of this work to enlarge upon all the implications of these theories. What we are concerned to show is that the maxim *dina de-malekhutha dina* was taken seriously. This is proved by the endeavour to define it in such a way as to equate the validity of Jewish law with the current rights of the sovereign.

[1] Rashbam in his commentary on B.T., *Bava Bathra*, 54b.

[2] J. Posen in his Ph.D. thesis, *Dina de-malekhutha dina* (London University, 1951), pointed out that Rashbam's view is the reflection of the *consensus fidelium* which plays an important part in medieval political thinking. Cf. F. Kern, *Kingship and Law in the Middle Ages*, p. 73.

[3] *'Or Zarua'*, *Bava Qamma*, 446–7.

[4] In the original version of Rabbenu Tam's *responsum* published by I. A. Agus, *Responsa*, 12, the first limitation is applied; in the quotation of R. Eliezer of Metz in *'Or Zarua'*, loc. cit., the second. Cf. also Rosh, *Nedarim*, 3. 11.

Whatever force the words retained after being defined was to be regarded as sanctioned by the authority of talmudic law. The maxim at least assured the political allegiance of the Jews, as well as their acceptance of the prevailing financial burden of taxes and customs imposed upon the population. The observance of public law, including regulations concerning the monetary system (a sensitive organ of public life in the Middle Ages), was explicitly included in the definition.[1]

During the period in question, Jews had not yet given up their claim to regulate their relationship with the authorities on the basis of mutually acknowledged legal principles. In the case of a violation of their rights they even attempted a form of collective resistance. In twelfth-century France and thirteenth-century Germany we find that the authorities tried to confine the Jews to the localities of their rule. This was regarded by the Jews as illegal, and running counter to well-established rules according to which Jews were free to move 'like the knights'.[2] Jews resented and fought such infringements of their legal status, and Rabbenu Tam forbade his contemporaries to assist any such arrogation of the right to restrict it on the part of local authorities.[3] In other localities, where such open resistance was perhaps not feasible, halakhists resorted to the device of *reservatio mentalis*. Any oath which was forcibly extracted from Jews, to the effect that they would not quit a certain locality, could be countered by giving the oath a conditional interpretation.[4] This is, incidentally, an excellent example of medieval morality: the fact that one had been forced to undertake an obligation was not in itself sufficient reason for regarding the obligation as invalid. In order to invalidate it, it was necessary to resort to the dubious device of a subjective interpretation of the words used in uttering the enforced oath.

However, such occasional overt or covert clashes with the authorities cannot blur the overall picture of Jewish loyalty. We find this also expressed theoretically. The saying of the Fathers,

[1] See *infra*, p. 63.

[2] *Tosafoth, Bava Qamma*, 58a.

[3] The passage occurs twice in *Teshuvoth Maharam*, Lemberg edn., 114, and *Teshuvoth Rabbi Ḥayyim, 'Or Zarua'*, 179. Both texts are slightly corrupt. See Finkelstein, *Jewish Self-Government in the Middle Ages*, pp. 46–47, 106.

[4] *Tosafoth, Bava Qamma*, 113a.

'Pray for the welfare of the State', was interpreted as applying also to the Gentile State.[1] Moreover, the injunction seems to have been practised by the Ashkenazim in the Middle Ages in its literal sense: Jews prayed for the welfare of their rulers.[2]

This is, however, only part of the truth, and it is necessary to know the whole truth in order to grasp the complexity of the Jewish situation. For, as distinct from their political loyalty to the country in which they dwelt, Jews harboured deep reservations as to the ultimate significance of secular States which, seen in the perspective of the messianic hope, were but ephemeral. As we have previously noticed, a reversal of the existing order was envisaged in the messianic age, when the dispersed and humiliated Jewish nation was to come into its own. The entertaining of such hopes, and the prayer for their fulfilment, might well be considered as conflicting with a profession of loyalty, and this was indeed inferred by hostile parties in disputes with Jews, as we shall see later.[3] Nevertheless, although the contradiction could not be resolved logically, both sentiments (the messianic hope and the wish for the well-being of their temporal Gentile rulers) were genuinely held by Jews. This is only one of the many contradictory features which are characteristic of religious tenets in general and are especially inherent in Jewish religious tradition, reflecting the paradoxical character of the Jewish situation.

The *modus vivendi* of the Jewish community *vis-à-vis* political institutions around it was eased by the fact that the Jews had relinquished their role in political life. With regard to juridical institutions, however, it was the State (i.e. the sovereigns of the respective countries) who forbore to insist that Jewry obey the full authority of the prevailing system of law. It was one of the main features of Jewish autonomy in this age that the Jews were allowed to adhere to their own jurisdiction, which was based on talmudic

[1] *Maḥzor Vitry*, p. 505. The commentary belongs to R. Jacob b. Samson and was published separately by A. Berliner, 1897.

[2] The 'Prayer for the King' as a part of the Sabbath Liturgy is mentioned only in *Kol Bo* (fourteenth century), Venice edn., 1567, 11a; *'Abudarham* (fifteenth century); Singer, *Transactions of the Jewish Historical Society of England*, iv, pp. 102–9. However, there are indications of prayers of this kind in R. Ṭoviah b. 'Eliezer's commentary; Jellinek, *Liqquṭey Jellinek*, at the end of the commentary.

[3] See Chap. IX.

law.[1] Capital offences were exceptions to this rule and were dealt with by non-Jewish courts.[2] Relationships between Jews and non-Jews were, of course, entirely subject to non-Jewish authorities. Consequently, Jews lived under a plurality of systems of law and jurisdiction.

The existence of such a plural system, varying according to the social qualifications of the litigants, comes as no surprise to the student of medieval institutions. But the position of the Jew *vis-à-vis* juridical institutions is not adequately defined by the statement that he was subject to different systems of law and jurisdiction. More important is the fact that he accepted this state of affairs because, living as he did in a foreign country and under foreign rule, it was unavoidable. Moreover, as the state in question was regarded as merely transient, it was not to be inferred that any part of the Jewish law could, as a consequence, be abrogated. Talmudic law was considered as valid *in toto*, its implementation being dependent on circumstances. Similarly, the acknowledgement of any other system of law to which a Jew might have had to submit was merely to comply with necessity. This reservation *vis-à-vis* Gentile laws and jurisdiction did not stem from an objection to their contents. It is true that Jews sometimes took exception to certain details of judicial procedure; they abhorred the various kinds of ordeal, and made every effort to be exempted from them when summoned before a Gentile court.[3] On the other hand, they took it for granted that Gentile judges sometimes applied the same rules of law and justice as did judges of their own faith, and even conceded that Gentile jurisdiction was sometimes superior to that of Jewish courts.[4] Moreover, an appeal to a non-Jewish court made with the consent of both parties was not always ruled out. In France such

[1] O. Stobbe, *Die Juden in Deutschland während des Mittelalters*, 3rd edn., pp. 140 ff.; J. E. Scherer, *Die Rechtsverhältnisse der Juden in den deutsch-österreichischen Ländern*, pp. 170–1; Kisch, *Germany*, pp. 172–3; Finkelstein, *Self-Government*, pp. 6 ff.

[2] Scherer, op. cit., pp. 171–2; Kisch, op. cit., pp. 185 ff.

[3] Stobbe, op. cit., p. 153; Scherer, op. cit., p. 163; Kisch, op. cit., pp. 139, 266–7.

[4] This is implied in the quotation of Rashi on Exod. xxi. 1, from B.T., *Giṭṭin*, 88b, that even if the Gentiles' 'law is the same as the Israelite law you must not resort to them'. See *Sefer Ḥasidim*, ed. Wistinetzki, 1301.

a practice was explicitly sanctioned at the time of Rabbenu Tam.[1] Nevertheless, this again must have been more of a concession to accepted usage than a ruling arrived at on halakhic principles. For talmudic tradition contained an unqualified prohibition of appealing to non-Jewish courts, and Rashi, quoting it in his commentary on the Pentateuch (Exod. xxi. 1), underlined its uncompromising character.[2] The reason for this prohibition, and for Rashi's emphasis, is the linking of jurisdiction with religious concepts and ceremonies. Indeed, the interweaving of religion and law which is so characteristic of the Jewish tradition itself is the main reason for the adherence of the Jewish community to its own legal system. The acceptance of an alien jurisdiction was considered as the discarding of an integral part of the Jewish heritage. Hence an appeal to non-Jewish courts in cases which concerned Jewish litigants tended to be regarded as the final resort only, if the Jewish opponent refused to appear before a Jewish court or to abide by its decision.[3]

In theory the Jewish legal system was regarded as self-sufficient, but in practice the Jewish courts and jurists (i.e. the halakhists) did not entirely disregard legal rulings and enactments emanating from non-Jewish sources. If non-Jewish authorities ruled on the question of the payment of debts following the devaluation of the currency, as is reported to have occurred at the time of Rabbenu Tam,[4] were the Jewish courts to disregard this ruling and have recourse to the Jewish law for regulating the payment between Jewish creditors and debtors? Or, if a Jew acquired certain rights as affecting a fellow Jew resulting from a contract with a non-Jew,

[1] Finkelstein, *Self-Government*, p. 153.

[2] Finkelstein's conjecture (op. cit., p. 156, n. 1) that this concession is a result of the evaluation of Christianity as a non-idolatrous religion is untenable. The real nature of the attitude to Christianity as we have observed it in the previous chapters excludes this view. However, in *'Or Zarua'*, *Bava Qamma*, 1–4, there is a clear attempt to reconcile this practice with the sources on casuistic lines. Some similar device must have likewise served Rabbenu Tam in his harmonization.

[3] In this case an appeal to non-Jewish courts was sanctioned by R. Joseph *Ṭov 'Elem* on the basis of an ingenious interpretation of a passage in B.T., *Bava Qamma*, 92b. See *Semag*, p. 189b. This was made dependent theoretically on permission granted by a Jewish court.

[4] *Teshuvoth Maharam*, Prague edn., 358; *Sefer ha-Terumoth*, 46. 8.

could these rights be contested on the grounds that they were based on a non-Jewish legal ruling?[1] In such cases the halakhists usually accepted the consequences of the Gentile ruling as binding also for internal Jewish practice. This was not regarded, however, as an infringement of the Jewish legal system. It was in order to assimilate such foreign elements that the above-mentioned maxim *dina de-malekhutha dina* was mainly applied. It meant that legal rulings of non-Jewish origin were regarded as valid within the Jewish system also. Although some elements of alien origin did penetrate into the system of Jewish law in this way, its workability and authority have remained unimpaired. The alien elements became part and parcel of the system. The principle of *dina de-malekhutha dina*, so far from being an implement undermining the institutions of Jewish law, became an instrument of its preservation: it served as a method of adaptation to the requirements of the non-Jewish environment.

How far the integrity of the Jewish legal system was preserved, at least in theory, can best be understood by considering the halakhists' stand on those points of the law which concerned mixed litigation, i.e. when one of the parties was a Jew and the other a non-Jew. Talmudic law, as all other legal systems of antiquity, was pluralistic, preserving different rulings according to whether both the litigants were Jews, or one was a Jew and the other a Gentile. We shall consider presently the difference in standards. So far as the Middle Ages were concerned, the double standard had scarcely any application. For litigation between Jews and non-Jews was dealt with by non-Jewish courts. The fact that this part of the Jewish law was not in use did not, however, mean that it was abrogated. As we have previously mentioned, the halakhists did not possess any authority to pronounce such formal abrogation. Moreover, although this part of the law was not practised, it was taken into account in so far as it had legal or ritual consequences for internal Jewish affairs. Talmudic law, for instance, established different procedures for conveying property from one Jew to another and for conveying it from a Jew to a non-Jew, or vice versa. Whereas in the first case the payment of money was decisive, in the

[1] Eliezer b. Nathan of Mainz, iii, p. 63b.

other the seizure of property paid for signified the acquired right of possession.[1] As business dealings with non-Jews were conducted according to non-Jewish rules, this had no practical significance. But where matters of ritual were concerned, this distinction was not discarded. Property conveyed from a Jew to a non-Jew entailed different obligations according as to whether, at a given moment, it was to be regarded as belonging to the Jew or the non-Jew. Thus, if the property in question was a cow in calf which gave birth while in the possession of a Jew, it involved the obligations laid down in Num. xviii. 17–18. According to this the Jewish owner was obliged to give the first-born calf to one of priestly descent. As, however, priests had had no real function since the destruction of the Temple, this was regarded as a formal duty only and legal means of avoiding it were sought. A fictitious sale to a Gentile was recommended, and practised in the Middle Ages. Yet even in connexion with such a fictitious transaction the legal formulas had to be observed in all their niceties.[2]

This distinction also had a bearing upon litigation between two Jews where one of them acted as the agent of the other in dealings with a non-Jew. If the non-Jew, by an oversight, left an unexpected profit in the hands of the Jewish agent, the question arose, whose was the benefit—the agent's or his employer's? The decision was dependent upon legal considerations, taking into account the mode of acquisition when one party is a non-Jew. Such cases were indeed brought before Jewish judges, who dealt with them on the basis of accepted legal propositions, even if they had moral misgivings as to the equity of their ruling.[3]

This instance brings us to the subject of the moral attitude of Jews in their contact with Gentiles.

The sociological notion of a dual standard, 'internal ethics' and 'external ethics', has been exemplified by Max Weber in reference to

[1] B.T., *Bekhoroth*, 13a–b.

[2] *Tosafoth*, *'A.Z.*, 71a.

[3] Rabbenu Tam, *Sefer Ha-Yashar*, Berlin edn., 53. 2, 54. 2; *Maharam*, Prague edn., 252–4; *'Or Zarua'*, *Bava Qamma*, 415. Failure to mention the moral point of view is no proof of lack of moral scruples. Halakhists used likewise to adhere strictly to the legal point in question also when dealing with litigation between Jews.

the medieval Jewish community, whose members acknowledged obligations towards each other different from those recognized towards individuals of the Gentile community.[1] Although Weber pointed out that this was a universal social phenomenon—the members of any cohesive social unit observing different moral standards among themselves from those observed by it in relation to strangers—he was right in depicting the medieval Jewish community as an extreme case in point, in order to demonstrate this sociological rule.

In order to arrive at a balanced appreciation of the Jewish situation, it is necessary to enumerate its main features. The Jewish community in the Middle Ages belonged to general society in so far as its political position and its economic functions were concerned. Politically, it was dependent on the protection of those who were the upholders of law and order in the various localities. Economically, it fulfilled a desirable function for at least some sections of Christian society. Socially, however, medieval Jewry remained unintegrated. Historical research has established the existence of common features and reciprocal influences in the sphere of social and even of religious life among Jews and Christians. There was also frequent and varied contact between the two communities. Similarity, reciprocal influence, and frequent contact are not, however, tantamount to social integration; to achieve this, members of different groups which live within the same social framework must be consciously aware of some common values. Such a consciousness does not necessarily efface the boundaries between the different groups, which may well preserve their particular cohesion and exclusiveness. But the acknowledgement of values held in common with the members of other groups does engender the consciousness of a common responsibility, and secures a minimum of moral consideration by each for the other.

Medieval society was deficient, where the Jews were concerned, in that, although it included groups of Jews, the system of values on which it rested excluded them from participating in it. Conversely the Jewish community, in spite of being a part of another society, retained *in toto* its own system of values which presupposed

[1] M. Weber, *General Economic History*, pp. 359 f.; see also pp. 357 ff.

the existence of a self-sufficing and separate Jewish society. The historical roots of this state of affairs go back to the first centuries of the Christian era, but its graver consequences were revealed in the Middle Ages only, when both communities lived in close proximity as sections of the same society. The situation can best be characterized by stating that, in the absence of a common source of moral authority, the communities were unable to base their relationship on a mutually acceptable scale of values. In establishing a practical attitude towards the members of the other community, both Jews and Gentiles relied on their own religious tradition. Since both traditions were particularistic, each attributing a greater spiritual and moral worth to its own adherents, a double standard of ethics was the inevitable result.

An example of this double standard is the problem of taking interest on money-lending. As is well known, the Catholic Church regarded the taking of interest as morally indefensible.[1] It therefore forbade it to its own members, as being pernicious to their spiritual welfare. This prohibition applied in principle to Jews as well, but in practice society at large condoned the taking of interest by Jews—their spiritual welfare being of no concern to Christians. Similarly, a double standard was to be observed in Jewish morality in this regard; it was not blameworthy to take interest from a non-Jew.[2] Among Jews themselves, the taking of interest was considered as infringing the biblical prohibition. Thus each society regarded the members of the other from the point of view of their usefulness. Christian society was interested in the facility of borrowing money, and it used the Jews as a means for an activity which it regarded as morally reprehensible. Jews, who relied mainly upon money-lending for their livelihood, took interest from Gentiles without compunction. Moral and legalistic

[1] Bibliography and a good summary of the problem in J. Parkes, *Community*, pp. 269 ff.; J. T. Noonan, Jr., *The Scholastic Analysis of Usury*, Cambridge, Massachusetts, 1957.

[2] Talmudic tradition contained some reflection on the taking of interest even from non-Jews, B.T., *Bava Meṣi'a*, 70b–71a, but this carried no weight against the accepted practice. Cf. *Tosafoth*, *Bava Meṣi'a*, 70b; see also *supra*, Chap. II. In the Middle Ages only Judah *He-Ḥasid* could dream of an occupation not involving the taking of interest, cf. *Sefer Ḥasidim*, 1958. See S. Stein, 'The Development of the Jewish Law on Interest, &c.', *Historia Judaica*, xvii, 1955, pp. 3–40.

considerations entered into the picture only when the taking of interest concerned dealings between one Jew and another.

Although the interrelationship between Jewish and Christian society was based on considerations of expediency, it does not mean that every individual approached the members of the opposite society merely with a view to his personal advantage. Such an attitude is usual in respect of itinerant traders, but it would have been intolerable here in view of the close intercourse which prevailed between Jews and Gentiles as a result of their continuous contact with each other. If, therefore, a universal standard of morality equating internal and external ethics could not be achieved (and this in any case lay beyond the aspirations of medieval society, Jewish and Gentile alike), neither could Jewish relationship with the outer world be left uncontrolled and subject only to the decision of the individual. Indeed, mere self-interest must have impressed upon the Jew the need to exercise moral restraint in his relations with Gentiles. A characteristic story is told by Rabbi Me'ir of Rothenburg of a Jew who warned his Jewish partner to state the real value of a silver vessel that he was about to sell to a Gentile because he 'is my friend (*'ohavi*), and I do not want to mislead him'.[1] No moral principle need be assumed in order to account for such behaviour: the value of goodwill in a business relationship, based on integrity, is reason enough. Permanency in business relationships between Jews and Gentiles is well attested in the sources, a special term (of Arabic origin) *ma'arufya*[2] being applied to the non-Jewish member of this relationship. It meant that a Jew acquired the right to be the only one in his community satisfying all the financial and commercial needs of a Gentile. One of the sources even mentions a covenant (*berith*) being concluded between Jews and Gentiles.[3] What is meant is probably a permanent association or partnership for business transactions, such as was not uncommon between traders in the Middle Ages. In the course of such continuous contact not only friendship, but also a feeling of common humanity might well have sprung up

[1] *Maharam*, Prague edn., 482.

[2] Cf. Hoffmann, *Der Geldhandel*, p. 95; Zimmels, *Beiträge*, p. 111.

[3] *Sefer Ḥasidim*, 1266.

between Jew and Gentile. Such a feeling is the only real basis for the growth of a natural morality.

Although opportunities for such associations between Jews and Gentiles were not lacking, they were not extensive enough for the development of a systematic morality or comprehensive scale of values. The individual was able to derive guidance for his moral behaviour from his immediate human contact with members of the other camp. We shall find examples of this when describing the attitude of the *Ḥasid*. For the theoretical evaluation of moral standards, however, the *Ḥasid* and his contemporaries relied upon the traditional ideas by which the reflective thinking of those generations was moulded.

What were the sources from which ideas could be drawn for the moral control of relationships with the outer world? A consideration of this problem demonstrates at once how perplexing the situation was. The different legal systems which regulated the relationships between Jews and non-Jews on the one hand, and between Jews and fellow Jews on the other, must have encouraged different notions as to moral conduct in the respective relationships. The ruling of the non-Jewish courts could have exercised but slight moral influence, if any, on the members of the Jewish community. Since Jews submitted to non-Jewish courts solely because of their sanctions, it is doubtful whether Jews were able or willing to accept Gentile standards for their moral conduct. In spite of occasional appeals by Jews to these courts, the prevailing opinions concerning their rulings are deprecatory. The belief that Jewish law was of divine origin, whereas Gentile law was a purely human invention, linked any evaluation with the most fundamental theological tenet of Judaism. The moral conduct of the Jew towards Gentiles, if it was not to be determined solely by expediency and prudence, could have been influenced only by principles derived exclusively from Jewish sources.

The talmudic tradition, which was the chief guide for the medieval Jew, contains many wholesome maxims urging fairness and loving-kindness towards all human beings, irrespective of their religious or national affiliation. 'We support the heathen poor along with the poor of Israel, visit the heathen sick along with the sick of Israel, and bury their dead along with the dead of Israel in the interest of peace' (B.T., *Giṭṭin*, 61a). Similarly, the moral duty of refraining from any kind of deceit or false pretence included in the notion of *genevath daʿath* was explicitly imposed upon the Jew in his relations with Gentiles also.[1] These maxims were often quoted in the Middle Ages, not only in an apologetic connexion but also for the purpose of genuine admonition.[2]

Similar to the function of these maxims is that of the notion of *Ḥillul ha-Shem* and *Qiddush ha-Shem*, i.e. the desecration or sanctification of the Holy Name. These terms appear in the Talmud, *inter alia* in connexion with the controversy as to whether or not a Gentile's property is directly under the protection of Jewish law. According to Rabbi ʿAqiva's view, the law does not recognize any difference between Jew and Gentile so far as the protection of his possessions is concerned. However, his contemporary, Rabbi Ishmael, seems to have held the view that, fundamentally, the law concerns itself only with relations between Jew and Jew.[3] The protection of the Gentiles' property therefore has to be secured by a supplementary principle. This principle is that of the sanctification of the Holy Name. It is derived from the concept of the Jewish religious mission: Jews are under an obligation to affirm the ideal of their religion in a world that would deny it. The term *Qiddush ha-Shem* implies, indeed, the obligation of the Jew to sacrifice his life rather than transgress the main precepts of his religion.[4] In the context mentioned above it appears as the source of obligation for exemplary moral behaviour. If a Gentile found a Jew dealing unfairly in business, it would reflect on the Jew not merely as an individual but as a representative of his faith. The wish to make the Jewish religion attractive, or at least to avoid its being discredited by the behaviour of its adherents, thus became the motive of an appeal for morality.

Medieval halakhists had no need to resort to this principle for the protection of a Gentile's property. They accepted, perhaps

[1] B.T., *Ḥullin*, 94a.

[2] Eliezer b. Nathan of Mainz, iii, p. 40a; *Sefer Yere'im*, p. 50a; *Wikkuaḥ Rabbi Yeḥiel*, Thorn edn., p. 10.

[3] B.T., *Bava Qamma*, 113a–b.

[4] We shall deal with this aspect of the term in Chap. VII.

with one exception,[1] Rabbi 'Aqiva's view that the Gentile's property is directly protected by law. Nevertheless they often invoked the notion of *Qiddush ha-Shem* and *Ḥillul ha-Shem*, sometimes to strengthen the binding power of the law and sometimes to fill a gap not covered by the law. Although the property of the Gentile was protected by the law, some cases arose in which it was possible to justify a legal course of action which ought to be rejected on moral grounds—as for instance the above-mentioned instance where a Jew derived a profit as the result of the oversight of a Gentile. The principle of *Qiddush ha-Shem* served in such cases as a corrective to the law. As this principle was applicable in relationships with Gentiles only, it can be said with some justification that the concern for fairness in relations with outsiders was supported by a motive which was lacking in internal relations. It was in this sense that the following passage of the Tosefta was quoted: 'It is more blameworthy to steal from a Gentile than from a Jew, because of the desecration of the Holy Name.'[2]

Such ethical teachings do credit to their authors, and even more to those who lived by them. We have no means of assessing the extent to which they were in fact followed. It would be rating human nature too high to assume that the average Jew was guided by these principles in his dealings with Gentiles. Several weighty factors counteracted moral striving. No moral teaching could change the realities of religious rivalry, social segregation, and the plurality of legal systems. All these must have encouraged a double standard of behaviour. Those who were reluctant to be guided by the ideal of a higher morality had the letter of the law on their side. Nobody could be compelled to accept the demands of morality if he was not prompted to do so by his own conscience. This was emphasized on a particular occasion by one of the great authorities, himself a person of high moral stature. Two Jewish litigants appealed to Rabbi Me'ir of Rothenburg for a decision in a case where a profit made by dealing with a Gentile was contested. One of the litigants seems to have suggested that his opponent return

[1] *Sefer Yere'im*, p. 50a–b. The passage is not, however, entirely clear. For a positive attitude, *Semag*, p. 58b; *'Or Zarua'*, *Bava Qamma*, 445; *Teshuvoth R. Ḥayyim*, *'Or Zarua'*, 253.

[2] *Sefer Ḥasidim*, 1414; *Semag*, p. 58b.

the whole of the gain to the Gentile as an act of calculated *Qiddush ha-Shem.* Rabbi Me'ir of Rothenburg, however, retorted that 'if he wishes the Holy Name to be sanctified, he must do so at his own expense and not at that of others'.[1]

The most that the moralists could do was to remind their congregants and readers of their responsibility as members of a religious minority, which was likely to be judged by the deeds of each individual. This was particularly apposite where individuals were inclined to find justification for acts which, on closer examination, were revealed as transgressions not merely of morality but also of the law. That such cases were not lacking is self-evident even when one disregards the peculiarities of the situation, but the accepted double standard made the drawing of a line between the permissible and the forbidden somewhat precarious. We have been able to follow with some sympathy the use of *reservatio mentalis* by Jews who were compelled to take the oath on an obligation which was illegally imposed upon them. Once the institution of *reservatio mentalis* was accepted, it was inevitable that unscrupulous individuals would make use of it to allay their consciences. We are told of a case where the burghers of a town exacted an oath from Jews to refrain from clipping the current coins. As tampering with coins was an almost universal malpractice in the Middle Ages, it is perhaps understandable that the Jews felt less compunction concerning the practice itself than concerning the transgression of their oath (for which they had a superstitious reverence). They sought the remedy in a *reservatio mentalis*, and even dared to approach a halakhic authority for a decision which would legalize their behaviour. The case was brought to the attention of Rabbi Me'ir of Rothenburg and drew from him a most severe condemnation.[2]

Rabbi Me'ir reinforces his moral indignation with rational exposition. His reasoning contains all the elements which might furnish a Jew with motivations for law-abiding and moral behaviour in his relations with Gentiles. First, the law which protects the value of the currency is a valid law (*dina de-malekhutha dina*), 'and even without the precept of this king it would be law'. Secondly,

[1] *Maharam*, Prague edn., 326. [2] *Maharam*, Lemberg edn., 246.

debasing the coinage is tantamount to stealing another's property, and this is forbidden equally in respect to a Jew and a non-Jew. Thirdly, an oath given in a just cause is fully valid, and *reservatio mentalis* is irrelevant and dishonest. Transgression of the oath entails a clear case of *Ḥillul ha-Shem*. Finally, such practices on the part of a Jew are likely to endanger innocent individuals as well as communities. For the latter argument Rabbi Me'ir adduces the plight of the Jews in France and in England, whose expulsion he attributes to similar malpractices, although this is historically incorrect.

This famous *responsum* of one of the greatest authorities of the Middle Ages is a summary of the teachings of medieval Judaism concerning Jewish-Gentile relations. But in order to assess its historical importance, we have to consider it against the background of its context. Moral teachings had to be upheld in the face of a situation which was fraught with temptations to evasion and self-justification. Lofty as were the sentiments, their formulation bore the marks of the situation. They are far from forming the elements of a universalistic ethic. They took social duality for granted. They made a praiseworthy attempt to create motives for moral behaviour towards members of a society with which no community of religion, and hardly any common humanity, was acknowledged. This is why their practical achievements cannot be rated very highly.

Within the framework of the medieval situation limited variations only were possible. The situation itself could be transcended through a softening of the religious antagonism, by a perception that Jews and Christians held certain religious and human values in common. Many generations, however, were to elapse before this came about. So far as the Jews were concerned, it was first achieved (earlier than on the Christian side) in the teaching of Menaḥem Ha-Me'iri at the beginning of the fourteenth century. We shall see later when, and under what conditions, his teaching and its theoretical consequences bore fruit in practice. Where such an equation of common values was not achieved, the basic situation of dualistic character persisted.

PART II

SOME TYPES AND ATTITUDES IN MEDIEVAL TIMES (TENTH TO FOURTEENTH CENTURIES)

VI

APOSTATES AND PROSELYTES

SINCE, in the period in question, Jews and Gentiles lived in such close proximity, there was always the possibility that individuals might change from one religion to the other. The only way of preventing such occurrences was by maintaining a rigid standard of mutual exclusiveness. As we have seen, however, Christianity kept its doors wide open for the whole of the Jewish community (although in practice it was only individuals who crossed the threshold) and, as we shall see presently, Jewish teachers adopted the same attitude towards Christians, the only difference being that the likelihood of all Christians converting to Judaism was even more remote; indeed, it was at most a messianic hope.[1] One of the most characteristic features of the social situation was the readiness of either community to welcome as members those outside it, on condition that they changed their religion. As we are here particularly concerned with the attitude of the Jews, it will be necessary to examine what were the consequences of this situation: to what extent did cases of apostasy and proselytization occur, and what was the Jewish attitude towards them?

Our sources do not allow us to come to a conclusion concerning either the absolute or the relative numbers of Jews who embraced Christianity in the Ashkenazi community of the Middle Ages. We have sufficient indications, however, to determine the sociological character of such apostasies as did occur. Their most striking feature is that they were isolated cases. The only contradictory source is Rabbenu Tam, who mentions that twenty apostates divorced their wives 'in Paris and *Francia*'.[2] It is more likely, however, that this is the total of a number of cases which occurred at different times rather than a reference to one event. The fact

[1] See *infra*, p. 80, nn. 1–3.

[2] The word *Ṣarefath* is used, probably meaning the province Île-de-France. Cf. H. Gross, *Gallia Judaica*, pp. 369, 468; Krauss, in *Jewish Studies in Memory of G. A. Kohut*, p. 407.

that two localities are mentioned suggests this interpretation, even more so the fact that the men alone, and not their wives, are said to have become converts to Christianity. Had a mass conversion taken place, such division according to sex would have been most unlikely. It is true that in times of persecution whole groups were sometimes baptized, either forcibly or with consent under threat of force.[1] Such converts, however, not being genuine, made every effort to return to the Jewish fold.[2] Whether to accept baptism *post factum*, or to extricate oneself from it at a price which must sometimes have involved danger to life, was again a question to be decided by the individual.[3] The Jewish community was well aware of the existence of *'anusim*, i.e. forced converts. In prayers for the welfare of the Jewish community these were specially mentioned.[4] It was deemed especially meritorious to assist them in their attempt to escape from Christianity.[5] All this is well in keeping with the assumption that the apostates were more or less isolated individuals. Neither voluntary nor forced converts played a part, so far as we know, as a distinguishable social unit in Christian society in France or Germany as they did in Spain.

That apostasies occurred in individual cases only does not mean that they were not frequent enough to be of great significance for the Jewish community. We have abundant proof in the sources to the contrary. The preoccupation of the halakhists with the legal problems arising from the status of the convert may be adduced as the first indication of this. Even more important was the stand taken by the halakhists on the questions discussed. The general trend prevailing in their discussions was to designate the apostate (*mumar* or *meshummad*[6]) as a 'sinning Jew' who, by his baptism,

[1] The best-known case is that of the First Crusade, cf. Graetz, *Geschichte der Juden*, 4th edn., vi, pp. 82–92; J. Parkes, *Community*, pp. 65–78.

[2] On the permission granted by the Emperor Henry IV to those forcibly baptized during the First Crusade to return to Judaism, and the Church's opposition to this, see Graetz, op. cit., pp. 92–93, and Parkes, op. cit., pp. 79–81.

[3] Cf. *Sefer Ḥasidim*, Berlin edn., 1891, 200, 201, 209.

[4] *Maḥzor Vitry*, p. 179.

[5] *Sefer Ḥasidim*, quoted *supra*, n. 3; see *infra*, pp. 69 f., for the motivation of the halakhist's decision concerning the apostates.

[6] These two terms already appear in alternation in the non-censored talmudic sources. See W. Bacher, 'Der Ausdruck Mumar in den Handschriften des Babylonischen Talmud', *Zeitschrift für hebräische Bibliographie*, xii, 1908, pp. 39–40.

neither lost his Jewish identity nor exempted himself from any obligation incumbent on a Jew by virtue of his birth.

We first encounter this tendency in the decision concerning the possibility of the apostate's returning to the fold after baptism, even if this had been voluntary. That the apostate might return, and was indeed obliged to do so, was never even questioned. Doubts arose only as to whether, having returned, he could be fully rehabilitated. In a strictly halakhic sense the question concerned only those of priestly origin (*kohanim*) who retained some prerogatives, such as that of being called first to the reading of the *Torah* and administering the priestly benediction on the days of festivals. There existed a tradition from the time of the Second Temple that the priest who participated in idol worship should be excluded for ever from taking part in any sacred function.[1] Some gaonic sources applied the same rule to the apostate.[2] This view was also upheld by one of the early Ashkenazi authorities, Rabbi Eliezer Ha-Gadol. He decided in a particular case that a *kohen* who, having apostatized, returned to Judaism should not be allowed to repeat the priestly benediction.[3] But this decision was repudiated by his greater contemporary, Rabbenu Gershom *Me'or Ha-Golah*.[4] The latter based his decision on moral grounds. The doctrine of repentance, *Teshuvah*, the universal applicability of which was an established Jewish tenet, in this case overruled what was merely a relic of an antiquated moral code. This code ascribed to those of priestly descent a sacred quality by virtue of their birth, regardless of personal merits or demerits. Moreover, once this sacred quality had been impaired it could not be regained by means of repentance. Rabbenu Gershom explicitly rejected this proposition. He extended the efficacy of repentance to those of priestly descent also, and assured the apostate full rehabilitation. The wording of Rabbenu Gershom's *responsum* clearly shows his motive in reaching this conclusion: any restriction on the rehabilitation of penitents would

[1] B.T., *Menaḥoth*, 109a.

[2] *Ḥemdah Genuzah*, 54; *Tosafoth*, *Menaḥoth*, 109a.

[3] I. A. Agus, *Teshuvoth Ba'aley Ha-Tosafoth*, 3. However, this authority did grant the *kohen* the right to be the first-called to the reading of the *Torah*.

[4] The *responsum* is printed in Eidelberg, *Teshuvoth Rabbenu Gershom Me'or Ha-Golah*, 4.

deter apostates from finding their way back to Judaism. To regain the lost members of their community, moreover, was the supreme objective of the Jews of the time. Rabbenu Gershom's decision was reiterated by Rashi and many other halakhic authorities.[1]

The principle that the apostate remained a Jew was upheld even in the case of one who persisted in his apostasy, although this led to grave consequences so far as his Jewish relatives were concerned. If the apostate was regarded as a Jew, his wife was still a married woman and could not remarry unless he consented to divorce her according to Jewish law. In such cases all possible means were used to bring pressure upon the apostate to divorce his wife.[2] Very often this seems to have been achieved, though certainly not always. In the latter cases the apostate's wife was doomed to a perpetual state of unmarried life. In spite of this it was, apparently, never suggested that the apostate, by severing himself from the Jewish community and its religion, had become a Gentile and that his wife should therefore be able to remarry without divorce. In gaonic times it was proposed by some correspondents of the *Ge'onim* that the apostate, being no longer a Jew, had become incapable of divorcing his wife according to Jewish law.[3] This view seems to have been adopted by R. Nathan, author of the *'Arukh*, and by his brother R. Abraham of Rome.[4] Characteristically, however, this proposition was tacitly disregarded by later authorities.

The consequences of the apostate being regarded as a Jew were not restricted to his wife alone. Since the levirate marriage (Deut. xxv. 5–10) had not been abolished, the widowed sister-in-law of the apostate, if she was childless, was bound, in theory, either to marry him or to induce him to submit to the ceremony of *ḥaliṣah* (in which the shoe of her brother-in-law was drawn off). Since in this case it was out of the question to apply the original intention of the law, namely the marrying of the widow by her brother-in-law,

[1] I. Elfenbein, *Teshuvoth Rashi*, 168–70; *Tosafoth, Menaḥoth*, 109a.

[2] The practice of compelling the apostate through the agency of non-Jewish authorities to divorce his wife is mentioned—and sanctioned—by *Mordekhai, Giṭṭin*, 450. The attempt to induce the apostate to do so by paying him is mentioned in *Teshuvoth Maharam*, Prague edn., 1022.

[3] *Ḥemdah Genuzah*, 51, 88.

[4] Cf. my article in *Tarbiz*, xxvii, 1958, p. 219.

there was every reason to seek a solution that would exempt her from this formal bond. Some gaonic authorities did indeed try to achieve this, at least in some cases. Their argument was that the *Torah* speaks of brothers, who are duty-bound to marry each other's childless widows. The apostate, however, had forsaken his Jewish brotherhood, and was therefore not considered a possible husband to succeed his deceased brother.[1] This argument was rejected by Rashi, for no other reason than that of consistency in defining the apostate as a Jew.[2] It was in this connexion that Rashi quoted the maxim 'although he has sinned he remains a Jew', which has, since then, become a standard ruling in connexion with the definition of the status of the apostate. In its original talmudic context this sentence appears in an aggadic setting only, and not in relation to apostasy.[3] By using it in this striking manner, Rashi ensured the almost uncontested adoption of his definition.[4] Behind this clear-cut statement lies an emphasis on the unchangeable character of the Jew, an emphasis that would contest any possible justification for obliterating Judaism by baptism.

That Rashi's definition had a polemical aim is evident from the use that he made of it in another connexion, viz. that of lending money on interest to an apostate. As many apostates continued to have economic relations with the members of their former community, and as money-lending became more and more the main basis of Jewish economic existence, the question was of practical importance. There was, therefore, a strong incentive to seek a justification, based on some halakhic authority, for taking interest from an apostate. This was found on the following grounds: since taking interest was forbidden between Jews only (Deut. xxiii. 21), the apostate who severed himself from his brothers was to be regarded as a 'stranger', to whom the prohibition did not apply.[5]

[1] The gaonic sources are collected in B. M. Lewin's *'Oṣar Ha-Ge'onim*, vii, pp. 34–37.

[2] *Teshuvoth Rashi*, 173.

[3] A. Berliner, 'Zur Charakteristik Rashis', *Gedenkbuch zur Erinnerung an David Kaufmann*, p. 271; cf. p. 204 in my article quoted *supra*, p. 70, n. 4.

[4] The halakhic consequences of this dictum were not always accepted; cf. my article quoted *supra*. The definition itself, however, remained uncontested.

[5] This reason is given as grounds for the permission by later authorities only, Rabbenu Tam in *Teshuvoth Maharam*, Prague edn., 799; Eliezer of Metz, *Sefer Yere'im*, p. 73b, *infra*. The permission itself, however, seems to have originated

Once again Rashi reiterated that a Jew, 'even though he has sinned, remains a Jew', and so forbade the taking of interest from an apostate.[1]

Rashi's decision was not universally accepted. As the taking of interest was an economic necessity some of the halakhists tried to maintain the more lenient view, which was not entirely without halakhic authority.[2] But the extent to which Rashi's view influenced the thinking of the following generations can be gathered from the manner in which his definition was applied to the status of the apostate in relation to the law of inheritance. There was unanimous agreement concerning the right of the Jewish community to deny the apostate the inheritance of his Jewish relatives' estate. Some of the privileges granted to the communities by the non-Jewish authorities contained an explicit acknowledgement of this right.[3] The halakhists, for their part, tried to point to the legal source of this accepted ruling. Some of the *Ge'onim*,[4] and Rabbenu Gershom *Me'or Ha-Golah*,[5] declared the disinheritance of the apostate to be a biblical law. They cited the biblical instances of Ishmael and Esau, who were both virtually disinherited in favour of their respective brothers, Isaac and Jacob.[6] The same rule was to be applied to any relative who apostatized. This argument must have had a strong appeal, especially since its legal consequence was in accord with accepted practice as well as with the prevailing attitude towards the apostate. Nevertheless, it was rejected—probably by Rashi himself,[7] and certainly by the great tosaphists

from earlier sources. Cf. *Teshuvoth Ha-Ge'onim*, Mantua edn., 285. The wording of this source (based on earlier tradition) was echoed in the statement of Rabbi Eliezer of Metz.

[1] *Teshuvoth Rashi*, 175.

[2] See *supra*, p. 71, n. 5.

[3] J. E. Scherer, *Die Rechtsverhältnisse der Juden in den deutsch-österreichischen Ländern*, pp. 155–9; G. Kisch, *Germany*, p. 202.

[4] Lewin, *'Oṣar Ha-Ge'onim*, ix, pp. 28–35.

[5] *Teshuvoth Rabbenu Gershom*, 58.

[6] The *responsa* quoted above, nn. 4–5. Rabbenu Gershom's *responsum* is, indeed, a mere transcription of the gaonic sources: cf. the editor's note on p. 134.

[7] Rashi (*Teshuvoth*, 174) deals with the opposite case; whether the apostate's possessions should be inherited by his relatives. He decides in the affirmative, and states his decision in the way of a generalization: 'We do not find that the *Torah* denies the [right of] inheritance from sinners.' Cf. my article quoted *supra* (p. 70, n. 4).

Rabbi Eliezer ben Joel and Rabbi Isaac ben Asher.[1] These authorities asserted that the disinheriting of the apostate was based upon a talmudic enactment contrary to biblical law. The reason given was once again based on the fundamental consideration that a Jew cannot change his status by becoming an apostate, and once again it was Rashi's definition, based on the above quotation, that turned the scales.

The popular view did not, however, accept the view that baptism did not affect the Jew's character *qua* Jew. Indeed, in contrast to the ruling of the gaonic period[2] the practice won acceptance that the repentant convert must undergo a ceremony of purification in the ritual bath in the same way as a proselyte. This practice, so far as I am aware, is first mentioned in the thirteenth century, but it may well be earlier.[3]

That the halakhists occupied themselves with legal problems involving apostates is no proof that apostasy was recurrent, for even the odd case would have necessitated legal decisions. However, our sources also indicate that certain customs and rules of behaviour evolved which were incumbent upon those who had 'lost' their relatives or associates by baptism. Rabbenu Tam speaks of the custom of distorting the names of the apostates so as to endow them, by a slight change, with a derogatory meaning. *Yehudah* was changed into *Yehudaḥ*, *Avraham* into *Avedan*, &c.[4] On the authority of the same rabbi we learn that it was an accepted rule not to observe the customs of mourning when a relative died as a convert. Some halakhists held that such conduct was halakhically unjustifiable, especially if the converts were minors who might have been baptized by one of their parents ('for what does it matter if a minor was put into the water?'). Rabbenu Tam, however, testified that 'to refrain from mourning is the usage' (*minhag*); 'better that they [sc. the relatives] should be merry and rejoice'

[1] *'Or Zarua'*, *Bava Bathra*, 103–5; cf. also *Teshuvoth Ha-Rosh*, 17. 10.

[2] Lewin, *'Oṣar Ha-Ge'onim*, vii, pp. 111–12.

[3] R. Me'ir of Rothenburg refers to the practice in *Mordekhai*, *Kethubboth*, 306; *Sefer Ḥasidim*, 209, too, may have known it. See *Sefer Ḥasidim*, ed. R. Margalioth (Jerusalem, 1957), 203, editor's note. See *Nimmuqey Yosef* on *Yevamoth*, 47b.

[4] *Sefer Ha-Yashar*, Berlin edn., 25.

(*sasim u-semeḥim*). The reason for such an unnatural reaction is given in terms which are a testimony to the attitude of faithful Jews towards conversion. 'For there is more delight in his death than in his life. Had he lived, he would ultimately have worshipped idols and gone the way of idolaters.'[1]

The prevalence of such customs was not limited to the France of Rabbenu Tam's generation. The great authority of thirteenth-century Germany, Rabbi Judah *He-Ḥasid*, refers to the same customs.[2] He deals also with many other problems arising out of apostasy. We learn of iniquitous sons who threatened their elders that if they were not allowed their own way they would apostatize.[3] On the other hand, the question of rescuing apostates who wished to return to the fold, but were prevented from doing so, is also a recurrent topic.[4] Perhaps the most significant item in Rabbi Judah *He-Ḥasid*'s account is that he finds it necessary to prescribe not only the conduct becoming to a son whose father (or to a father whose son) had become converted to Christianity,[5] but also the attitude of a disciple whose master has apostatized. 'One whose master (*ha-rav*) apostatizes should not quote in his name the interpretations (*ṭeʿamim*) he has heard from him.'[6]

This at once raises the question of what motives there were which might have induced apostasy. The question is also linked up with the social standing of those who were potential converts. Cases of forced conversion can be disregarded in this connexion, though this might sometimes have created the type of convert who was neither a convinced Christian nor a Jew of sufficient ardour to take risks in order to keep his faith or to return to it. The above-mentioned 'iniquitous sons' who used the threat of baptism in order to extract concessions from their parents are likewise a hint of the existence of unprincipled converts. We have a vivid description, dating from the thirteenth century, of a type of convert who was neither Jew nor Christian, but adopted the way of life of either community according to convenience. R. Me'ir of Rothenburg tells us that 'there came a Jew who had been baptized and

[1] *'Or Zaruaʿ*, 2. 428.
[2] *Sefer Ḥasidim*, 192–3.
[3] Ibid., 857, 1376, 1704, 1876, 1897.
[4] Ibid., 183, 200, 201.
[5] Ibid., 183, 1506, 1572.
[6] Ibid., 791; cf. also 790, 1476.

then repented, not with his whole heart, but hypocritically, like those utterly worthless folk who wander round the countryside, appearing now as Jews, and now conducting themselves according to the customs of idolaters [i.e. Christians]'.[1] That some of the converts were at heart Jews or quasi-Jews is borne out by the fact that they tried to gain access to such means of salvation as the Jewish religion had to offer. We learn of converts who contributed to Jewish charity, and who wished to be owners or part-owners of the Scroll of the *Torah* used in the synagogue service.[2] No less significant is the fact that Rabbi Judah *He-Ḥasid*, who relates such cases, is not entirely negative in his attitude towards such overtures. True, he tells the story of a rabbi who was offered a large donation by a convert but refused to take it.[3] To him, however, this appears to have been an act of pious self-abnegation on the part of the rabbi. For in another passage he explicitly condones the acceptance of charity from an apostate.[4] His ruling as to an apostate's sharing the ownership of a Scroll of the *Torah* is even more astonishing: it would depend on whether or not the apostate was likely later to remove the Scroll from the community. Another consideration is whether the apostate's family would not be discredited by his being mentioned as part-owner of the Scroll. Our author adds, however: 'Sometimes it is a source of gratification for the family; for people will say that, although he is an apostate, his heart is towards Heaven' (*libbo la-Shamayim*), that is to say, at heart the apostate remained a Jew.[5]

Although the existence of the opportunist convert to Christianity is frequently attested, he is not the only type, and perhaps not even the most conspicuous. Christian sources tell us of many Jews who accepted Christianity through conviction,[6] and we have no

[1] *Mordekhai, Kethubboth*, 306.
[2] *Sefer Ḥasidim*, 190, 679, 1476.
[3] Ibid., 1702.
[4] Ibid., 1701.
[5] Ibid., 190. In another paragraph (1476), however, his attitude is entirely negative. Such contradictions are not uncommon in *Sefer Ḥasidim*. Cf. J. Freimann in the introduction to *Sefer Ḥasidim*, Frankfurt, 1924, pp. 10–12; F. Y. Baer, 'The Religious-Social Tendency of *Sefer Ḥasidim*' (Hebrew), *Zion*, iii, 1938, p. 38.
[6] See the instances in L. Lucas, 'Judentaufen und Judaismus zur Zeit des Papstes Innocenz der Dritte', *Festschrift zum siebzigsten Geburtstag Martin Philippsons*, pp. 25–38; S. Grayzel, *The Church and the Jews in the XIIIth Century*, pp. 17–20.

reason to doubt this even though such sources were both prone to exaggeration and apt to be taken in by false converts. The Jewish sources are, naturally, disinclined to dwell upon the motives of those who embraced Christianity genuinely. Nevertheless, they casually reveal the existence of the latter type. We read of a convert who refused to undergo the act of *ḥaliṣah* even when offered substantial remuneration, participation in any Jewish procedure being held by him to be an act of *heresy*.[1] We have also the account of one who 'apostatized of his own free will . . . he studied the books of their erroneous teachings . . . and became a priest like one of the priests of the Gentiles'. Later, this same man, by a second conversion, 'repented and returned to Judaism'.[2] This latter phenomenon must certainly be regarded as more exceptional than the first.

It is obvious that some genuine conversions must have occurred at a time when the whole of society lived in a state of religious tension. The psychological motivation of religious conversion is in any case a complicated process. In countries where the whole material and spiritual culture was pervaded by Christian thought and symbolism, the appeal of Christianity to a Jew must have been of a very complex character. To embrace Christianity meant accepting the whole scale of values which prevailed in the ruling society. As medieval civilization was expressed almost entirely in religious terms, it is very likely that a Jew who was captivated by the values of Christian society experienced this process subjectively in the form of religious conversion.

It is therefore also obvious that it was not only persons of marginal attachment who were attracted towards Christianity, as might have been the case in other epochs and other areas of the Jewish Diaspora. Some of the converts in the Middle Ages came from among the most eminent, both socially and intellectually. It was the loss of these, even though they might number a few only, and not the loss of those of dubious character and position, that caused the community to be in a state of permanent defence against Christianity.

[1] *Teshuvoth Maharam*, Prague edn., 1022. The word *heresy* is used in the source, which is, however, of the fourteenth century.

[2] *Teshuvoth Ba'aley Ha-Tosafoth*, 3. It was on this case that the decision of the two early halakhists mentioned *supra*, p. 69, nn. 3–4, turned.

If apostasy from Judaism might, perhaps, be explained in terms of the social attraction of members of a religious minority to the majority, the converse phenomenon presented by proselytes to Judaism defies such an interpretation. No assertion can be made about the numbers of Christians who turned to Judaism or of the frequency with which this occurred. That it happened occasionally amongst the Ashkenazim in the Middle Ages is clearly attested in the sources, and the occurrence was frequent enough to induce the exponents of Judaism to evolve an attitude towards it.

In this case, too, the first reference point of orientation was talmudic tradition. This entailed defining the conditions upon which the proselyte could be accepted, fixing the procedure to be followed during the initiation, and also evaluating the act and its consequences for the Jewish community. The condition was the acknowledgement of the *Torah*, in its entirety, through religious conviction. The procedure included circumcision, and a ritual bath, for men; for women, the latter only.[1]

Medieval conditions were different from those reflected in the talmudic sources. In talmudic times, acceptance of the Jewish faith and integration into the Jewish community were sometimes achieved in stages, and not always in accordance with the halakhic precepts, which were themselves not uncontroversially defined in every detail.[2] In the Middle Ages, to become a proselyte meant to be formally accepted by a Jewish court. This was done mostly in the face of opposition to proselytization by the non-Jewish authorities.[3] That the practice of accepting proselytes was continued in spite of this is proof enough that it was not conceived as a mere formal duty, but arose out of the Jew's urge to see his own religious truth conveyed to others.

By defining conditions and procedure, the Talmud can be said to have held the door open to accepting proselytes. The medieval Jewish authorities were anxious that this should continue to be so,

[1] Summed up in Maimonides, *Hilkhoth 'Issurey Bi'ah*, chaps. 13–14.

[2] See the talmudic sources of Maimonides' decisions cited in the reference given in the previous note.

[3] Scherer, op. cit., pp. 12, 46. Grayzel, *Church*, pp. 22–23; Kisch, *Germany*, pp. 199–200. The danger of participating in the acceptance of proselytes is often reflected in the Hebrew sources. Cf. *Zikhron Berith La-Ri'shonim*, p. 132; *Sefer Ḥasidim*, 214; *Teshuvoth R. Ḥayyim, 'Or Zarua'*, 142.

in spite of certain adverse reflections on the value of proselytes from the point of view of internal Jewish life. Such reflections were not lacking in talmudic literature, and some of the medieval halakhists seem to have identified themselves with them. Among them we find the great tosaphist, Rabbi Isaac.[1] The same author, however, found it necessary to guard himself against the possible inference that proselytes should never be accepted. Such a conclusion could easily have been drawn from the passage in B.T., *Yevamoth*, 109b, where there is a strong condemnation, almost amounting to an anathema, of those who accept proselytes: 'Evil after evil comes upon those who accept proselytes.' The above-mentioned tosaphist commented on this sentence that it applies only to those who encourage Gentiles to become Jews or those who accept converts without first warning them of their religious responsibility. If a Gentile persisted in his wish to become a Jew after being duly warned of the implications, he was to be accepted.[2] The door was thus left open for proselytes.

Although it was possible for Gentiles to become proselytes, was it also desirable? Liberal thinkers, starting with Moses Mendelssohn, have read into the talmudic tradition an unequivocal tendency to discourage proselytization. We shall examine the motives underlying this interpretation in Chapter XIV. In any case, that was not what the talmudic sources seem to have conveyed to the Ashkenazi exponents of Judaism in the Middle Ages. The desirability of *gerey ṣedeq*, 'righteous proselytes' (i.e. those who became Jews through conviction), was indeed taken for granted. It is sufficient to quote the description by the tosaphist, Rabbi Joel ben Isaac, of an actual case of conversion: 'And the Spirit went forth from the Lord and rested in the heart of that man, Rabbi Abraham, son of Abraham our Father, and it came to pass that when the Spirit rested on him . . . .'[3] The use of the sonorous biblical style, exceptional in the writings of the halakhists, is in itself an indication of a favourable attitude towards the event so described. Even more so are the actual terms used. To conceive of the act as the descent of God's Spirit into the heart of the proselyte undoubtedly pre-

[1] *Tosafoth*, *Qiddushin*, 70b.
[2] *Tosafoth*, *Yevamoth*, 109b.
[3] *Ravyah*, 549.

supposes a positive evaluation of the conversion. It may be, of course, that we have here to do with a special case of a proselyte of exceptional virtue. Indeed, he is described as such: 'And he drew nigh unto the work of the Lord to seek God and to study the Book and the holy tongue . . . and he was a man whole-hearted and upright, dwelling in tents',[1] i.e. the tents of learning. This, however, is not the only instance of a proselyte who endeavoured to obtain a sound knowledge of the Jewish religion. Another tosaphist, a disciple of Rabbenu Tam, relates the story of a proselyte who was taught the Bible and the Mishnah by the tosaphist's brother 'by day and by night'.[2] We shall also hear, later, of a proselyte, Rabbi Abraham, who was able to offer an original interpretation of one of the talmudic sources concerning proselytes.[3] It is true that the average proselyte was regarded as unacquainted with the details of Jewish law.[4] As the proselyte usually joined the Jewish community in his adult years, it was no easy matter for him to make up for the Jewish education he had missed. Nevertheless, we have to picture one type of proselyte of this time as resembling the instances mentioned above. The proselyte whom we first mentioned knew Latin, but not Hebrew. He was about to study the latter language, and he made use of his Vulgate as an aid. It is very likely that, as a Christian, he was one of the clergy,[5] but it was this kind of person who would have been inclined to ponder religious matters and conceivably to have come to the conclusion that the Jewish tradition was the true interpretation of the Old Testament which served as a basis for both the Christian and the Jewish religions.

We should, however, pause here, in order not to lose sight of the historical basis. We have no account of the mental process by which any proselyte arrived at his decision. We may, however, assume that it was an experience on an exclusively religious level, even more so than in the case of the Jew converted to Christianity.

[1] Ibid.

[2] *Sefer Ha-Yashar*, Berlin edn., p. 107.

[3] *Tosafoth*, *Qiddushin*, 70b.

[4] Rashi on B.T., *Niddah*, 13b; *Sefer Ḥasidim*, 986, 1011.

[5] Surmised by Aptowitzer, *Mavo' le-sefer Ravyah*, p. 447. Similar is the case of Bodo, cf. B. Blumenkranz in *Revue d'histoire et de philosophie religieuses*, xxxiv, 1954, pp. 401–13.

For a positive attitude towards proselytizing we may quote some additional sources: Rashi, in his commentary on the Pentateuch and the Prophets, depicts the day of redemption as being preceded by the adherence of proselytes to the Jewish people.[1] True, this feature of the messianic prospect was not his original contribution. It has its source in the Talmud.[2] But its repetition by so outstanding a commentator, who spoke also for his own contemporaries, is not without significance.

This attitude appears even more clearly in the explicit reference to the messianic era by the great authority of the thirteenth century, Rabbi Moses of Coucy. In admonishing his hearers and readers not to deal fraudulently with non-Jews, he uses the following argument: since, according to the Talmud, the dispersion of the Jewish people among the nations of the world was for the purpose of attracting proselytes, it is incumbent upon each Jew to act in an exemplary moral fashion. 'But if they behave unfairly towards others, who would join them? [sc. the Jews].'[3] Rabbi Moses expected the coming of the Messiah in the year 1240,[4] some four years after his preaching tour in Spain. At least the fact that he expected proselytes to be joining the Jewish community in the near future is a clear indication of his positive attitude towards them.

The tosaphists could not, of course, disregard the ambivalence which prevailed in the talmudic sources as to the desirability of proselytes. With some of them, the negative attitude might have gained the upper hand. In any case they had to cope with these sources and to find some way of integrating them into their thinking. The most famous dictum in the Talmud against proselytes is that of Rabbi Ḥelbo, in B.T., *Yevamoth*, 47b: 'Proselytes are as

[1] Deut. xxxiii. 19; Isa. xliv. 4–5.

[2] The comment on Deut. xxxiii. 19 is from *Sifrey* (cf. A. Berliner, *Rashi 'al Ha-Torah*, 1866, p. 361); for Isa. xliv. 5 Rashi himself indicates as his source *'Avoth de-Rabbi Nathan*, [36]; Isa. xliv. 4 reflects B.T., *Pesaḥim*, 87b.

[3] *Semag*, p. 152b.

[4] This year was mentioned as a messianic year; cf. Zunz, *Zur Geschichte und Literatur*, p. 87, note *a*; cf. H. Breslau, 'Juden und Mongolen im Jahre 1241', *Zeitschrift für die Geschichte der Juden Deutschlands*, i, 1887, pp. 99 ff.; ii, 1888, pp. 382 f. Our source is therefore an additional proof for the messianic hope attached to this date. Cf. T. Gilath, 'Two *Baqqashoth* of Moses of Coucy' (Hebrew), *Tarbiz*, xxviii, 1958, pp. 54–56.

bad for Israel as a scab.' This would call for an explanation even if it had not been contradicted by the prevailing opinion. Of the seven interpretations offered in the *Tosafoth*[1] which summarize the views of known and unknown authorities since the time of Rashi, three succeeded in twisting the meaning of the sentence into the opposite of its obvious intention. According to these three explanations, Rabbi Ḥelbo had no derogatory meaning in mind when comparing the proselytes to a scab. It may be (and this is Rabbi Abraham the Proselyte's own interpretation) that he wanted to extol the convert's strict adherence to the *Torah* in contrast to the moderate observance of the Jews themselves. It is true that not all the opinions mentioned tend to neutralize the negative purport of the talmudic dictum. But we have good reason to attribute a greater significance to the positive explanations than to the negative ones. For some of the expositors might well have followed the usual path of interpretation, which is to expound the meaning of the text without necessarily identifying oneself with it. On the other hand, those who converted the sentence into the opposite of its meaning will rightly be suspected of having possessed strong convictions of their own, which prompted them to soften Rabbi Ḥelbo's assertion.

Jewish society, being isolated from but at the same time in a permanent state of tension *vis-à-vis* Christian society, is best characterized by its attitude towards apostates and proselytes. Not only does Jewish society maintain its claim to retain its own members within its fold, but it also dares to hope to win adherents from other faiths, and sometimes even to take action with that aspiration in view. No better proof could be adduced for the fact that medieval Jewry was convinced of Judaism's truth, its superiority, and its religious mission.

[1] *Qiddushin*, 70b.

VII

THE MARTYRS

As a proof of the truth of their religion theologians—the Christian ones to a greater extent than the Jewish—adduced the constant readiness of the faithful to sacrifice their lives rather than renounce their faith.[1] The modern historian is not called upon to judge the merits of such claims: the fact that two rival religions are both able to lay claim to the same proof would appear to invalidate the argument. Nevertheless, in any account of the objective historical process such as it is the historian's task to render, the phenomenon of martyrdom must occupy a unique place. Martyrdom marks the highest manifestation in the history of any religion. It is a sign that the individual identifies himself with the tenets of his religion to such a degree of consciousness that their renunciation would make life no longer worth living for him.

This alone would justify us in placing martyrdom in the same sociological category as other corresponding phenomena. For not only religious movements, but other social groups also, achieve a degree of loyalty which endows their adherents with a readiness to make the supreme sacrifice. Nevertheless, religious martyrdom has its own special characteristics, and in the case of any given religion it is the result of a distinct historical development. The origin of Jewish, and Christian, martyrdom is to be found in Judaism's uncompromising repudiation of ancient polytheism. The first martyrs in this special historical sense were the *Ḥasidim* of the Hasmonaean period, who furnished an inspiring example

[1] The origin of the term *martyr* has been much discussed; cf. Dornseiff, 'Der Martyr, Name und Bedeutung', *Archiv für Religionswissenschaft*, xxii, 1924, pp. 133–53. However, with the full emergence of the martyrs into history, it acquired the notion of witness to the truth of Christianity. See H. von Campenhausen, *Die Idee des Martyriums in der alten Kirche*, 1936, pp. 55 ff.; T. W. Manson, 'Martyrs and Martyrdom', *Bulletin of the John Rylands Library*, xxxix, 1956–7, pp. 463–84. On the other hand, even if it is true that the Christian notion of the martyr was derived from Jewish sources, no equivalent term was evolved in Judaism. In the talmudic literature the term *harugey malekhuth* is used, in the Middle Ages *qedoshim*.

for later generations, whether among Jews or Christians.[1] The Christians continued the Jewish attitude, and for the first centuries of the Christian era the adherents of both religions defied the might of the pagan Roman Empire.[2]

A new phase of development commenced when the role of Jewish martyrdom had to be maintained in the face of coercion and violence on the part of the Christian society amidst which Jews lived. This phase began immediately after the establishment of the Christian Church as a ruling authority in the fourth century. Its climax, or, indeed, its most manifest and passionate form, was reached in the period which is our present theme, the tenth to fourteenth centuries.

The moral duty of being prepared to 'Sanctify the Holy Name', i.e. to sacrifice one's life rather than transgress the main precepts of the *Torah* or renounce fidelity to the Jewish religion, was itself a part of the Jewish tradition. Rules for the conduct expected of a faithful Jew in an emergency were discussed at length in the Talmud.[3] The later halakhists endeavoured to determine these rules according to the accepted hermeneutic methods of their discipline. Here, even more than in other spheres of religious life, Halakhah was merely a regulating factor.

This can best be illustrated by examples. In the Talmud there is a controversy as to whether the duty to sacrifice one's life arises only when the act of compulsion occurs publicly. Rabbi Ishmael—and possibly later authorities—held that, unless ten Jews were eye-witnesses to the act of compulsion, one might, and perhaps even should, submit to force and even worship idols rather than be the cause of one's own death.[4] When considering which of the talmudic views was to be accepted as the binding rule in practice, the tosaphists rejected the lenient view as entirely inconceivable. 'Far be it from us', they said, 'that we should follow Rabbi Ishmael's

[1] E. Bickermann, *Der Gott der Makkabäer*, Berlin, 1937, pp. 36–39.

[2] The current view, according to which the Jews enjoyed complete religious freedom while the Christians suffered martyrdom at the hands of the Roman Empire, has been disproved, conclusively in my opinion, by F. Y. Baer, 'Israel, the Christian Church, &c.' (Hebrew), *Zion*, xxi, 1956, pp. 1–49.

[3] B.T., *Sanhedrin*, 74a–b; B.T., *'A.Z.*, 27b; Pal. T., *Shevi'ith*, 4. 2.

[4] B.T., *Sanhedrin*, 74a, and B.T., *'A.Z.*, 27b, 54a; cf. *Tosafoth*, *'A.Z.*, 54a; *Kethubboth*, 19a.

opinion.'[1] Such a passionate interjection in the course of a halakhic discussion is unusual. That it occurs here is evidence that the halakhists were deeply involved emotionally. For the Ashkenazi Jews it was, indeed, inconceivable that one should submit to religious compulsion merely because there was not a substantial number of witnesses.

A very similar attitude is evinced in the approach of the Ashkenazi halakhists to other, related questions. Is one allowed to go beyond the letter of traditional teaching, and face martyrdom even where the religious coercion does not involve the specific transgressions which make resistance to it a religious duty? Is one allowed to take one's own life, and even the life of one's children, in order to avoid religious compulsion and the temptation to apostasy? These questions were not explicitly mentioned in the talmudic sources, and the halakhists had to find their answers by means of inference. Halakhists of a different background, as for instance Maimonides, when they dealt with the first point, gave a rationally based answer, limiting both the duty and the permissibility of martyrdom to the minimum prescribed in the sources.[2] The answers of the Ashkenazi halakhists were preconceived and emotionally predetermined. They invariably inclined in the direction of stringency, even at the cost of making severe demands on the moral strength of the individual.[3]

The real source of readiness for the fate of the martyr derived from the attachment of the individual to the religious tradition which made possible the existence and continuance of the community to which he belonged. The initiation of every Jew into the knowledge of Jewish tradition may be said to have been simultaneously a preparation for possible martyrdom. The tradition contained special elements which aimed at inculcating into the

[1] *Tosafoth*, *'A.Z.*, 54a. Similarly the *Tosefoth R. 'Elḥanan*, *'A.Z.*, 18a (ed. B. Frankel, 1901), when discussing the question whether one may commit suicide in order to escape forced conversion, close the discussion with an exclamation rather than with an argument. See also *Tosafoth*, *Pesaḥim*, 53b.

[2] Maim., *Hilkhoth Yesodey Ha-Torah*, 5. 4.

[3] *Tosafoth*, *'A.Z.*, 27b; *Semag*, *'Aseh*, 3; *Tosafoth*, *'A.Z.*, 18a; *Tosefoth R. 'Elḥanan*, *'A.Z.*, 18a; *Sefer Ḥasidim*, 249. However, Rashbam, in his commentary on Eccles. vii. 15–16 (ed. Jellinek, 1855), seems to approve the more lenient view.

individual the need to remain faithful to Judaism even at the cost of his life. Stories and legends of saintly persons who had done so were transmitted and taught in various forms.[1] The story of Hannah and her seven sons, who sacrificed themselves in defiance of the idolatrous king at the time of the Hasmonaean uprising, was well known.[2] Of special appeal was the story of Rabbi ʿAqiva and the other 'Ten Martyrs' of talmudic times, who were familiar figures to every Jew however superficial his religious education.[3] A poetic version of the death of the 'Ten Martyrs' was included in the liturgy for the Day of Atonement and for the Fast of the 9th of Ab.[4]

The factors making for this willingness to submit to martyrdom were not exclusive to Ashkenazi Jewry. They were present in all the dispersed communities of traditional Jewish society, and they proved powerful enough to evoke the moral courage necessary to face martyrdom, so long as attachment to tradition was not enfeebled through the undermining influence of rationalism or of other spiritual or social factors. The Ashkenazi Middle Ages were not exposed to such subversive forces. This does not mean, of course, that every Jew in the Ashkenazi sector of Jewry, i.e. northern and north-eastern Europe including England, was a potential martyr. Cases of surrender due to fear of death, or under the threat of torture, are found alongside the records of the heroic acts of the martyrs.[5] Notwithstanding this, the Ashkenazi Middle Ages outshine all other periods of Jewish history as an epoch of heroic steadfastness. Everything known to us points to the assumption that the proportion of those who stood the test, compared with those who failed to do so, was greater in the Ashkenazi Middle Ages than in any other period of Jewish martyrdom.

[1] We shall find them reflected in the Hebrew records of the Crusades. These were published by Neubauer and Stern, *Hebräische Berichte über die Judenverfolgungen während der Kreuzzüge*, 1892, with a German translation. A more complete collection is that of A. M. Habermann, *Sefer Gezeroth 'Ashkenaz we-Ṣarefath*, Jerusalem, 1946. This collection will be quoted below.

[2] It is mentioned in Habermann, *Gezeroth*, pp. 34, 102.

[3] R. ʿAqiva, or the 'Ten Martyrs', are often mentioned in the records, see Habermann, *Gezeroth*, pp. 31, 49, 73, 104.

[4] Zunz, *Die synagogale Poesie des Mittelalters*, pp. 139–44.

[5] Habermann, *Gezeroth*, pp. 36, 43, 56–57, 80, 96; cf. the previous chapter.

Although this is true, it is not the merely numerical assessment of the potential or actual victims that conveys to us the spirit of martyrdom, i.e. the motivation and subjective experience of the martyrs in any given period. To understand the latter, we must determine the characteristics of the religious spirit which manifested themselves in the martyrs' demeanour, and in their mental reaction to their lot. In the case of the Ashkenazi martyrs, these characteristics seem to be two.

The first is a state of intense religious excitement and susceptibility towards spiritual stimuli. For those generations, the world to come was not an abstract concept but a living reality. Not only was contact between the two worlds held to be possible through prayer and religious experience, but they were also directly interdependent on each other.[1] This world, in fact, is nothing more than the plane upon which decisions made above are carried out. The martyr is able to apprehend, almost concretely, the celestial reward which awaits him when he has fulfilled the supreme religious duty. He is convinced that his death is only a temporary phenomenon.

> For the time being the enemy will slay us . . . and yet we shall live and flourish, our souls will be in Paradise [reflected] in the great shining mirror for ever and ever. . . . Above all, do not question the justice of the Holy One, Blessed be He, and Blessed be His Name. . . . Happy shall we be if we do His will, and happy everyone who is slain and slaughtered and dies for the Sanctification of His Name. Such a one is destined for the World to Come, and shall dwell in the same regions as those righteous men, Rabbi ʿAqiva and his companions, the pillars of the world, who were slain for the sake of His Name. Furthermore, for such a one the world of darkness is transformed into a world of light, the world of sadness into a world of joy, and the fleeting world into one that shall exist for ever and ever.[2]

The martyrs try to avert catastrophe by all measures to which both worldly and celestial powers are likely to respond. They pray and fast, they distribute their possessions amongst the poor in order to soften the celestial wrath, even though at the same time

[1] F. Y. Baer, 'The Religious-Social Tendency of *Sefer Ḥasidim*' (Hebrew), *Zion*, iii, 1938, pp. 15–17.

[2] Habermann, *Gezeroth*, p. 31.

it is difficult for them to comprehend the sins which might have incited Heaven against them.[1] They also employ every conceivable worldly means of saving themselves. They apply for protection to the authorities, and seek refuge with benevolent neighbours and rulers.[2] In many instances they part with all their possessions to purchase the doubtful protection of burghers and bishops.[3] They also use their money to bribe the leaders of the Crusaders when they enter their homes.[4] In some cases they fortify themselves in their quarters and buildings and fight back their attackers as fiercely as they can.[5] No way of escape is left unattempted.[6]

When all fails, however, the martyrs know that their ultimate destruction has been decreed by celestial judgement. They now abide by this, not only because it is inevitable, but also because it is the 'Judgement of Heaven',[7] whose justice cannot be fathomed by the human intellect, but whose wisdom is never doubted. Although the martyrs themselves are hardly in a position to speculate upon the reason for Heaven's choice of themselves for this supreme sacrifice, at least their chroniclers are free to do so. It was the *élite* of all generations which had to atone for the past deeds of Israel; it was their task to create a fund of good will for coming generations; they had been chosen particularly, because of their capacity to fulfil the highest duty, which also entailed the highest reward.[8]

The second characteristic of the martyrs' attitude is more closely linked with the subject of our inquiry. This is the attitude towards the religion in whose name force is used. Although the persecutions which occasioned the martyrdom were not initiated by the heads and officials of the Church, and indeed very often were expressly

[1] Ibid., pp. 28–30, 53.

[2] Ibid., pp. 27, 40–41, 50, 93.

[3] Ibid., pp. 26, 27, 51, 53, 95, 98.

[4] Ibid., pp. 29, 53, 93–94, 99.

[5] Ibid., pp. 30, 99, 101.

[6] P. Browe, 'Die Judenbekämpfung im Mittelalter', *Zeitschrift für katholische Theologie*, lxii, 1938, thought to find in this activistic attitude a special feature of the Jewish martyrs, in contradistinction to the passivity of the Christian ones. The longing for martyrdom was, however, not entirely unknown in Jewish history either—cf. *Sefer Ḥasidim*, 251; cf. also I. Caro's *Maggid Meysharim* (Amsterdam edn., 1708), p. 38b. Cf. Graetz, *Geschichte der Juden*, 3rd edn., ix, p. 300.

[7] Habermann, *Gezeroth*, pp. 31, 33, 44, 54, 77.

[8] The motivations are variously stated; see Habermann, ibid., pp. 25, 48, 52–53, 61, 73.

disavowed by them,[1] the martyrs were in effect confronted by the —probably self-appointed—representatives of the Christian religion. The Jews were at any rate approached in the name of the rival religion. The alternative to surrender was death. In this situation most Ashkenazi Jews chose death, very often at their own hands. The ancient tradition of martyrdom became, once again, a reality. In its extent, as well as in its intensity, it probably surpassed all that was known of ancient Jewish martyrdom. During the First Crusade whole communities in the Rhineland cities perished, at each other's hands or those of the Crusaders.[2] The deeds of these great martyrs became a paragon for the generations to come. The descriptions of the scenes of mass-suicide and massacre leave no doubt that these acts were carried out and endured with the full consciousness of martyrdom, i.e. with the manifest purpose of testifying to the truth of the faith to which the victims adhered and to the emptiness of that in whose name their assailants compelled them to sacrifice their lives. Expressions are to be found, both of the positive affirmation of the one faith and of the absolute repudiation of the other. Such affirmations of Judaism referred to the fundamental tenets in which the Jewish religion differed from Christianity. They testified to the absolute oneness of God, the formula of the *Shema'* being the last words uttered,[3] a pattern which was exemplified in the classical story of Rabbi 'Aqiva's martyrdom.[4] The verb *le-yaḥed* became almost a technical term for sacrificing one's life as a witness to the Faith.[5] The theme of absolute adherence to the Jewish faith also found more figurative expressions. The

[1] Grayzel, *Church*, pp. 76–82; Parkes, *Community*, pp. 87–88.

[2] The story of this episode has been frequently told; see, for example, the sympathetic account in Parkes, op. cit., pp. 61–81. A thoroughgoing analysis and appraisal is to be found in F. Y. Baer's article 'Gezeroth Tatnu', *Sefer 'Assaf*, Jerusalem, 1953, pp. 126–40.

[3] Habermann, *Gezeroth*, pp. 25, 33, 49, 74, 100.

[4] B.T., *Berakhoth*, 61b; Pal. T., *Berakhoth*, 9. 5. According to both versions, however, 'it was the hour of the recital of the *Shema'*', i.e. R. 'Aqiva repeated the formula as part of the daily liturgy. With the later martyrs, it became part of the ritual of self-sacrifice.

[5] The expression has, already sometimes in talmudic literature, the connotation of 'to declare the unity of God' (Jastrow's *Dictionary*, i, p. 572). The expression recurs very often in the records and it sometimes tends to be a synonym for *Qiddush ha-Shem,* see, for example, Habermann, op. cit., pp. 55, 73.

Sanctification of the Name by trusting in God and by acquiescing in His inscrutable will finds recurrent expression in the declaration of faith which preceded the act of self-sacrifice.[1] Although the terms used in this connexion are drawn from tradition, when applied by the martyrs to their own resolve they acquire a heightened ardour, and shine forth as the expression of a genuine, deeply religious experience.

Just as the supreme ordeal of Jewish martyrdom evoked expressions of loyalty and attachment to the martyrs' own conception of faith, so it inspired hatred against the alien religion. It called forth expressions of denial, in word and gesture, which were normally suppressed or not even consciously felt. Some expressions, again, refer to differences in dogma and tenet; others are reactions to the visible symbols of Christian religion, coming to the surface in moments of religious coercion and of heroic rejection of Christianity. The rejection of the Christian belief in the divinity of Jesus—always, for Jews, an uncompromising and fundamental rejection—came to the fore again when endeavours were made to force its acceptance, and all that it implied, upon Jews. Expressions of contempt and derision for one who was, in their eyes, nothing but a human being and not one to be revered and exalted sprang to the lips of the martyrs.[2] In their indignation at the attempt to compel them to forsake the only living God in the name of one they thought a human nonentity, the martyrs used language that went to excess and was found, by later generations, to be unrepeatable.[3]

The worst paroxysms of hatred and denial of the other's religion were evoked in each party by the sight of the other's religious symbol. This phenomenon occurs on both sides. Whenever Christian persecutors forced their way into the Jewish quarter, they

[1] Expressions of trust (*livṭoaḥ*) in God are recurrent in the records, see Habermann, op. cit., pp. 38, 39, 42. F. Y. Baer, in his article in *Sefer 'Assaf*, emphasized the mystical aspect of the religious experience reflected in the records of the martyrology. This does not, however, neutralize in this case, though it does in many others, the more simple concept of Jewish faith, on the level of which the conflict with Christianity was experienced.

[2] Habermann, op. cit., pp. 31–32, 36, 80, 103–4.

[3] See the introduction by the editors of the German translation quoted on p. 85, n. 1. That the editors refrained from translating these expressions is understandable, but the argument that they are in the nature of technical terms in the original texts is an apologetic assumption.

would rush into the synagogue and tear up the Scrolls of the *Torah*,[1] rightly recognizing in them the central religious symbol of the Jewish faith. This desecration of the sacred trust of God's *Torah* was bewailed by the narrators of the persecutions no less than the death of the martyrs themselves. We may well believe the chroniclers that these acts on the part of the aggressors heightened the determination of the victims not to submit to conversion. Those attacked felt themselves bound to act in a similar way towards the religious symbols of their attackers. They could do so only at the risk of immediate death, but this was a price that they were ready to pay. Many cases are related of Jews accepting the offer of their lives on condition of baptism, merely in order to gain the opportunity of spitting at the crucifix or demonstrating their utter rejection at the very moment of their seducers' victory. In the same way it became a form of ritual for the Jewish martyrs to speak words of utter denial and contempt when offered their lives in exchange for accepting the Christian faith—an act which then became a challenge to the persecutor to carry out physical destruction.[2]

The attitude of the Jewish martyrs, perhaps more than any other factor, bears out the assertion that the Jewish community at this time conceived its position and religious mission in terms of its own antagonism to Christianity. Those who testified under the stress of martyrdom to their passionate repudiation of Christianity must also have been conscious of their attitude towards it in times of mutual forbearance. Considerations of expediency, backed by an ideology of relative tolerance achieved on the level of reflective thinking, permitted both communities to exhibit this practical forbearance towards each other. In times of crisis, such a basis of co-existence collapsed. On the Christian side, destructive instincts were awakened against a religious minority which was physically unprotected. From the Jewish side came the response of absolute refusal in the sphere of religious antagonism.

The Jewish readiness for martyrdom is not to be explained in psychological terms only: dissimilarity of belief and customs made

[1] Habermann, *Gezeroth*, pp. 35, 53, 76, 102–3.

[2] See the passages quoted on p. 89, n. 2.

the formal acceptance of the Christian religion, without a genuine conversion to it, a proposition that, at conscious and intellectual levels, could not be entertained. We shall find in later generations, when the extreme exclusiveness of the Ghetto reduced religious tension to a minimum, that this mental dissimilarity served as the main motive for choosing death in preference to Christianity.[1] There is no doubt that already in the Middle Ages this factor also played its part. This is particularly apparent in the behaviour of those who, at the moment of crisis, could not summon the strength to make the supreme sacrifice, and accepted baptism as a way of saving their lives. Most of them could not adapt themselves to the new environment into which they had been forced against their will and conscience. When conditions were restored to relative normality they made every effort, as we have seen above, to disentangle themselves, and to return to the Jewish community. In some cases those converted under threat of death later underwent psychological agonies which led them to self-destruction in frightful circumstances.[2]

However, revulsion from the alien world of Christianity is not the whole story. The purpose of the martyrs in laying down their lives was to fulfil a positive role also: that of bearing witness to the truth of their own religion. Talmudic Halakhah, in restricting the duty of the Sanctification of the Holy Name to cases of public religious compulsion, defined this latter term as 'in the presence of ten Israelites'.[3] No significance, apparently, was to be attributed to the presence of Gentiles. Such indifference towards the non-Jewish world is a long way from the outlook of the medieval martyrs. In the records of their deeds it is repeatedly emphasized that the act was performed publicly, *le-ʿeyney kol*,[4] i.e. before the very persons who had resorted to compulsion. The act of self-sacrifice is not one to be performed between God and His servants or, for that matter, among the members of the community of those servants. Such an attitude might have prevailed in the late talmudic

[1] See Chap. XII.

[2] Habermann, op. cit., pp. 36–38, 78.

[3] B.T., *Sanhedrin*, 74b. However, the original definition of R. Yoḥanan speaks of ten human beings (*beney 'adam*) and the inference of R. Jeremiah is not necessarily correct. In Pal. T., *Shevi'ith*, 4. 2, no such restriction is mentioned.

[4] Habermann, op. cit., pp. 73, 77, 78.

period, as well as later, in the sixteenth to seventeenth centuries.[1] In the Ashkenazi Middle Ages, the act of martyrdom was deliberately and pointedly directed at the Christian world. The Christians were to be made aware of the true faith. It is not explicitly mentioned that with this is associated the hope that Christians might accept Judaism. It was hoped, however, that Christians would recognize the errors and aberrations which drove them to do violence to those possessed of real religious truth.[2] At any rate, it may be asserted that the religious attitude of the adversary is not outside the concern of the martyr. Martyrdom was accepted in defiance of the adversaries' assumptions, and carried with it the wish to testify to the truth in the name of which such defiance was maintained.

[1] See my article 'Beyn Tatnu le-Taḥ–Taṭ' to appear in the Jubilee Volume for Prof. F. Y. Baer.

[2] Habermann, *Gezeroth*, p. 43.

VIII

THE *ḤASID*

THE impact made on the Jewish community during the Crusades by threats of physical force brought to the fore those sentiments and attitudes which were normally latent in Jewish religious and historical consciousness; and we may reasonably assume that, as a consequence, these events had some repercussions on Jewish everyday life. It would, however, be fallacious to attribute every change which may be observed in the relationship between Jews and Gentiles from that time onwards to the effect of the Crusades, and indeed such a fallacy is only too common in Jewish historiography: the sequence of cause and effect is more complicated. The Crusades are themselves rightly regarded as an expression of the religious upheaval which convulsed the Western world from the eleventh century onwards. This awakening of the religious spirit affected Christians and Jews alike. Parallel to the Cluny movement in the Christian world was the readiness for martyrdom in the Jewish communities,[1] and the religious revival of the Franciscans had its counterpart in Jewish history in the *Ḥasidim* of the age of Rabbi Judah *He-Ḥasid*[2] (1146–1217).

That the Jewish and the Gentile phenomena belong to the same historical current, however, is a historical fact that has been ascertained *post factum*; we owe the awareness of it chiefly to the profound insight of F. Y. Baer.[3] The actual participants in the events, whether Jewish or Christian, were hardly aware of a common religious consciousness, nor did any such concept serve as a unifying link between them. On the contrary, the intensity of their religious sentiments and experiences strengthened the attachment

[1] F. Y. Baer, 'The Religious-Social Tendency of *Sefer Ḥasidim*' (Hebrew), *Zion*, iii, 1938, pp. 4–6.

[2] Baer, op. cit., pp. 6–8. Gershom G. Scholem, *Major Trends in Jewish Mysticism*, 1941 edn., pp. 83–84.

[3] Apart from the previous note, see his article 'Rashi weha-Meṣi'uth ha-historith shel zemanno', *Tarbiz*, xx, 1949, pp. 320–32.

of both sides to their own respective traditions. Their adherence to their inherited religious symbols became even closer, and the aversion aroused by the outward manifestations of the alien religion grew more acute. The religious intolerance of the twelfth and thirteenth centuries found its expression not only in the nightmare of the Crusades but also in the enactments of the Church against Jewry; the violence of the Jewish recoil from these led to exclusiveness and dissociation from anything which seemed to them to represent the religious world of Christianity. This trend became most conspicuous in hasidic circles as exemplified in the book of Rabbi Judah *He-Ḥasid*, *Sefer Ḥasidim*.[1]

The *Ḥasid* is, perhaps, best characterized by his combination of spirituality and religious and ethical spontaneity.[2] For the *Ḥasid*, spirituality makes contact with the supernatural world real. The *Ḥasid*'s theoretical as well as his practical orientation is determined mainly by stimuli he may receive through dreams and apparitions, which are ordinarily beyond the perception of the senses and are not controlled by reason.

Historically, as well as psychologically, there is a strong link between this trait and that of religious and ethical spontaneity. The *Ḥasid* is not fully satisfied by the ordinary level of religious aspiration and ethical conduct, which is based on the precepts of the *Torah*. He not only goes beyond the expected standards of behaviour in accepting more stringent criteria, but also discovers a new source of religious and ethical guidance: that of spontaneous feeling. The immediate promptings of the heart are relied upon as a trustworthy guide. Unlike the halakhists, the *Ḥasid* does not feel obliged to find for his decisions a formal justification in tradition. The *Ḥasid*'s mind is, of course, moulded to a very great extent by the normal sources of Jewish tradition.[3] His actual expositions,

[1] Many editions of *Sefer Ḥasidim* exist. If not otherwise stated, my quotations refer to that of Wistinetzki (1891).

[2] Cf. F. Y. Baer, *Zion*, iii, 1938, p. 12. I follow Baer in his evaluation of *Sefer Ḥasidim*. The full significance of the hasidic attitude towards Christianity can, however, be realized only within the framework of the whole problem of Jewish-Christian relationships.

[3] This is evident from the many allusions to the Halakhah. The *Ḥasid* is not a halakhist, inasmuch as he does not aim at creative activity in this field. The reason for this must be sought in his religious and ethical aspirations, which

however, are not presented as the interpretation of tradition, but are proffered as the fruits of the *Ḥasid*'s religious impulse. These religious and moral precepts are sometimes covered by the notion of *din Shamayim* (the Law of Heaven), which means that, beyond the written law of the *Torah* (which includes the whole of Jewish tradition), there exists an additional source for religious and moral criteria, according to which one is judged in Heaven, although a terrestrial judge would not adopt them as a standard.[1]

This direct approach of the *Ḥasid* to the problem of religious and moral conduct naturally created a new relationship with the non-Jewish world. The *Sefer Ḥasidim* contains a list of precepts concerning contact with Christian ceremonies or implements: the Jew should avoid physical contact with them; he ought not to go into a church or even into its courtyard; he who goes into one has to seek atonement for so doing, and he who keeps away will be rewarded.[2] The Jew should not go near a church, and if he builds a house next to one the windows should not be placed opposite it.[3] The Jew should refrain from doing anything which could be interpreted as respecting or supporting idolatry. Even the appearance of bowing to a church should be avoided.[4] A Jew who meets a Gentile going to church should not change money for him, as the latter might use it for contributing to the maintenance of the church.[5] 'One should not teach a cleric the [Hebrew] alphabet, one should not play before him pleasant tunes lest he play them in church.'[6]

The precepts of the *Ḥasid* differ from those of the Talmud and of his contemporary halakhists not only in their strictness and bigotry: even the method and motive of the *Ḥasid* are different from those of the halakhist. The *Ḥasid* seldom bases his decisions on literary sources, and hardly ever elaborates them on rational lines.[7] His decisions are the expression of spontaneous emotions.

lie beyond the limits set by the Halakhah. See Baer, loc. cit., and Scholem, *Major Trends*, p. 94.

[1] See Baer, op. cit., pp. 11–13. It is perhaps noteworthy that the same term appears also in connexion with the martyrs (cf. *supra*, Chap. VII) where it has a different meaning.

[2] 1356–9.

[3] 1353.

[4] 1354.

[5] 1363.

[6] 348.

[7] Of the above-mentioned precepts of the *Ḥasid* only 1354 could be paralleled from B.T., *'A.Z.*, 12a; see the editor's note.

One who went into a church heard, on leaving, a *Bath Qol* (a Divine Voice) calling to him 'and thou hast cast me behind thy back' (1 Kings xiv. 9).[1] The sage who, in the spring, saw a blossoming tree in the courtyard of a church—and felt prompted to say the blessing which is prescribed at the first sight of reawakened nature[2]—declares emphatically: 'I shall not say the blessing over *this* tree.'[3] It was regarded as a miracle when, at the burial of a pious man who had never entered the house of an idol, the horses drawing the hearse ignored the coachman's intentions and avoided taking a road in which an idolatrous image would have been encountered.[4]

It is genuine religious exhilaration which engenders aversion towards the visible symbols of an alien religion. Revulsion becomes especially acute when the symbols of the two religions are liable to trespass upon each other. We are told the story of a Jewish community which refused to celebrate its own day of fasting and prayer simultaneously with that of the Christians. Although the Jews accepted the Christians' suggestion that it was their duty to pray for rain to avert drought and famine, yet they preferred to fast and pray on a different day.[5] The *Sefer Ḥasidim* rules that one should not put Hebrew books into a cupboard which contains books belonging to a Christian cleric.[6] It also prohibits the use for religious purposes of any material or instrument which has had any contact with a Gentile ceremony. Lime and sand left over from building a church should not be used for the building of a synagogue.[7] Rivers which are used for the purpose of ordeals, during which the Christian clergy recited religious formulas, must not be used for Jewish ritual ablutions.[8] The parchment of Gentile books, even if the writings have been erased, must not be used as

[1] 1357.
[2] B.T., *Berakhoth*, 43b.
[3] 581.
[4] 1356.
[5] 402.
[6] 668.
[7] 1630. The *Ḥasid*'s ruling has a parallel in the talmudic discussion in B.T., *Sanhedrin*, 47b, concerning the shroud prepared for a dead person. ("Abbaye rules . . . designation is a material act. . . . Rava says . . . designation is not a material act.') The parallel was not, however, referred to (nor is it noted by the editor). The accepted Halakhah is that designation does not count. In 726, where the *Ḥasid* deals with a similar problem, he refers explicitly to B.T., *Sanhedrin*, 47b, and states his intention of complying with 'Abbaye's view although it is not the accepted Halakhah.
[8] 1369.

material for Jewish prayer-books.[1] Melodies which were employed in Christian services were to be excluded from Jewish worship,[2] and so on.[3]

Only a few of these precepts can be explained as inferences from talmudic regulations, even assuming a very strict interpretation.[4] Most have to be understood as the expression of a religious hypersensitivity which regarded any object used for religious ritual as itself partaking of the nature of that ritual. The sanctity or profanity of the object adheres to it in a phenomenological sense, and cannot be erased. This is the explanation for precepts which forbid giving to a Gentile objects which have been used in a religious ceremony by a Jew. A cup over which a Jew has habitually made a benediction should not be given to a Gentile to drink out of: 'I would not degrade it from its holiness',[5] runs the reasoning, in explicit terms. In the same way the citron (*'ethrog*) which was used in the ritual of the *Sukkoth* festival should not subsequently be sold to a Gentile.[6] The *Ḥasid* was indignant that Jews complied with the request of a prince to open the holy ark that he might see the *Torah* Scroll therein.[7] The prohibition of allowing Gentiles to do work which, while not precisely constituting the performance of the Jewish ritual, is nevertheless a preparation for it belongs to the same category.[8]

This extension of the talmudic prohibitions entailed a diminution of the business dealings of those who complied with them; such prohibitions could be fulfilled only at the cost of economic sacrifice. The *Ḥasid* would not pawn his books with a Gentile, rather forgoing a possible loan.[9] If he inherited Christian books, he would not desire the financial benefit of selling them and preferred to burn them.[10] The story is told of a *Ḥasid* who encountered

[1] 1348.

[2] 348.

[3] Cf. 1370, 1348 (adaptation of religious poems from the Christian to the Jewish service), 1792.

[4] Attempts were made by traditional commentators to account for the *Ḥasid*'s sources; see the edition of *Sefer Ḥasidim* by R. Margalioth, 1957, e.g. 238, 432.

[5] 728, 1636.

[6] 1635.

[7] 1563.

[8] 1539. The *Ḥasid* allows the *Sukkah* to be built by a Gentile in an emergency, but generally he seems to oppose this. Cf. 340–1, where, however, other halakhic considerations enter into the matter. Cf. the later authorities quoted by the editor on 340.

[9] 689.

[10] 1351; cf. 1635.

difficulties in collecting debts from a cleric. The latter, knowing the aversion of the Jew to following him into the church, hid himself there from his creditor. 'And the Jew did not follow him there'.[1] A Jew who refrains from joining a procession to meet the king, because of the presence of Christian images and the burning of incense which is performed during the procession, likewise forgoes some advantages.[2] The *Ḥasid* must not employ the services of a Christian cleric in the repairing of his books.[3] If the Jew is himself a craftsman, he must refrain from binding the books of a Christian cleric.[4] Potential loss is involved in the acceptance of the view of Rashbam, which would prohibit a Christian from taking the oath when in debt to a Jew.[5]

The main cause of loss, however, was undoubtedly the prohibition of dealing in the objects of Christian worship. The *Book of the Ḥasidim* does not resort to the distinctions found in the casuistic method of the tosaphists to qualify the prohibited and the permissible. It resorts to the method of casuistry only when religious interests are at stake; for instance, whether the prohibition to enter a church may be suspended in order to save the life of a fellow Jew.[6] Another example is the case where a religious commandment would be neglected if one refused the assistance of a Gentile in its preparatory stages.[7] Economic considerations did not carry sufficient weight with the *Ḥasid* to effect a change in the laws of segregation.[8]

These demands are the expression of an extreme attitude. They represent a special code, for the use of an *élite*, rather than the rules followed by the average Jew. We have no means of ascertaining the absolute or relative number of those who associated themselves with the *Ḥasidim*. But everything known about their rulings indicates that they were more or less isolated individuals rather than a community, or even a fully fledged sect.[9] The decisions of

[1] 1362. [2] 1361. [3] 682. [4] 681.
[5] 1265. Cf. *supra*, Chap. III. [6] 1032. [7] See *supra*, p. 97, n. 8.
[8] The *Ḥasid*'s adherence to the prohibition of dealing in the sacred objects of Christian worship is evident from his moralizing on this point. Cf. 1349; see Baer, op. cit., pp. 37, 41.
[9] Baer, op. cit., p. 6, speaks of a 'movement' of the *Ḥasidim*. The term, however, remains undefined by him, and the view implied in it has not been substantiated.

the *Book of the Ḥasidim* are generally offered to individuals, and only very seldom to a whole community. From the book it appears that dealing in Christian ritual objects was a commonplace occurrence, despite admonitions to the contrary. In one family some members comply with the prohibition, and some do not.[1] In the author's view, the money acquired by transgressing the prohibitions is cursed and 'it is preordained that that money should be lost again'.[2] 'And should you observe that "those who deal with clerics" are rich people, you may be assured that they will not continue to be so until the end of their days.'[3] Of course, punishment may come upon them after their death. In contrast to the story of the *Ḥasid* who was spared from encountering the Christian images at his burial, there is the story of a man who used to supply the clergy with jewellery for the churches; when he died it happened to be the day of a procession, and the Gentiles encountered his funeral with their images. 'So people said it was a just and fitting retribution'.[4]

Nevertheless, even those who aspired to the ideal of the *Ḥasid* in every detail did not sever themselves from all social contact with Gentiles. Economic relations in the course of trading and money-lending were a necessity for the *Ḥasid* also. Neither were reciprocal services between Jews and Gentiles excluded, as the above-mentioned instances show. The *Ḥasid* performed work for a Gentile, and entrusted his own work to a Gentile.[5] In the *Ḥasid*'s house as well as in the houses of other Jews Gentile servants were to be found.[6] There were, perhaps, some individuals who refrained from taking any food prepared by a Gentile,[7] but this was not in order to be an example to others. The *Ḥasidim* accepted the halakhic rule that bread prepared by a Gentile may not be forbidden to the Jewish public.[8] In an emergency, the *Ḥasid* was prepared to use a Gentile's services in the preparatory stage of a

[1] 1350.

[2] 1233. The curse applies also to any other possession acquired in an unfair way.

[3] 1349.

[4] 1359.

[5] See *supra*, p. 98, nn. 3–4. That Jews and Gentiles should perform services for each other is objected to only if some ritual consideration is involved.

[6] 159, 184, 614 (servants or slaves?), 1075.

[7] 1075.

[8] 1940.

ritual act.[1] There were also social contacts of a more intimate kind, as for instance the interpretation of a Gentile's dream by a Jew,[2] as well as reciprocal medical care.[3] The *Ḥasid* objected to any of these contacts only if they involved the transgression of a prohibition.[4] The acts of contact themselves were not regarded as forbidden. Even religious discussions were not excluded, except on grounds of expediency when the Jewish disputant or others attending the controversy might be weakened in their Jewish faith. 'But if you are wise and you know that you will prevail over him', it is one's duty to participate in the discussion.[5]

As the Jews continued their social contact with Gentiles, they were in need of guidance as to how to behave towards them in matters both legal and moral. The author of the *Book of the Ḥasidim* did not refrain from advising the Jews on these matters, generally following the rulings of the halakhists of former generations. Nevertheless, his rulings have some special features. Since contemporary Gentiles were regarded by him as idolaters, the 'alien law' of the Talmud applied to them as a matter of course.[6] The author also accepted the negative evaluation of Gentile morality, which is adduced in the Talmud as a reason for some of the rules of segregation, and applied it to his contemporaries. The bitter experience of Jews who, during persecutions, had hidden themselves in the houses of 'princes who pretended to be their friends' but ultimately had been slain by them served him as additional proof of the truth of the traditional view; and he was able to accept the ruling of the Mishnah that 'one should not stay alone with a Gentile, as he is liable to commit murder' as applicable also to his own generation.[7]

Sometimes the author refused to generalize, and judged each Gentile or Jew according to merit. The two prevalent ways of thought concerning an alien group, the spontaneous and the reflective, which are referred to in Chapter V, are emphasized here with special clarity. In judging individual cases, the *Ḥasid* was well able to set aside the social affiliation of the object of his attention;

[1] See *supra*, p. 97, n. 8.
[2] 389.
[3] 1455, 1470.
[4] 1352.
[5] 811.
[6] This is evident, for instance, from 1216 and 1021, where an exemption is granted to a Gentile of exceptional qualities.
[7] 250, 1848.

thus his moral judgement, unaffected by a strong group-bounded bias, remained fair. But when dealing with Gentiles in general he became the prey of stereotyped characterizations, and individual experiences lost their corrective influence.

Awareness of this differentiation makes it possible to reconcile contradictions between the various attitudes of the *Ḥasid*. Sometimes it would appear that no common bond of humanity existed between Jew and Gentile, as, for instance, when the saving of a Gentile's life was not regarded as justifying any desecration of the Sabbath that might be committed in the course of such an action. The rescuer had to undergo days of fasting, in order to expiate his 'sin'.[1] On the other hand, the life of a Gentile was sacred, and if Jews and Gentiles 'agreed between themselves to stand by each other, and the Gentiles do so with their whole heart, the Jews in turn should stand by the Gentiles'.[2] If a Jew was known to be conspiring against a Gentile with the intention of killing him, it became incumbent on every other Jew to help the Gentile to foil the Jewish plotter.[3] In these cases no reasoned argument for the decision was put forward. It is, however, the very absence of a rational argument that testifies to the genuineness of this moral obligation. In other instances the obligation of integrity and loyalty towards the Gentiles was based on grounds of expediency. Robbing a Gentile was worse than robbing a Jew, for the robber 'will cause many of the privileges granted to the Jews in that town to be abolished'.[4] 'He who borrows from a Gentile and does not intend to repay him is desecrating the Holy Name, for people will say that all the Jews are thieves and knaves.'[5] The term *Ḥillul ha-Shem*, the desecration of the Holy Name, signified in hasidic usage that the individual or the community was in imminent danger because of the immoral act of a Jew. Only occasionally did the original content of the term, with its religious and missionary implications, assert itself: as, for instance, in connexion with the false oath. He who swears perfidiously desecrates the Name of Him in whose Name he swears.[6] Sometimes the *Ḥasid* ignored the

[1] 1777; cf. also 496 *ad fin.*, 1544.
[2] 1849. [3] Ibid. [4] 23, 632.
[5] 1248; see also 1216, 1247.
[6] 1401, 1403. See Baer, op. cit., pp. 40–41.

utilitarian reasons completely, and condemned wrongdoing for its ethical reprehensibility: 'for the Holy One, Blessed be He, does justice to wronged Jews and Gentiles alike'.[1] Sometimes he appended the latter consideration, as if on second thoughts, in obligations which were originally phrased as obligatory to Jews alone. In travelling, one should give precedence to anybody who carried a burden—'even to a Gentile'.[2] 'One should not mislead anyone, not even a Gentile.'[3] This last instance is a quotation from the Talmud.[4] The addition of the words 'even a Gentile' is a pointer to the nature of this moral attitude. The obligations were binding, in the first place, in respect of the members of the inner group. For their application in respect of those who did not belong to the group special reasons had to be adduced, and special emphasis was required.[5]

The attempt of Rabbi Judah *He-Ḥasid* to go beyond the Talmud in regulating relations with Gentiles, especially in the field of ethics, is not an isolated example. A generation later, Rabbi Moses of Coucy, the author of the great compendium of Halakhah and morals known as *Sefer Miṣwoth Gadol* (*Semag*),[6] developed a similar attitude, though taking a different line of thought. Rabbi Moses is primarily a halakhist, but his great work has a frankly educational and moral aim. The admonitory passages which are scattered throughout the book are intended to strengthen the precepts which had first been established and justified on halakhic grounds. The halakhic material is authenticated by the method of the tosaphists, of whom Rabbi Moses was one. As preacher and moralist, he does not restrict himself to addressing the chosen few or an exclusive *élite*. He speaks to all the 'dispersions of Israel', i.e. to the communities of France and Spain which he visited as an itinerant preacher in the years 1236–40.[7] In his capacity of a religious leader of the whole community, he is debarred from making extravagant demands on his own congregants. In contrast to Rabbi Judah *He-Ḥasid*, he

[1] 133. [2] 1003. [3] 1232, 1431.

[4] B.T., *Ḥullin*, 94a. For the exact meaning of the term *genevath da'ath* used here, see *supra*, Chap. V. [5] See *supra*, Chap. V.

[6] I quote according to the Venice edn., 1547.

[7] Graetz, *Geschichte der Juden*, 2nd edn., vii, pp. 62–64; Urbach, *Ba'aley Ha-Tosafoth*, pp. 384–8.

accepts the current view that allows business dealings in Christian ritual objects.[1] However, in connexion with the participation of Jews in Gentile banquets he goes out of his way to take a strict stand, even on points which were contested by other authorities.[2] His inclination to stringency is no doubt influenced by his experiences during his stay in Spain, where the problems of intimate relations, including sexual relations, between Jews and Gentiles were acute. The great preacher singled out the biblical example of Daniel, who refrained from partaking of the meals of Gentiles. Not so his own contemporaries, 'who did not pay attention to this and drank from the wine of the Gentiles and the princes, and their own deputies were the first to sin. Thus I preached in Spain.'[3]

A new note was struck by Rabbi Moses when he was dealing with the problem of moral relations between Jews and Gentiles. The starting-point in his approach to this, as to all other problems, was the talmudic tradition. He therefore had to accept the principle that, according to the basic law, moral obligations between Jew and Gentile were not the same as those between Jew and Jew. He was inclined to eliminate this moral stumbling block even from the talmudic sources by means of interpretation. For instance, he limited the application of the talmudic controversy as to whether the property of a Gentile was protected by law to the case of a Gentile who injured a Jew,[4] without any recognizable authority for this assertion. He consequently assumed that normally, even in talmudic times, it was never disputed that the property of a Gentile enjoyed the same protection as that of a Jew. However, not all discrepancies of the Gentile's legal status could be thus explained away. Rabbi Moses, as a compiler of the halakhic sources, faithfully repeated the controversies of his predecessors, Rabbenu Tam and Rashbam, concerning a Gentile's property which had come into the possession of a Jew by an oversight.[5] His arrogation of a superior moral approach found expression in the concluding

[1] *Semag*, p. 10a–b. He is not amongst the more lenient halakhists, and some prohibitions remain valid. His method, however, is casuistic, and he accepts the exemptions authorized by his predecessors.

[2] In prohibiting beer manufactured by Gentiles he went farther than the tosaphists. *Semag*, pp. 54d, 57a. Cf. *Tosafoth*, *'A.Z.*, 31b.

[3] *Semag*, p. 54c.

[4] Ibid., p. 58b.

[5] Ibid., p. 167d.

sentence of the discussion: 'but we have already explained, concerning the remnant of Israel, that they are not to deceive anyone, whether a Christian or a Moslem'.[1]

The clue to the above sentence lies in the use of the biblical expression 'the remnant of Israel', which is applied by Rabbi Moses to his own generation. As we shall see, Rabbi Moses regarded his time as the period of the advent of the Messiah, and his generation as being that referred to by the Prophets as the residue of Israel who were considered worthy of redemption.[2] From this he inferred the existence of special obligations of a universal kind, as he explains in a noble passage:

> I have already preached to the dispersed community of Jerusalem which is in Spain, and to the dispersed communities in other Christian lands,[3] that, now that the dispersion has lasted all too long, Israelites should separate themselves from the vanities of the world and hold fast to the seal of the Holy One, Blessed be He, namely Truth, and not lie either to a Jew or to Gentiles, nor mislead them in any matter; but should sanctify themselves, even in that which is permitted to them, as it is said, *The remnant of Israel shall not do injustice and shall not speak what is false, neither shall there be found in their mouth the tongue of deceit* (Zeph. iii. 13). So that when the Holy One, Blessed be He, comes to save them, the Gentiles shall say, 'He has acted justly, for they are men of truth and the law of truth is in their mouths.' But if they behave deceitfully towards the Gentiles, they will say, 'See what the Holy One, Blessed be He, has done. He has chosen thieves and impostors for His portion.' Furthermore it is written, *and I will sow her unto me in the earth* (Hos. ii. 23). Now a man will only sow one measure in order to produce several measures. Thus the Holy One, Blessed be He, sows Israel in the lands so that proselytes shall be gathered unto them; but so long as they behave deceitfully towards them, who will cleave unto them?[4]

The concept of *Ḥillul ha-Shem* emerges here purged of any notion of utilitarianism and expediency. It has recaptured its original religious meaning, appealing to the bearer of the true faith to live by the moral standard demanded by the loftiest conception of the religious idea. At the same time, this appeal is

[1] *Semag*, p. 167d.
[2] See *supra*, Chap. VI.
[3] It is to be noted that this admonition is not limited to Spain, as is that of p. 103, n. 3.
[4] *Semag*, p. 152c–d.

wedded to the messianic expectation which, once again, became intense at this period in Jewish history. The tense, eschatological atmosphere lends special weight to the appeal. The *Ḥasid* now feels entitled to demand of his fellow Jews that they elevate themselves to the standard of moral perfection necessary to justify their redemption in the eyes of the Gentiles. This notion is also connected with the anticipation that, as a first step to redemption, Gentiles will accept Judaism and become proselytes.[1] Jews, therefore, must live an exemplary moral life, so as to attract the Gentiles to their community.

[1] See *supra*, Chap. VI.

IX

THE DISPUTANT

ALL that we have heard up to this point about the Jewish attitude towards Christianity has been derived from sources which were intended for internal Jewish use. The definition of the Jewish position was the product of the need for self-identification and for self-protection from the impact of the Gentile world. At the same time, it served to reconcile accepted practice with the traditional concept of the relationship between Jewry and the 'Nations'.

We may take it for granted that some of the arguments which contributed to internal clarification were also used in controversies with Gentiles. Such disputations did occasionally occur,[1] but the first literary account of one from the Jewish side dates from the middle of the thirteenth century. In the year 1240 a disputation took place in Paris between a Jewish apostate and four representatives of French Jewry. One of these was Rabbi Moses of Coucy, with whose teachings we have become acquainted in previous chapters. He assisted his colleague Rabbi Yeḥiel of Paris, who took the lead in the discussion on the Jewish side.[2]

This controversy, however, was not a voluntary one. It was forced upon the Jewish scholars by an apostate, through the agency of the Inquisition, which on this occasion concerned itself for the first time with Jewish teachings. Two accounts of the course of the controversy are extant, one in Latin, being the official record of the tribunal, and one in Hebrew attributed to Rabbi Yeḥiel of Paris.[3] The two accounts do not square with each other in their

[1] See E. E. Urbach, 'Étude sur la littérature polémique au moyen-âge', *REJ*, 1935, pp. 50–77.

[2] The story has been told repeatedly; cf. Graetz, *Geschichte der Juden*, 2nd edn., vii, pp. 104–7; Urbach, *Ba'aley Ha-Tosafoth*, pp. 371–5. See also next note.

[3] I. Loeb, 'La controverse de 1240 sur le Talmud', *REJ*, i, 1880, pp. 247–67; ii, 1881, pp. 243–70; iii, 1881, pp. 39–75; F. Y. Baer, 'Le-biqqoreth ha-wikkuḥim shel R. Yeḥi'el mi-Paris we-shel R. Mosheh ben Naḥman', *Tarbiz*, ii, 1931, pp. 172–7; Urbach, *Ba'aley Ha-Tosafoth*, p. 372. The Hebrew version (*Wikkuaḥ Rabbenu Yeḥi'el mi-Paris*) has appeared in many editions; I quote

details, and historical criticism has reached the conclusion that the Hebrew version is not a record of what was actually said at the time of the controversy, but a free reconstruction written for the benefit of Jewish readers, instructing them what a disputant would have been able to retort had he been free to speak his whole mind.

Nevertheless, the Jewish version does reflect the predicament and atmosphere of a public disputation, and furnishes an insight into the approach and technique which were apt to be used in such a situation. As far as the questions raised are concerned, there are no major differences between the official protocol and the Hebrew account.[1] They revolve about the points already raised in internal Jewish discussions. The main interest of our analysis will therefore be to ascertain how far the answers accepted for internal Jewish use stood the test of public disputation.

The resemblance of the questions posed during the disputation to those raised in internal Jewish discussion is to be explained, of course, by the fact that the accuser was a converted Jew who was well versed in the Jewish sources. The technique of his accusation is very simple. He takes the various dicta of the Talmud at their face value, and asserts that all that is said in them about Gentiles applies, without qualification, to Christians. In this way there emerges a picture of extreme hostility on the part of the Jews towards their Christian neighbours. 'You have permitted [Jews] to shed the blood of Gentiles.' 'It is permitted to steal and plunder the Gentile's possessions and [it is allowed] to cheat him.' 'Concerning the lost property of a Gentile, you say that it is forbidden to return it to him.' The Gentile is suspected by the Jew of practising fornication, adultery, and sodomy. The Jew is not allowed to make the Gentile any gift, nor is he even permitted to say, 'How handsome this Gentile is'; 'it is permitted to you to curse and to despise idolatry'; 'and we are as despised in your eyes as locusts and flies'.[2]

As it is certain that the apostate knew what the sources originally meant and how they were treated in internal Jewish discussions,

the first (Thorn, 1873). An inadequate translation into English is to be found in M. Brande, *Conscience on Trial*, 1952.

[1] Cf. Loeb and Baer as quoted in the previous note.

[2] *Wikkuaḥ*, pp. 8–9.

we cannot acquit him of the charge of basing his accusations on grounds known to him to be false. Some of the sources he misused, for none of them warranted the statement that a Jew was allowed to shed the blood of a Gentile.[1] He must further have been aware that the sentences quoted by him were not applied to contemporary Gentiles without qualification by any Jewish authority. The indignation of his Jewish opponents is therefore easily understandable. The situation appears the more tragically ironic in that the accusations were levelled at Rabbi Moses of Coucy, who, as we have seen, had done more than anyone else to neutralize the possible influence of the talmudic dicta on the conduct of Jews in their relationships with Christians.[2]

In any case, the refutation of the apostate's charges was not a difficult task. The defenders had only to point to actual practice to prove that Jews did not apply the ruling of the Talmud concerning idolators to contemporary Gentiles. 'None of the prohibitions binding on us in respect of those nations do we apply to you.'[3] The apologists enumerated the talmudic prohibitions which were in fact being ignored by Jews every day. The Mishnah says that one should not deal with Gentiles three days before their festivals: 'go to the street of the Jews and see how much business they do even on the day of the feast itself'.[4] Contrary to the prescription of the Talmud, 'we do sell cattle to Gentiles, we enter into companionship with them, we stay with them alone, we entrust our infants to them to be suckled in their own homes, and we do teach *Torah* to a Gentile, for there are many clerics able to read Jewish books'.[5]

The difficulties of the Jewish disputants commenced when they

[1] The dictum 'the best amongst the Gentiles should be slain', from Tractate *Soferim*, chap. 15, appears in an aggadic connexion and, whatever its meaning may be, it certainly does not imply permission to shed Gentile blood. See the variant readings in J. Müller, *Massekheth Soferim*, pp. 211–12, and *Tosafoth*, *'A.Z.*, 26b. As capital punishment lay outside contemporary Jewish jurisdiction, Jewish medieval authorities had little opportunity of dealing with the homicide of either a Jew or a Gentile. Occasionally the prohibition of both was stated: see *Sefer Yere'im*, 84a. The attitude of talmudic law to the murder of strangers is sufficiently treated by the Christian scholar G. Marx (i.e. Dalman, pseudonymously), *Die Tötung Ungläubiger nach talmudisch-rabbinischem Recht*, Leipzig, 1885.

[2] Cf. Chap. VII.

[3] *Wikkuaḥ*, p. 10.

[4] Ibid.

[5] Ibid.

passed from the stating of these facts to explaining them. These practices were, admittedly, at variance with the letter of the law, the validity of which was not denied. Neither could the Jewish apologists explain the legal devices with which the non-application of these precepts was justified in halakhic literature. For these devices had been evolved with regard to individual cases, every point of which involved a particular course of reasoning. Such reasoning could scarcely be understood, and certainly not appreciated, by anyone who was not initiated into the methods of the halakhic discussions. The apologists had therefore to look for an answer which was comprehensive enough to justify all the exemptions from the law, and which had a reasonable chance of being accepted, at least by an unprejudiced opponent. Such an answer was the distinction between contemporary Gentiles and those of talmudic times. As we have seen above,[1] such a distinction was repeatedly made by the halakhists in order to reconcile tradition with accepted practice. In these cases, however, it was limited to certain instances and was not meant to be of comprehensive application. The disputants, under the pressure of the polemic situation, extended the casual distinction to a broad generalization. All the segregative laws, it was claimed, were enacted with regard to the nations of antiquity only. Contemporary Gentiles, i.e. Christians, were altogether exempted from them.

Here, apparently, we are moving towards the establishment of a rule which would base the exemption of the Christians from the segregative laws upon a principle. The statement of the disputants was a shift from near-casuistic justification in the direction of a definite rule; such a rule was actually established, some fifty or sixty years later, by Rabbi Menaḥem Ha-Me'iri. But we have not yet arrived at an actual principle. For the seemingly comprehensive exemption is based upon a distinction which its proposer used as a polemical device, but which he could not genuinely have endorsed in practice.

The disputants claimed that all disparaging references to Gentiles in talmudic sources applied only to those 'seven nations' which are mentioned in the Bible as the aboriginal inhabitants of

[1] Cf. Chaps. III and IV.

the Land of Israel, and remnants of which survived as late as talmudic times.[1] But this statement is no more than an *ad hoc* device to be used in the course of controversy. There is no indication in the Talmud or in the later halakhic sources that such a view was ever held, or even proposed, by any individual halakhist. In fact, evidence to the contrary exists. For it was the accepted view in the Talmud that the nations among whom Jews lived at that time were not descendants of the seven nations. Only on this assumption was it possible to accept proselytes, the aboriginal inhabitants of the Land of Israel being excluded from the privilege of joining the Jewish nation.[2]

The motive for applying this argument is clear enough. In falling back, as it were, from the Talmud upon the Bible, the Jewish disputants gained common ground with their Christian opponent. If the disqualification of Gentiles mentioned in the Talmud applied to the 'seven nations' of Palestine, the blame for it, if blame was due, attached not only to those who adhered to the Talmud, but also to all who shared the belief in the divine origin of the Bible.[3] The 'seven nations' were singled out because of their idolatry and their licentious way of life. The enacting of segregative laws against these nations could not but be justified in Christian eyes. At the price of some slight disingenuousness, the Jewish disputants had scored a good point.

This disingenuousness may be judged leniently, first of all because it was occasioned by a controversy which was forced upon the Jewish disputants, and the outcome of which might have been disastrous to their whole community. It indeed turned out to be so, for the controversy in Paris ended with the confiscation and burning of the Talmud in Paris in the year 1242.[4] Moreover, even

[1] 'Take this as a rule: Wherever the [word] Gentile [is mentioned] in the Talmud, it refers to [a member of] one of the seven nations who made peace by accepting the condition of paying tribute.' *Wikkuaḥ*, p. 10. The last passage refers to the *'aggadah* in Pal. T., *Shevi'ith*, 6. 1, that makes Joshua, previous to his conquest, send word to the inhabitants of the Land of Israel that those who accepted the conqueror's rule would be spared.

[2] B.T., *Berakhoth*, 28a.

[3] The device of shifting the discussion from the Talmud to the Bible is applied by the Jewish disputants in regard to other questions also. *Wikkuaḥ*, pp. 2, 14–15.

[4] The exact date is much disputed; cf. Urbach, *Ba'aley Ha-Tosafoth*, pp. 375–6.

if the argument was not sincere, the conclusion to which it was intended to point, namely that the talmudical laws were not to be applied to contemporary Christians, was substantially correct. It is true that the conclusion, if based on the adduced reason, was more far-reaching than it would have been so long as it rested on the arguments of particular instances. For, on the assumption that the talmudic laws were concerned with the 'seven nations' only, the contemporary Christians would have been exempted from any of the allusions in valid talmudic law. But this was certainly not the intention of the disputants, any more than it was the intention of any other Jewish authority at the time. Consistency of thought, however, was not achieved or sought even in internal Jewish discussion.

To make use of *ad hoc* arguments, of whose truth the proposer himself was not wholly convinced, was an accepted practice in medieval polemics. We have good examples of it in our own text. The apostate referred to the talmudic saying that the serpent imbued Eve with its *zohamah*;[1] and Israel, in contrast to the nations, was purged from it when standing on Mount Sinai. To this he receives the answer: 'That applies only to those nations I have mentioned, the Canaanites, and the Egyptians who were immersed in lechery and did not stand at Mount Sinai or receive the *Torah*. You, however, did receive the *Torah*, and your Lord did not come to abolish our *Torah* and did not add to it or diminish it; so according to your own words your *zohamah* ceased to be, and the talmudic sages did not refer to you.'[2] The phrase 'according to your own words' discloses the dialectic employed. The defendant allows himself to answer the question in such a way as to make it acceptable to the questioner on his own assumptions. But the propounder of the reply himself does not commit himself to sharing the conclusions indicated.

Similar dialectical ambiguity is encountered in another distinction which was made by the disputants. It concerned the attitude of the Jews towards the ruling authority, the *malekhuth*. The apostate accused the Jews of being disloyal to the sovereign, since they

[1] B.T., *Yevamoth*, 103b. *Zohamah* is rendered 'sullying' or 'lust'. What it implies theologically is not quite clear.

[2] *Wikkuaḥ*, p. 11.

prayed for the downfall of the *malekhuth zadon*, i.e. the unrighteous kingdom.[1] The disputants replied that the prayer referred to the kings of ancient Egypt, to Nebuchadnezzar, king of Babylonia, and his like, 'who all of them slew people of Israel', and so on.[2] Now this part of the answer was certainly fictitious, for when Jews prayed for the coming of the Messiah and for the downfall of the 'unrighteous kingdom', they meant the whole secular world with its entire political edifice. But the concluding words were meant to point to a contrast: 'But as for this kingdom and the Pope, who command, with all their powers, to protect us, and who keep us alive and give us sustenance and refuge in their land of their own free will—for we have no portion and inheritance with them in this land, and through them (and the Creator) do we live—surely no one will believe that we should repay kindness with evil. Of this kingdom it is said: *pray for the peace of the realm*.'[3] Both gratitude for protection, and the prayer for the peace and well-being of the realm, were genuinely meant.

Controversies with Christians fulfilled the unintentional function of furthering the clarification of Jewish thinking about the Jew's position and status in the Gentile world. It may be that the Paris disputation gave occasion to those who took part in it to survey all that had been said until then concerning their relationships with Gentiles. In comparison with the sporadic utterances in halakhic contexts, the overall exemption of Christians from a particular category of the talmudic laws is certainly a step towards a measure of recognition for Christianity.

This more positive attitude towards Christianity here receives an additional impulse from the fact that the Christian opponents appear in conjunction with the apostate. The Jewish disputants have therefore to fight on two fronts: and there is a marked difference in tone and content according to whether the Jewish arguments are directed towards the Christian or at the apostate. Rage and hatred are levelled against the apostate, while what is said against the Christian is not only lenient in comparison, but even acquires an element of independent condonation and apology.

[1] *Wikkuaḥ*, p. 11.

[2] Ibid., p. 12.

[3] Ibid., pp. 12–13; cf. *supra*, Chap. V.

Of the apostate the Talmud states (*Rosh ha-Shanah*, 17a) that '*Gehenna* will be consumed, but they will not be consumed.' For apostates 'altered the Covenant, as they were of Jewish faith first, and bore it many days and then cast away the yoke'. 'But the Gentiles, who did not accept the Covenant, do not deserve *Gehenna* to the same extent.'[1] For the Gentiles, the disputant can suggest a way of salvation. 'If you keep the seven commandments of the Noachides, which were commanded to you, you will be saved.'[2] But the apostate is obliged to fulfil the 613 commandments of the Jewish law, and, if he fails to fulfil even one, 'he will be doomed to annihilation. For he originally accepted the Covenant.'[3] Even if these words were written only in order to annoy the apostate, the idea of tolerance, namely the accordance of a certain recognition to the Gentiles, is implicit in them. The situation created by the controversy may have advanced the thought of the disputants beyond the point up to which they had committed themselves in the first place.

If our analysis is valid, we have exposed a very significant historical coincidence. For the Paris disputation marks a transition, from the comparative tolerance of the Catholic Church towards the Jewish faith to the harassing practice of scrutinizing and censuring Jewish customs and tenets.[4] The same event assisted, or even compelled, the Jews to take a further step towards the idea of religious tolerance.

[1] *Wikkuaḥ*, p. 12. [2] Ibid. [3] Ibid.

[4] Graetz, *Geschichte der Juden*, 2nd edn., viii, pp. 116–20. S. Grayzel, *Church*, pp. 29–33.

X

MEN OF ENLIGHTENMENT[1]

In the present chapter we shall go beyond the boundaries of time and space within which we have moved hitherto. We shall also encounter a new type of personality in R. Menaḥem Ha-Me'iri.[2] Ha-Me'iri was active in Provence, at the turn of the fourteenth century.[3] He belonged to the group of rationalists who maintained the philosophical tradition derived from Spanish-Jewish sources. Ha-Me'iri took up a position in defence of philosophy during the controversy about Maimonides' teaching, which arose for the second time in the first decade of the fourteenth century.[4] It will not be surprising to find that his exceptional attitude towards other religions is connected with his philosophical outlook.

In spite of these facts, the teachings of Ha-Me'iri are not extraneous to our main theme. For whatever might have been the impulse which prompted him to conceive his theory of religious tolerance, both its application and its justification had to be achieved on the basis of the Halakhah. As a halakhist, Ha-Me'iri undoubtedly belongs to the Ashkenazi school, whose method had captivated the minds of the talmudists of Spain and Provence some hundred years before he was born.[5] Ha-Me'iri himself added to this method of interpretation some individual features of elucidation and paraphrase. Fundamentally, however, Ha-Me'iri follows

[1] I have treated the subject of this chapter in an article in *Zion*, xviii, 1953, pp. 15–30.

[2] For the biography of Ha-Me'iri see S. K. Mirsky, *Toledoth Rabbi Menaḥem Ha-Me'iri u-Sefaraw*, which appeared as a preface to Ha-Me'iri's *Ḥibbur Ha-Teshuvah*, ed. A. Schreiber, New York, 1950; M. N. Zobel, 'Qeṣath Peraṭim le-Toledoth Ha-Rav Ha-Me'iri', S. A. Horodezky Jubilee volume (*'Eder Ha-Yeqar*), Tel Aviv, 1947, pp. 88–96.

[3] The date of Ha-Me'iri's death is contested; see Zobel, op. cit., pp. 93–96, who supports the year 1315.

[4] Graetz, *Geschichte der Juden*, 2nd edn., vii, pp. 239–50; F. Y. Baer, *Toledoth Ha-Yehudim bi-Sefarad Ha-Noṣerith*, pp. 191 ff.; J. Sarachek, *Faith and Reason, the Conflict over the Rationalism of Maimonides*, 1935, pp. 167–201.

[5] See I. H. Weiss, *Dor Dor we-Doreshaw*, v, pp. 3–5.

the method of the tosaphists. Like them, he strives to arrive at a harmonization of the sources; and, in determining the Halakhah, he endeavours to reach conclusions which are not at variance with accepted practice.[1] We shall find both tendencies corroborated by many instances relating to our special problem. In contrast, however, to this correspondence with the tosaphists' aims and methods, we shall find that in evaluating contemporary Christianity and Islam Ha-Me'iri developed an attitude deviating from that of other halakhists down to his own generation.

Ha-Me'iri's personal view can best be summarized thus: he held that the exclusion of Christians and Moslems from the category of the idolatrous—an exclusion which had been suggested purely casuistically by earlier halakhists—was to be acknowledged as a firm and comprehensive principle. At first sight, the opinion of other halakhists and that of Ha-Me'iri might be taken as identical. Modern scholars, affected by an apologetic bias of their own, have read into the Ashkenazi halakhists' views the theory held by Ha-Me'iri.[2] It may, however, be possible to demonstrate the uniqueness of his attitude by several arguments.

1. *Verbal usage*. Ha-Me'iri, when he wished to differentiate between the nations of talmudic times and contemporary Gentiles, coined a new term, as was already observed by D. Hoffmann.[3] He called his contemporaries *'ummoth ha-geduroth be-darekhey ha-dathoth*, 'nations restricted by the ways of religion', and those of talmudic times 'nations not delimited by the ways of religion'.[4] We shall have to consider later the theological implications of this definition. It is, however, certainly not without significance that Ha-Me'iri expresses the exclusion of Christians from the category of idolaters not only in negative, but also by a definition in positive, terms. In this way he granted them a positive religious status. Indeed, the kind of expression used by Ha-Me'iri is different from

[1] Ha-Me'iri's standing with halakhists of recent generations is shown by the fact that they were the first to publish most of his works. An analysis of his method has not yet been attempted.

[2] D. Hoffmann, *Schulchan Aruch*, pp. 4–7. More explicitly H. Albeck in his introduction to Mishnah, *'A.Z.*, p. 322.

[3] Op. cit., p. 7.

[4] *Beth Ha-Beḥirah* on *'Avodah Zarah* (henceforth *B.H.–'A.Z.*), ed. A. Schreiber, 1944, pp. 46, 591, also p. 39. Other slight variations in *B.H.*, *Bava Qamma*, ed. K. Schlesinger, p. 320, and other passages quoted below.

that of the other halakhists, even when he has recourse to negative terms. 'We have already explained that all these things were said at the time [i.e. that of the talmudic sages] when those Gentiles were cleaving to their idolatry, but now idolatry has disappeared from most places. . . .'[1] No such clear-cut statement is to be found in the writings of other halakhists.

2. *The unqualified nature of the consequences.* The straightforward language of Ha-Me'iri is the unhesitating expression of an unqualified attitude. As we have seen in the first chapters of this book, other halakhists discarded the talmudic precepts under pressure of circumstances only, and as a concession to accepted usage. Contrary to this, Ha-Me'iri is almost glad to notice the obsolescence of the talmudic precepts. 'In our days nobody heeds these things, neither *Ga'on*, Rabbi, Disciple, *Ḥasid*, nor would-be *Ḥasid*.'[2] This exuberant and almost jubilant language is well in accord with the view expressed here. For in contrast to the other halakhists, who could give their assent to the disregarding of the talmudic precepts with reluctance only, Ha-Me'iri could do so whole-heartedly, since in his opinion it was not a concession but a clear case, based upon a firm principle.

3. *The exclusive application of the exemption.* The limited importance which was attached by the ordinary halakhist to the distinction between the nations of old and his Gentile contemporaries is apparent in the way use was made of this idea. As we have observed in the analysis of Rabbenu Gershom,[3] the distinction was used by him (as by other halakhists) as one of many casuistic devices to justify the disregarding of certain specific talmudic laws. Not so with Ha-Me'iri. He acknowledges the distinction as the only answer which could account for the contradiction between the law and accepted practice. Consistently, he renounces all the other ways of harmonizing them which had been put forward in halakhic literature down to his own time. After discussing the merits of these devices on logical considerations, he discards all of them as being neither useful nor necessary. For, having accepted the distinctions between the idolaters of old and the *'ummoth ha-geduroth*, 'you have no need of the forced justifications which you

[1] *B.H.–'A.Z.*, p. 28. [2] Ibid., p. 3. [3] See *supra*, Chap. III.

will find in the talmudic commentaries and the *Tosafoth*'.[1] These can only be the expressions of someone who is convinced of the truth of the one solution, validity of which entails the repudiation of all others.

4. *The extent to which this distinction is applied.* Even more conclusive is the extent to which Ha-Me'iri, in contrast to other halakhists, applied this rule. When a question arose concerning the halakhic justification of the making of gifts by Jews to Gentiles, which was prohibited in talmudic law, the halakhists had to resort to the implicit concession in the circumstance that some talmudic sources had, as they found, made an exception if the Gentile was a good friend.[2] Ha-Me'iri can dispense with this circumvention, and remarks: 'But in so far as we have to deal with nations which are restricted by the ways of religion and which believe in the Godhead, there is no doubt that, even if he [the Gentile] is not a friend, it is not only permitted, but even meritorious to do so.'[3] The tosaphists also had to find casuistic justification for disregarding the precept laid down in the Mishnah (*'A.Z.*, 1. 8): 'One should not let a house to a Gentile.'[4] Ha-Me'iri states simply: 'This prohibition applies fundamentally only to those idolaters who kept their idols in their house, and sacrificed to them there.'[5] The Mishnah forbade Jews to commit beasts to the care of Gentiles, who were suspected of perverted sexual practices. Once again the tosaphists had to account for the ignoring of this precept by their Jewish contemporaries.[6] Ha-Me'iri finds this disregard justified by his comprehensive distinction: 'It has been already stated that these things were said concerning periods when there existed nations of idolaters, and they were contaminated in their deeds and tainted in their dispositions . . . but other nations, which are restricted by the ways of religion and which are free from such blemishes of character—on the contrary, they even punish such deeds—are, without doubt, exempt from this prohibition.'[7]

Finally, Ha-Me'iri used his principle to escape the moral

[1] *B.H.–'A.Z.*, p. 28.

[2] *Tosafoth, 'A.Z.*, 20a, cf. *Pisqey Tosafoth* on the same passage, and *Haggahoth Ha-Rosh, 'A.Z.*, 1. 19.

[3] *B.H.–'A.Z.*, p. 46.

[4] *Tosafoth, 'A.Z.*, 21a.

[5] *B.H.–'A.Z.*, p. 48.

[6] *Tosafoth, 'A.Z.*, 22a.

[7] *B.H.–'A.Z.*, p. 53.

embarrassment which some talmudic passages had caused Jewish religious leadership for many a generation. We have noticed what means the other halakhists had adopted to neutralize reprehensible sentiments which seemed to require lower standards of morality in relation to Gentiles.[1] Ha-Me'iri could once again deal with the whole problem comprehensively and as a matter of principle. For all the instances in which, according to the Talmud, Gentiles were not on the same legal and moral footing as the Jews applied to peoples of remote times only, who deserved no better treatment. 'But everyone who belongs to the *'ummoth ha-geduroth* . . . is not included in this, and is to be regarded as a full Jew in respect of all this.'[2]

There is, therefore, no doubt that Ha-Me'iri elevated the idea of the distinction between the peoples of old and the Christians and Moslems of his time into a principle applicable whenever and wherever it was needed.

In endowing the distinction between the peoples of the two periods with the character of a principle, Ha-Me'iri definitely transcended the conventional methods of halakhic thinking. It was implicit in this method, as we have seen above, to avoid committing oneself to consistency. The question therefore arises, what had prompted Ha-Me'iri to introduce into the halakhic discussion a line of argument which was alien to it, and did not serve any practical purpose? For, as we shall see later, Ha-Me'iri did not intend to abolish any precepts concerning the relationship between Jews and Gentiles which were not already disregarded in practice and had not been justified by other halakhists. The difference between the two ways of justification was a theoretical one. While the other halakhists arrived at their arguments casuistically and piecemeal, Ha-Me'iri attained the same object with one simple maxim. But there is no doubt that the evolution and presentation of the maxim occasioned Ha-Me'iri a personal—one might say a spiritual—satisfaction.

[1] See *supra*, Chap. V.

[2] *B.H.*, *Bava Qamma*, p. 320; see also p. 120. Some passages relating to the problem of morality were already known before the publication of Ha-Me'iri's major work. They were, significantly, quoted by Bezalel Ashkenazi, *Shiṭṭah Mequbbeṣeth* on *Bava Qamma*, 38a, 113b.

Obviously, the concept of *'ummoth ha-geduroth*, which is Ha-Me'iri's main intellectual instrument in the achievement of his purpose, originated outside the province of Halakhah, in the sphere of philosophical and theological thinking. On the basis of Ha-Me'iri's exegetical and philosophical writings, we are fortunately able to describe the system of thought which served as a background to the evolution of this concept.

As mentioned above, Ha-Me'iri belongs to the 'rationalistic' school of the post-Maimonidean period. In accordance with the exponents of this school, he held that the ultimate destiny of man was intellectual insight into the essence of God.[1] In the field of practice, i.e. of the moral and ritual commandments, he would have been able to discover some parts of the revealed religion for himself.[2] Other doctrinal and practical elements of religion were, however, vouchsafed to man by revelation only. The intellectual aim of religion is to be valued more highly than the practical one.[3] But in point of temporal succession, practice has to precede the intellectual insight; and 'the latter is the fruit of the former, and is derived from it'.[4]

Every student of medieval Jewish philosophy will recognize in this train of thought the reflection of the ideas of Maimonides.[5] Ha-Me'iri was not only a champion of Maimonides in the controversy over his teaching; he also became his popularizer. But as regards the evaluation of other religions, he took up a stand independent of that of Maimonides, and indeed in diametrical opposition to it. Maimonides appraised the achievement of the two other monotheistic religions, Christianity and Islam, as historical extensions of Judaism, and conceived their historic task to be the dissemination of Jewish ideas in preparation for the messianic era, when the pure monotheistic doctrine of Judaism would be

[1] *Ḥibbur Ha-Teshuvah*, p. 540; cf. his commentary on Proverbs (Fürth, 1844), chap. 1 *ad fin.*, where he classifies man in a Platonic fashion. Some human beings are capable of manual work only, others also of social and moral achievement. A third category is capable of grasping the truth. In this, 'the purpose of Creation is fulfilled'.

[2] *Ḥibbur Ha-Teshuvah*, p. 256.

[3] Ibid., p. 540.

[4] Ibid.

[5] See *The Guide for the Perplexed*, 3. 54, and the *Eight Chapters* (introduction to Mishnah, *'Avoth*), chap. 5.

universally accepted.[1] But in their actual religious practices and tenets, he regarded them—Christianity even more than Islam—as contaminated with idolatrous elements. The talmudic laws concerning the relationship between Jews and Gentiles were, therefore, to be accepted as valid also with regard to contemporary Christians.[2]

This is the point where Ha-Me'iri went his own way. He taught that Gentile nations were also capable of founding religions, whose inferiority to Judaism was but comparative. This admission is an outcome of his theory of religion as summarized above. Since the Jewish religion itself contains practical as well as doctrinal elements —elements which could have been evolved without prophecy and revelation—it is quite plausible to assume the existence of nations who did in fact develop a religion of this type, based upon those pre-revelational elements. The doctrinal elements could have been achieved through philosophical reasoning, while the practical elements might have been evolved by that 'imaginative power' which, according to the theory of Maimonides, was the faculty of 'leaders of States and law-givers'.[3] Following up this theory, and by watering down, to some extent, the meaning of prophecy, Ha-Me'iri defined the nature of other religions, which stood in no need of a real prophet but rather of leaders to introduce political institutions and to give laws. Such institutions and laws could be arrived at, according to the theory, by the perfection of imagination: and 'this would be entirely sufficient for them, according to the nature of their religions'.[4] The Jewish religion adds to this its own special content, which imparts to its followers the distinction of being 'perfected by all kinds of perfections, perfections of virtues as well as those of intellectual and doctrinal ideas'.[5]

We are now in a position to determine the exact meaning of Ha-Me'iri's formula, so often used in a halakhic context,

[1] G. Tschernowitz, *Ha-Yaḥas beyn Yisra'el la-Goyim le-fi Ha-Rambam*, New York, 1950.

[2] See Maimonides' commentary on Mishnah, *'A.Z.*, 1. 1, and *Hilkhoth 'Avodath Kokhavim*, 9. 4. This paragraph is omitted in the censored editions. Cf. G. Tschernowitz, op. cit., p. 20.

[3] *The Guide for the Perplexed*, 2. 37.

[4] Ha-Me'iri's commentary on Mishnah, *'Avoth*, ed. S. Stern, 1854, Introduction, pp. 3b ff.

[5] Ibid.

'ummoth ha-geduroth and its opposite. By the first expression is meant the maintenance of juridical and moral institutions, i.e. the practical aspect of religion, which the nations could have evolved without any revelation in the strict theological sense of the term. In the same way they could arrive at a certain degree of theoretical insight, and Ha-Me'iri sometimes adds to the characteristics of the contemporary nations that they 'recognize the Godhead'[1] or that 'they believe in God's existence, His unity, and power, although they misconceive some points according to our belief'.[2] However, Ha-Me'iri's positive evaluation of Christianity stems in the main from his esteem for the maintenance of legal institutions and moral standards in society.[3]

This conception of an intermediate type, standing between Jews and idolaters, was not entirely novel. Talmudic literature contains the notion of *ger toshav*, meaning a Gentile who has given up idolatry, or observes certain fundamental commandments of the Jewish religion summed up in the 'seven precepts of the sons of Noah'.[4] This term, apparently, reflects the historical reality of the situation at the beginning of the era of the Second Temple; and the literary tradition may have facilitated the formulation of Ha-Me'iri's term. The notion of *ger toshav*, however, was fraught with associations which made it inappropriate as a definition to be applied to Christianity and Islam.[5] Moreover, a positive concept relating to contemporary Gentiles was insufficient for the evolution of Ha-Me'iri's theory. He needed a negative term to describe the ancient nations, in relation to whom the segregative laws of the Mishnah could be justified. The term *'ummoth ha-geduroth* met this requirement. In applying this term, Ha-Me'iri contrived to depict these peoples of his own imagination in as unattractive a light as possible. They are devoid of the doctrinal, as well as the practical, benefits of religion. 'They have no religion whatsoever,

[1] *B.H.–'A.Z.*, p. 46.

[2] *B.H.*, *Giṭṭin* (ed. K. Schlesinger, 1943), p. 246.

[3] Cf. the passages quoted above in connexion with his term *'ummoth ha-geduroth*.

[4] B.T., *'A.Z.*, 64b. According to a third opinion, the *ger toshav* observes all the precepts of the Jewish religion except the dietary laws. This view, however, was disregarded by later halakhists. See Maimonides, *Hilkhoth 'Avodath Kokhavim*, 10. 6; *B.H.–'A.Z.*, pp. 255–6.

[5] *B.H.–'A.Z.*, p. 214.

and they do not submit to the fear of the Godhead.'[1] On the other hand, 'they did not refrain from any iniquity',[2] 'and they were defiled in their deeds and corrupted in their nature'.[3] Some features of this description may have been derived from the Mishnah and Talmud, which attributed similarly abhorrent qualities to those against whom the segregative enactments were deemed to be necessary.[4] But the theoretical aspect of this description, viz. that these nations had neither faith nor religion, is the result of Ha-Me'iri's own philosophical conception. According to this theory, even the political and moral order in society is the product of the first grade of prophecy and philosophical insight, which such nations could never have possessed.

It is, however, possible to trace another direct source of this conception. It is once again Maimonides who, in his *Guide for the Perplexed*, propounded a theory of the biblical commandments. These commandments were said to have been enacted as a protection for Israel against possible contamination by a morally degenerate race, the Sabæans, who were supposed to have existed at the time of Moses.[5] This assumption, as well as details of its elaboration, Maimonides owed to Arabic sources.[6] For Ha-Me'iri, Maimonides' description became a model for imitation. Just as Maimonides had explained the necessity for the biblical laws by presupposing this fictitious race, so Ha-Me'iri found in the aforementioned nations of his own invention the reason for the mishnaic enactments.[7]

We may assume—although we have no proof of it—that Ha-Me'iri knew Rabbi Yeḥiel's tract on the Paris disputation which we have analysed in the previous chapter. From it he may possibly have derived the idea of an overall exclusion of the monotheistic religions from any equation with idolatry. Rabbi Yeḥiel had used the notion of the 'seven nations' to account for the need for the

[1] *B.H.–'A.Z.*, p. 39. [2] Ibid. [3] Ibid., p. 53.
[4] B.T., *'A.Z.*, 15b, 22a. [5] *The Guide for the Perplexed*, 3. 29.
[6] This was proved by D. Chwolson, *Die Ssabier und der Ssabismus*, 1851, i, pp. 691–9.
[7] Ha-Me'iri's dependence upon Maimonides is apparent from his use of the word *talisman* ('worship of idols, stars, and talismans', *B.H.–'A.Z.*, p. 59). This word is not found in the Talmud, but served Maimonides for the describing of his imaginary race. *The Guide for the Perplexed*, 3. 29.

talmudic enactments. Ha-Me'iri substituted for these his corrupt race which, although lacking all historical authenticity, has the advantage of not being contradicted by talmudic sources. Unlike Rabbi Yeḥiel, who used this concept as a polemical device only, Ha-Me'iri was convinced of the truth of his theory. It corresponded admirably with his own tolerant attitude towards Christianity.

Ha-Me'iri's concept included, by implication, Islam also. But Christianity was the religion familiar to him from extended experience. His tolerance towards Christianity becomes apparent from the circumstance that he arrived at his theory notwithstanding the fact that Christianity was specifically mentioned, in the version of the Talmud which he used, as one of the sects to which the laws of segregation applied.[1] The offending passage which, apparently, would exclude Christians from any business relations with Jews doubtless originated in Babylonia, where Christians constituted a negligible sect, contact with which could easily have been avoided. The passage seems to have been preserved also in the form of the talmudic text current in Arabic countries,[2] and it will therefore have confronted Ha-Me'iri with a formidable obstacle to his theory. But once again, heartfelt conviction proved stronger than the written word. Ha-Me'iri explained the words as possessing a meaning which had nothing to do with contemporary Christianity.[3] The latter was to be regarded as a religion whose adherents were more aptly to be classed with Jews than with idolaters.

The most impressive proof of this last assertion is to be found in a halakhic decision by Ha-Me'iri concerning apostates. In a previous chapter we have seen what was the attitude of the halakhists towards the apostate. They vacillated as to the degree to which an apostate could be regarded as a Jew; but nobody ever contemplated giving the apostate a positive religious status derived from his adherence to another religion. Ha-Me'iri is once again an

[1] *B.H.–'A.Z.*, p. 4. It is the passage referred to in Chap. III, p. 25, n. 2.

[2] This is the explanation of Maimonides' special mention of Christians (cf. p. 120, n. 2), in accordance with his usual practice of listing the cases treated by the Talmud. There is therefore no basis for M. Gutmann's apologetic contention that Maimonides' 'intolerance' is derived from philosophical, and not from Jewish, sources. See his *Das Judentum und seine Umwelt*, p. 155.

[3] He connected the word *noṣeri* with Nebuchadnezzar.

exception. He comments on the talmudic passage which includes the apostate (*ha-meshummad*) in the category of heretics towards whom no human obligation applies. His comment reads as follows:

> But all this applies only to one who still retains the name Israel. For everyone who retains the name of Israel and frees himself [from its obligations] and desecrates the [Jewish] religion incurs great punishment, for he becomes a heretic and he is like one who has no religion. But he who has left the fold altogether and become a member of another religion is regarded by us as a member of that religion in respect of everything except the marriage laws. And thus ruled my teachers also.[1]

This passage has no parallel in the whole of medieval Jewish literature. Nor could it have, for the supposition upon which it rests is the positive status of other religions. The enunciation of such a doctrine is the achievement of Ha-Me'iri, or rather of the enlightened circles in Provence to which he belonged, as the mention of 'my teachers' at the end of the passage indicates.

We may (tentatively) sketch in the social background which fostered this attitude among enlightened halakhists such as Ha-Me'iri and his master Reuben ben Ḥayyim.[2] These men based their Jewish beliefs upon the current philosophical system of rationalism. They thus felt themselves akin, in their approach, to Christian and also to Moslem believers who, like them, cultivated philosophical thinking. It is true that in their conclusions—and even more so in their premisses—they differed from each other. These differences came to light in the course of voluntary discussions which took place between representatives of the respective religions. Such discussions may sometimes have been, to a certain extent, fruitful ones. Ha-Me'iri relates, for instance, that the writing of his book *Ḥibbur Ha-Teshuvah* was inspired by discussions with a Christian scholar.[3] The spiritual intercourse between enlightened members of both camps will have brought about a certain degree of mutual identification, or at least a feeling of loose association. Ha-Me'iri stresses repeatedly that certain basic tenets of belief and morality are common to the sages of Israel and the nations. He refers to

[1] *B.H., Horayoth* (ed. A. Schreiber), on 11b. Cf. *B.H.–'A.Z.*, p. 61.

[2] Mirsky, *Toledoth*, p. 13; see p. 114, n. 2. What we know of his teachings suggests that he was an adherent of Maimonides' philosophy (see M. Toledano, *'Oṣar Ḥayyim*, 1935).

[3] *Ḥibbur Ha-Teshuvah*, p. 2.

those elements which, according to his theory, can be arrived at by simple reasoning. This association, based upon common ground, explains the wish of enlightened Jewish thinkers to win the recognition of their Christian opponents by emphasizing common values. Hence Ha-Me'iri's argument, in his internal Jewish polemics, on the merits of philosophical study: If Jews refrained from such studies, the Gentiles would say 'they are but a stupid and foolish people', rather than *this is a people wise and sage*.[1] The words in which the *Torah* (Deut. iv. 6) here urges Israel so to conduct themselves as to appear as a sage people could be explained in different ways. Those who regarded themselves as holding certain values in common with some non-Jewish social groups always tended to evince their Judaism through active participation in the pursuit of these values. But this entailed the conceding of at least some measure of justification to the whole system of one's opponents, and such a concession forms the basis of all religious tolerance. It is safe to believe that Ha-Me'iri arrived at such a justification for contemporary Christianity.

We shall have the opportunity of observing, in the latter part of this book, how ideas similar to those of Ha-Me'iri affected the relationship between Jews and Gentiles in the eighteenth century in all fields of social and even religious contact. In the case of Ha-Me'iri, however, the social application of his ideas was extremely restricted. To demonstrate this we must revert once again to Ha-Me'iri's halakhic writings. As we have seen, on the basis of his distinction between two kinds of Gentiles, he justified the non-observance of many segregative laws. These exemptions had already been established, in practice, previous to Ha-Me'iri's rationalization of them. The difference between Ha-Me'iri and the other halakhists was but this, that what others justified casuistically he justified on the strength of a principle. In the sphere of theory, his formulation of the principle is no mean achievement. As to practice, the principle found its limitations in Ha-Me'iri's

[1] Cf. Deut. xxxii. 6 and iv. 6. A similar argument is used by Samuel Ibn Tibbon, *Ma'amar Yiqqawu Ha-Mayim*, ed. M. L. Bisliches, Pressburg, 1837, p. 153. See also Ha-Me'iri's conciliatory remarks about the Gentiles' philosophical teachings, in *Ḥoshen Mishpaṭ* ed. D. Kaufmann, *Jubelschrift zum 90. Geburtstag Zunz*, p. 162.

own adherence to established usage. In addition, there is no reason to suppose that, in adopting the principle of religious tolerance, Ha-Me'iri overcame the emotional attachment to his own religious group and his antipathy to others. We should not, therefore, look for consistency in the application of Ha-Me'iri's principle.

This will become apparent if we quote Ha-Me'iri's ruling concerning business dealings in Christian sacred objects. From Ha-Me'iri's principle, a clear-cut permission to deal in these objects can be deduced. For, if Christianity was *ex hypothesi* excluded from idolatry, its ritual vessels should not fall under the category of *tiqrovoth ʿavodah zarah* (offerings made to an idol). But, in striking contrast to Ha-Me'iri's practice of concluding the discussions about similar problems with the reiteration of his principle, in this case he avoids mentioning it.[1] There are clear signs in the wording of his discussion that he does so intentionally, and in full consciousness of his logical inconsistency. On one occasion he attempts to escape from the problem by relating such customs as the lighting of candles and the provision of bread for clerics to the idolatry of ancient times; adding that, in his own day, such customs existed only in those places where idolatry survived.[2] We may, however, be sure that Ha-Me'iri did not fail to note that these problems were not mentioned in the Talmud, but were introduced into the halakhic discussions by authorities who, like himself, lived in a Christian environment. In any case, in his own time dealing in Christian sacred objects might well have been permitted. This permission, however, was merely hinted at, and not explicitly granted. Neither was a negative decision arrived at; and the reader is left wondering what the actual opinion of the author was. It would seem to be not far from the truth to assume that Ha-Me'iri was reluctant to reach a final decision, but hovered between applying his principle and adhering to traditional practice. Or, in the language of psychology, the author is involved in a conflict between consistency of thought and his emotionally conditioned repugnance to the visible symbols of the alien religion.

[1] *B.H.–ʿA.Z.*, pp. 32, 189. The introductory passage in his *Qiryath Sefer* (ed. D. Hakohen Nahar, 1863) is a commentary on Israel's plight in Exile: it does not refer to any peculiar event as Zobel assumes. Cf. pp. 90–91.

[2] Ibid., p. 32.

It cannot be doubted that Ha-Me'iri felt quite clearly that his principle might lead to far-reaching consequences. In theory, the principle could have been applied to the dietary laws also, in so far as they are accepted in the Halakhah as serving the purpose of segregation. Other halakhists, who dealt with the segregative laws casuistically, had no need to state that the dietary laws continued to be valid. Ha-Me'iri felt this to be necessary, and he explicitly stated that 'concerning prohibitions of food and drink . . . and other prohibitions of this sort . . . all the nations are alike'.[1]

Neither is there any doubt that, emotionally, Ha-Me'iri felt himself attached to the symbols of the Jewish religion and retained, like any other Jew of the Middle Ages, his aversion to the Gentile world. He certainly had no intention of demolishing the social barrier between the two worlds. Signs of such feelings sometimes escape him unintentionally. Thus, for instance, he discards a logical conclusion which would lead him to permit Jews to partake in a meal together with a Gentile—provided that no prohibited food was used. He closes his discussion by saying that, if this conclusion were valid, 'we would almost become one people'.[2] A similar attitude appears when he discusses the problem of whether Gentiles may help in burying the dead—a contingency which was envisaged in the Talmud as arising if the death of a Jew occurred on the first day of a Jewish festival.[3] He concludes his remarks on this point with the significant observation: 'For the doing of all this by the Gentiles is a great shame and affront, and it is only right that these things should be done by Jews. Let the saints be honoured.'[4]

Again, Ha-Me'iri does not dispense with independent Jewish communal institutions. The non-Jewish authorities are, traditionally, accorded honour for maintaining order in society.[5] Ha-Me'iri also has expressions of gratitude for the protection which the Jewish nation receives from Gentile rulers.[6] But this does not lead him to the conclusion that Jews should not have their own

[1] Ibid., p. 59. [2] Ibid., p. 132. [3] B.T., *Beṣah*, 6a.

[4] *Magen 'Avoth* (ed. J. Last, London, 1904), p. 38; cf. also *B.H.*, *Beṣah* (ed. J. Lange, K. Schlesinger), p. 36.

[5] See his commentary on *'Avoth*, 3. 2. His comments are similar to those quoted *supra*, Chap. V, p. 51, n. 1. [6] *B.H.–'A.Z.*, p. 39.

juridical institutions and the like. The talmudic dictum *dina de-malekhutha dina*,[1] moreover, is limited by Ha-Me'iri to the right of the authorities to impose taxes and customs. The juridical system is explicitly excluded from the area covered by this dictum, on the ground that otherwise 'the whole Jewish law would be invalidated'.[2]

Neither do we find in Ha-Me'iri any weakening of the consciousness of being in Exile. He does not cherish any illusions about the real position of Jewry in dispersion. Ha-Me'iri was an eye-witness of the expulsion of the Jews from France in the year 1306. He knew also, from earlier experiences, the constant dread to which the caprice of rulers and the unruliness of the masses subjected the Jews. He occasionally mentions a case of the actual expulsion of Jews from a given place, as well as other signs of disfavour on the part of the population.[3] We meet with the expression of sentiments prompted by the feeling of being in Exile, especially in his commentary on the Psalms. He admits that he is inclined to explain some passages as referring to the Exile and the redemption, even where other interpretations would have been acceptable.[4] And he explicitly includes the Moslems and Christians among the nations to whom Scripture refers in predicting the punishment, at the end of days, of those who have dealt with Israel unjustly during their Exile.[5]

One is certainly not entitled to conclude that Ha-Me'iri's idea of tolerance overcame his feelings of solidarity with his own people, or even that it diminished sensibly his resentment against others. Nor, indeed, could this be expected, considering the circumstances in fourteenth-century France. That he was nevertheless able to evolve a principle of tolerance, and to do so at a level that would make of it an intellectual conception, must be counted as a very remarkable achievement indeed.

[1] See *supra*, Chap. V.
[2] *B.H.*, *Bava Qamma*, pp. 321–2; *B.H.–'A.Z.*, p. 41.
[3] *B.H.*, *Beṣah*, p. 38; *Magen 'Avoth*, p. 37.
[4] Pss. xxxv, lxii, ed. J. Cohn, pp. 75, 120.
[5] Ps. cl (ed. Cohn, p. 293).

PART III

FROM EXCLUSIVENESS TO TOLERANCE
(SIXTEENTH TO EIGHTEENTH CENTURIES)

XI

GHETTO SEGREGATION

ASHKENAZI Jewry, as defined in our introductory chapter—the Jews of France and Germany, and their descendants in central and eastern European countries—underwent great changes between the fifteenth and seventeenth centuries. First, a considerable shift occurred on geographical lines. France, after having revoked earlier decrees of expulsion, finally expelled her Jews in 1394. In Germany total expulsion never took place; indeed, because of the manifold distinct sovereignties into which German territory was divided, such a thing was hardly to be expected. Nevertheless, local evictions, vexatious legislation, and repeated massacres did diminish the number and lower the status of the German Jews. There was a definite shifting of the Jewish population eastward during the period in question, the route of migration being Bavaria, Austria, Bohemia, Poland, Lithuania, and the Ukraine; the latter formed the extreme easterly boundary of Jewish settlement.[1] Whether the bulk of the Jewish population in Poland was ethnically of Ashkenazi stock is contested amongst historians. There is a theory that there was a large influx of proselytes from the Khazar kingdom[2]—on the borderland of Europe and Asia—in the sixth to tenth centuries. As far as historical consciousness was concerned, however, Polish Jewry clearly regarded itself as a branch of Ashkenazi Jewry. The fact that Yiddish was used exclusively as the everyday language is sufficient proof of this. The upper social strata which became, in time, representative of Polish Jewry certainly were, or at least regarded themselves as being, of Ashkenazi origin and affiliation. It was the avowed intention of the great halakhist, Rabbi Solomon Luria (died 1573), in his treatise

[1] For general reference see S. M. Dubnow, *Weltgeschichte des jüdischen Volkes*, Berlin, 1925–8, v–xi; idem, *History of the Jews in Russia and Poland*, Philadelphia, 1916, i.

[2] See A. N. Pollack, *Khazaria*, Tel Aviv, 1951 edn., pp. 219–28, 250–75; D. M. Dunlop, *The History of the Jewish Khazars*, Princeton, 1954, pp. 261–3.

Yam Shel Shelomoh to defend the Ashkenazi tradition against the influence of the Sephardi halakhists.[1] Their writings, particularly the *Shulḥan 'Arukh* of Joseph Caro of Safed (died 1575), were reaching Poland at about that time. A similar attitude may be discerned in the books of Luria's contemporaries, the Rabbis Moses Isserles and Mordecai Yaffe.[2] To the extent that historically orientated thinking is apparent in Polish Jewry, it clearly reflects the consciousness of being linked with the Ashkenazi tradition.

No justification, therefore, is necessary for the inclusion of Polish Jewry in a study that aims at tracing the development of Jewish-Gentile relations within Ashkenazi Jewry. We shall, in fact, fail to find any marked difference between German and Polish Jewry in this period, and we must regard both as the historical descendants of Ashkenazi Jewry of the Middle Ages. Whatever divergencies we may find in contrast to medieval Jewry must be attributed to historical factors. These divergencies range from the extent of contact with the outer world to the most subtle variations in mental attitude.

Let us begin with the ecological aspect. Although Jews always preferred to live near to one another, it was only in this period that a fully fledged ghetto developed. The principal characteristic of this institution was its obligatory nature. In the Middle Ages Jews were accustomed to settle together because of mutual dependence and attachment to the same communal institutions. Later, in the ghetto period, close settlement was forced upon them by legislation.[3] This entailed physical hardship, the ghetto being usually small, without provision for expansion, and located in the worst part of the town. Jews made attempts at improving these living conditions as far as possible. But, contrary to what might be expected, the institution of the closed Jewish quarter was not in itself resented by Jews.[4] It was accepted as a provision appropriate to a group of their status, and as corresponding to their social and

[1] See his introduction to *Yam Shel Shelomoh* on *Bava Qamma* and on *Ḥullin*; see S. A. Horodetzky, *Le-Qoroth Ha-Rabbanuth*, Warsaw, 1910, pp. 123–44.

[2] See Horodetzky, op. cit., pp. 81–116, 145–74.

[3] L. Wirth, *The Ghetto*, Chicago, 1928, chaps. 2–3. I. Abrahams, *Jewish Life in the Middle Ages*, Philadelphia, 1896, pp. 62–68.

[4] Abrahams, op. cit., pp. 63–67.

religious needs; moreover, it provided a measure of security. Jews were content to be recognized as a socio-religious unit, distinct from the general population. The ghetto became, in fact, the home of exclusively Jewish activity, possessing all the characteristics of a distinct civilization. The Jew whose work took him out of the ghetto and among Gentiles for the day or the week felt as if he were leaving his natural environment and entering a strange world. Only on returning home in the evening, or at least for the Sabbath, did he find any satisfaction beyond the goal of earning a living. Even those who left the ghetto as individuals or as small groups and settled among Gentiles—as very often happened, especially in Poland at the time of the intensive colonization of the Ukraine—did so out of necessity, and cherished the memory of the full-blooded Jewish life that they had left. The ideas and values with which they were imbued while living in the ghetto continued to be their guide; and it seldom occurred that even an isolated Jew lost all contact with one of the more or less extensive Jewish centres. It was there that he contributed to the maintenance of Jewish institutions, and there that he obtained satisfaction of his religious and social needs. For the high holidays, at least, even the most isolated Jew joined one of the Jewish communities for prayer and fasting.[1] In this fashion he demonstrated that he was a member of the Jewish community, at least as regards the most prominent form of religious expression.

This description of the intensely Jewish life of the ghetto provides the first indication of the kind of Jewish-Gentile relationship that we shall encounter. It is a relationship dominated by Jewish exclusiveness. This exclusiveness and the new Jewish-Gentile relationship are interdependent. Reasons of method, and nothing else, oblige us to proceed from a description of the one phenomenon—Jewish exclusiveness—to the other, namely Jewish-Gentile relationships. The logical corollary of the socially introverted Jewish ghetto life was the Jewish indifference to conditions and events in the outside world. The tense Jewish feeling and apprehension

[1] I have described the ghetto institutions more fully in my book *Tradition and Crisis: Jewish Society at the End of the Middle Ages*, Jerusalem, 1958 (Hebrew, English translation in preparation).

regarding Christianity, which were the principal characteristics of the Middle Ages, had disappeared during the ghetto period. We shall be able to examine this radical change when we inquire into those fields where such tension had earlier expressed itself. We shall then discover that tension—even aggression—gradually weakened, and was replaced by indifference and apathy.

The doctrinal differences between Judaism and Christianity in medieval times constituted the primary demonstration of the existence of a mutual awareness of diversity. These differences remained, of course, during the ghetto period. The sixteenth- and seventeenth-century Jew, no less than his twelfth-century ancestor, realized that Christianity constituted a denial of Judaism, and vice versa. But when he had occasion to define the Jewish faith or to expound its tenets, he did not—as had formerly been the case—do so in terms of a comparison with Christianity.

Polemics against Christianity virtually ceased in the sixteenth century. The last compendium summarizing Jewish arguments against Christianity was compiled by Yom-Ṭov Lipmann Mühlhausen in Prague, at the beginning of the fifteenth century.[1] If we are prepared to regard the book of Isaac Troki, *Ḥizzuq 'Emunah*, as a Jewish product in spite of its having been written by a Karaite, the date of the latest treatise may be placed some hundred and fifty years later, that is, in the second half of the sixteenth century.[2] Characteristic of the period, however, is not so much the lack of special tracts dealing with Jewish-Christian polemics, but the conspicuous absence of references to the relationship between Judaism and Christianity. Controversies between Jews and Christians naturally occurred, from time to time, even during this later period. Indeed, in view of the manifold relations between Jews and non-Jews, it was inevitable that different religious beliefs should become a subject of conversation and polemics. For example, Rabbi Judah

[1] His *Sefer Niṣṣaḥon* was first published by a Christian, Theodor Hackspan, Altdorf, 1644: in 1709 an edition appeared, published by Jews in Amsterdam; cf. Judah Kaufmann, *R. Yom Ṭov Lipmann Mühlausen* (Hebrew), New York, 1927, pp. 61–69.

[2] Troki's book was also first published by a Christian, Wagenseil, as *Tela ignea Satanae*, Altdorf, 1681, with a Latin translation. On Troki see A. Geiger, 'Isaak Troki, ein Apologet des Judentums am Ende des sechzehnten Jahrhunderts', *Nachgelassene Schriften*, Breslau, 1885, iii, pp. 178–223.

Loeb of Prague (known, from his initials, as Maharal—died 1609) mentions his controversies with Christians.[1] Rabbi Ḥayyim Ya'ir Bacharach tells us about a conversation of his uncle, the Rabbi of Mannheim, with Karl Ludwig, the Elector of Pfalz, in which the former defended the behaviour of his congregants, who had admittedly bribed Christian judges in lawsuits with non-Jews.[2] Bacharach himself sharply ridicules a 'great Gentile scholar' who, during a discussion, tried to prove that the observance of Sunday, not Saturday, was intended in the biblical injunction to observe the Sabbath.[3] Even Rabbi Judah Pochowitzer, in late seventeenth-century Poland, argued with Christians whom he encountered.[4] Rabbi Joseph Stadthagen was well equipped to hold his own in a controversy with an apostate which was forced upon him.[5] And Rabbi Jonathan Eybeschütz boasted of the pointed rejoinders he had made in discussions with highly placed Christians.[6] But it is significant that, with one exception, the controversies reported above were accorded only brief and incidental mention in the writings of the scholars concerned.

We shall analyse later the teachings of Rabbi Judah Loeb of Prague and shall find that his exposition of Jewish exclusiveness was based on the ancient dichotomy of Israel and the nations as a whole. The contrast between Judaism and Christianity in particular played almost no part in his thinking. Indeed, were we to ignore those passages which deal with Christianity in his writings, his entire philosophy would lose nothing of its completeness. The same is true of the others. Their references to Christianity are almost incidental—*curiosa* rather than a basis for comparison and a means of clarification. In the voluminous moral and qabbalistic treatise of Rabbi Isaiah Horowitz (died 1628), *Sheney Luḥoth Ha-Berith*, which probably influenced subsequent generations more than any other book of its kind, Christianity is mentioned only in a few casual instances. Commenting on Gen. xlix. 10, he

[1] An account of an oral discussion with a Christian is to be found in his *Neṣaḥ Yisra'el*, chap. 25.

[2] Ḥayyim Ya'ir Bacharach, *Responsa*, 136.

[3] Ibid., 219, Frankfort edn., p. 206b.

[4] *Derekh Ḥokhmah*, 182.

[5] A. Berliner, *Religionsgespräch gehalten am Kurfürstlichen Hofe zu Hannover, 1704*, Berlin, 1914.

[6] *Luḥoth Ha-'Eduth*, Altona, 1755, p. 752, and in *Tif'ereth Yisra'el*, chap. 69.

utters a warning against the well-known christological exegesis that would read into the verse a prediction of the coming of Christ.[1] Despite the fact that Rabbi Horowitz was one of the most prolific and ingenious interpreters in his own particular field, he added nothing original when discussing points of controversy with Christianity. Indeed, one gets the impression that he contented himself with merely repeating what he had learned of the subject in his youth.

Judaism now became, more than ever, a closed system of thought. As is well known, Ashkenazi Jewry produced at this time no comprehensive thinkers, with the sole exception of Rabbi Judah Loeb of Prague (Maharal). Instead, the period was prolific with preachers who moralized and admonished. It is not easy to convey their method of thinking and presentation—the *derush* in the post-talmudic sense. Preachers of this age took the tenets and teachings of Judaism for granted, and did not consider it necessary to provide proofs for them. Only occasionally did they furnish rational explanations of one or other religious belief or institution. True, they were expected to have something novel to say in their preaching or writing—to discover a new content in a given biblical or talmudic passage, but at the same time not to depart from accepted beliefs. Their real purpose was to admonish their listeners not to be led astray from the path of duty by worldly temptations, or by their own evil inclinations. The path of duty was clear to all, and scarcely questioned. If a question did arise, it could be solved by reference to the new compendia of Halakhah or by consulting one of the halakhists, many of whom were then public officials of their communities.[2] Similarly, there was little room for doubt as to fundamental beliefs.

The closed system of thought evinced by the preacher was in harmony with the general position of Jewry and Judaism from the sixteenth to the eighteenth centuries. If Judaism had been constrained to define its teachings in relation to any other creed, it could never have allowed itself to sink into the lethargy of a mental attitude which accepted Jewish fundamental beliefs as uncontested

[1] *Shelah*, Warsaw edn., ii, 32a. Cf. 16a and i, 43a.
[2] See my *Tradition and Crisis*, chaps. 17–18.

truth. The question which posed itself to the Jew of that time was not why, and in what, the Jewish and Christian religions differed. If any such question arose, it took the form: What are the special features and qualities of the Jew, and why is his destiny unique? Jews were able to answer this question by drawing on their biblical and talmudic traditions. The 'Aggadah, with its mystical exposition of Jewish destiny, was common knowledge amongst the Jewish masses. Rashi, and especially his commentary on the Pentateuch, was the text universally used, even by beginners. But Rashi's original intention, i.e. to state the Jewish point of view in contrast to the Christian, was completely ignored by students of his commentaries. Rashi seldom refers to Christianity explicitly. On the whole, he included it in the term *'ummoth ha-'olam* or under similar talmudic expressions differentiating between Israel and all other nations.[1] Rashi's contemporaries, themselves combatively inclined towards Christianity, had no difficulty in grasping his controversial intention against that religion in particular. A reader who lived between the sixteenth and the eighteenth century, over five hundred years later, would be more likely to interpret his terminology literally.[2] Thus the original dichotomy of Israel and the nations reasserted itself. As the differences involved did not concern the two religions but dealt with one nation in contrast to all the others, they were more likely to be racial in origin rather than a matter of doctrinal dissension. The theories of Maharal to be discussed later in this chapter will serve us as a good example of this. But even if Jewish peculiarity was defined in terms of belief or dogma, the notions as a whole might have been conceived of as an antithesis. Gentile beliefs were thus construed *in abstracto*, as being opposed to those of the Jews. 'Jews believe in *creatio ex nihilo*; the nations do not.'[3] Such statements are quite common in the quasi-philosophical and homiletical literature of the time. Their authors were therefore fighting a

[1] See *supra*, Chap. II.

[2] This is apparent in the way in which Rashi's commentary was dealt with by the many supercommentaries written during our period. Besides the *Gur 'Aryeh* of Maharal which will be quoted later on, see *Ḥokhmath Shelomoh*, by Solomon Luria.

[3] Moses Isserles, *Torath Ha-'Olah*, part 2, chap. 21.

fictitious opponent rather than a real adversary. In fact, differentiation between Judaism and Christianity as opposing creeds disappeared almost entirely at this period. From that time on, Judaism became largely indifferent to Christianity.

The indifference of Judaism to Christianity is all the more astonishing, in that profound changes had occurred in Western Christendom with the Reformation, which presented an opportunity for a restatement of the Jewish position *vis-à-vis* the Christianity so transformed. As a matter of fact, Jewish writers of that time took very slight cognizance only of what was happening in Christianity. Luther himself did attract some attention. As is well known, he thought at first that his purification of Christianity would remove the obstacles to the conversion of the Jews. On the other hand, some Jews at first judged Luther to be a Christian rebel, on the verge of becoming a Jew himself. In Worms two Jews, perhaps sent by the local Jewish community, approached Luther with the intention of offering him a helping hand in finding his way to Judaism.[1] Indeed, by 1525 information about Luther's anticipated turn towards Judaism had filtered as far as Jerusalem.[2] However, even where Luther was concerned Jewish interest appears to have been essentially directed at what were taken to be signs of the coming of the messianic era—these seemed to be implied in the shock suffered by the world of 'Edom', i.e. the supreme power of the Pope—rather than at the conversion of Christians to Judaism.[3] Once the upheaval of the Reformation had subsided, Jews ceased to interest themselves in the religious differences and controversies of the Christian world.

The only Jewish author of our period to expound Judaism as a comprehensive conception was Rabbi Judah Loeb of Prague.[4]

[1] See Graetz, *Geschichte der Juden*, 3rd edn., ix, pp. 196–8; R. Lewin, *Luthers Stellung zu den Juden*, Berlin, 1911, pp. 15–20.

[2] See the letter from Jerusalem published by G. Scholem in *Qiryath Sefer*, vii, 1931, pp. 444–6.

[3] See Lewin and Scholem, opp. citt.

[4] It is only quite recently that Maharal's theory has attracted the attention of scholars. See A. Gottesdiener, 'Ha-'Ari Shebbeḥakhmey Prag', *Azkarah* (Jerusalem), iv, 1937, pp. 253–443; Martin Buber, *Beyn 'Am le-'Arṣo*, Jerusalem, 1944, pp. 78–91 (German version: *Israel und Palästina*, Zürich, 1950, pp. 100–15). B. Z. Bokser, *From the World of the Cabbalah. The Philosophy of Rabbi Judah Loew of Prague*, New York, 1954. A doctoral thesis on the pedagogical thinking of

In his voluminous writings, he touched upon all aspects of Judaism, and devoted special attention to the origin of Jewish exclusiveness and its metaphysical significance. The divine election of Israel, Israel's historical fate, and messianic destiny were fully treated by him. One might have thought that here, at any rate, was a man who would have been concerned to define the place of Judaism in comparison with Christianity. Indeed, Maharal did occasionally refer to Christianity and, as mentioned, he no doubt had some contact with Christian disputants. But his remarks about Christian dogmas and concepts were hardly an integral part of his philosophy.[1] Most Christian arguments against Judaism reached him through Jewish writers. These arguments may not have lost their essence in transmission, but they certainly could not have conveyed the same forceful impression as their protagonists would have made by word of mouth. Thus, in writing his supercommentary, *Gur 'Aryeh*, on Rashi's commentary on the Pentateuch, Maharal dealt but incidentally with biblical exegesis which had been the subject of Christian-Jewish disputes;[2] the same was the case in his philosophical and homiletical writings. Reading his books, one feels that the controversy was conducted in a vacuum, since the author was not confronted with an actual opponent. Other themes that seem to reflect the attitude of Christian controversialists concerning Judaism—for instance, the loss of Jewish political independence and the infliction of the Exile[3]—probably originated in the inner Jewish speculations of an earlier period. By the time of Maharal, the seemingly endless *Galuth* had evoked profound thought among Jews, quite apart from the polemical use to which it had been put by Christians. As Maharal took it upon himself to deal fully with the position of the Jewish people in the

Maharal has been written by F. Kleinberger of Jerusalem, and I have consulted it with considerable profit.

[1] Bokser, op. cit., pp. 147–78, listed the passages which may be regarded as touching on Jewish-Christian differences. He failed, however, to differentiate between polemics proper and material which had originated from polemics. That is why he attributed to him so much controversial intention.

[2] He commented on Gen. ii. 23; xlix. 10; Deut. xviii. 15; rejecting the Christian exegesis of these passages; all of these had been mentioned in Lipmann's *Niṣṣaḥon*, which no doubt served Maharal as source for them.

[3] This topic recurs repeatedly and it is the central subject of *Neṣaḥ Yisra'el*.

world, he could not escape the necessity of explaining the seeming contradiction in their status. On the one hand, they were the Chosen People, and, on the other, were subjected to Exile and to consequent trials of all kinds. As these questions had already been treated in the Talmud and the Midrash, which Maharal took as a starting-point for his own remarks, he appeared merely to be interpreting the traditional sources. Indeed, it is not at all clear whether Maharal was always aware that, in attempting to find an answer to such questions, he was in fact dealing with Christian argumentation.

Maharal used the vocabulary and the concepts of medieval philosophy[1] and tried to define Judaism in terms of its eternal significance. He was concerned primarily with the character of the Jewish religion. It was his basic premiss that the innate spiritual make-up of the Jew—both of the individual and of the Jewish nation—was the clue to an understanding of his destiny. It therefore followed that the difference between Jewry and the nations was fundamentally not one of creed and faith, but one of inner nature. The difference between the Jewish way of life and destiny, and the life and destiny of other nations, was not the result of Jewish acceptance of the *Torah*, as is clearly suggested by tradition; but rather the fact that the Jewish people accepted the *Torah* was itself the result of their unique nature. To quote Maharal's own words:

> The fact that Jews are imbued with the Spirit of God and with an abundance of prophecy to a greater extent than nations that do not possess the Spirit is comparable to the fact that the human race possesses a superior quality of mind, thanks to a predisposition inherent in it, in greater measure than in the other creatures which do not possess mind. And if it be claimed that it was without a special predisposition of the nation that it received those superior qualities, that is, the divine qualities of prophecy and the Divine Spirit, then it is also possible that an animal might obtain a human mind without a peculiar predisposition. But this certainly cannot be so. And in the same way it is impossible that Israel should have acquired these things without some special

[1] Bokser styles Maharal a qabbalist. The *Qabbalah*'s influence on him, however, expresses itself more as a general trend than in an adaptation of terms and concepts.

spiritual characteristic. And proof that all sublime things require such a character is to be found in Chapter 1 of *'Avodah Zarah*, which runs: 'R. Yoḥanan said: "[The Lord] offered the *Torah* to every nation and language, but they did not accept it." We do not read that God sent them prophets; the meaning is that He examined their character, to see if they possessed predisposition to the *Torah*, and did not find it in them, and this constituted their refusal.'[1]

Maharal may thus be said to have followed the same trend of thought as did Judah Ha-Levi in the Middle Ages.[2] But he outdid his medieval predecessor in eliminating all historical and theological criteria from the definition of Judaism and from the delineation of the Jewish character. Neither the clash between Judaism and Christianity, nor the doctrinal differences between them, meant much to him. He accepted the traditional view of 'Jewish' and 'Gentile' qualities. Jews were merciful, chaste, &c., in contrast to other peoples.[3] At the same time, Maharal became the severest critic of contemporary Jewish practices. He found fault with communal life, with religious standards, and, in particular, with educational methods and objectives.[4] He saw these deficiencies—chiefly wrangling and envy—not only in the light of his own lofty Jewish ideals, but also in comparison with other peoples.[5] However, his criticism did not affect his basic conception that Jews were, essentially, of a superior religious and moral calibre to others. Their inadequacies were incidental only, and attributable to the trials of Exile;[6] at a different level, Jewish deficiencies had a direct relationship to the Jews' superior spiritual nature.[7] That is why failure indicated greater inadequacy, and was

[1] *Gevuroth Ha-Shem*, chap. 72. Cf. *Tif'ereth Yisra'el*, chap. 1.

[2] See Julius Guttmann, *Die Philosophie des Judentums*, Munich, 1933, pp. 144–8. Hebrew translation, Jerusalem, 1953, pp. 119–22.

[3] *Gevuroth Ha-Shem*, chap. 45; *Tif'ereth Yisra'el*, chap. 1; *Gur 'Aryeh* on Gen. xxiv. 22 and Deut. ii. 9.

[4] More direct is the criticism voiced in his sermon *Derush Na'eh, Derush 'al Ha-Torah weha-Miṣwoth*. The passages concerning education are collected in S. Assaf, *Meqoroth le-Tholedoth Ha-Ḥinnukh be-Yisra'el*, i, pp. 45–51; concerning other subjects, see Gottesdiener, op. cit. iv, 1937, pp. 320–6.

[5] See especially *Neṣaḥ Yisra'el*, chap. 25, where he records his conversation on this subject with a Gentile, and accepts the latter's criticism and stresses that Jews fall short of other peoples in this respect.

[6] *Neṣaḥ Yisra'el*, ibid.

[7] *Gevuroth Ha-Shem*, cnap. 5.

the more severely punished.[1] This theory likewise accounted for the Jewish Exile; at the same time, it provided an assurance of continued divine grace and ultimate redemption. The Exile itself was an unnatural state of affairs, which could not last.

Maharal is an excellent example of the medieval thinker who adopted a group of ideas and adhered to them despite the contradictory evidence of reality. He thus succeeded in becoming the most outspoken critic of contemporary Judaism and, at the same time, the most eloquent apologist of Jewish existence. No other thinker considered the Jewish nation a *species per se*, to which no parallel could be found. It is safe to assume that it was the isolation of Jewish life from that of the outside world which made such theories both possible and acceptable.

[1] *Gur 'Aryeh* on Exod. ii. 14.

XII

THE ATTITUDE OF ESTRANGEMENT

WE shall now examine the effects of the altered status of Jewish society. This new status caused a change in the Jewish attitudes to Jewish-Christian relations, no sphere of which remained untouched.

Let us first examine the attitude towards proselytes and apostates. There can be no doubt that, at this juncture, Christian acceptance of the Jewish religion ceased to be a motive in Jewish thinking and feeling. There were, it is true, some cases of Christian conversion to Judaism during this period; and naturally these could not have occurred without the approval of Jewish courts. Jews were occasionally accused of having deliberately influenced proselytes to accept Judaism, a charge which cannot be entirely refuted.[1] On the other hand, this assertion could have been true regarding isolated individuals only, who remained under the influence of earlier Jewish missionary trends and took advantage of the fact that the law providing for the acceptance of Gentiles into Judaism had never been abrogated. But public sentiment had long since veered away from proselytization; indeed, it was now opposed to it. Ample evidence is available to substantiate this.

The first indication that proselytizing had ceased is the absence of instructions and legal decisions on this subject in contemporary halakhic and moralistic literature. A comparison of the *Sefer Ḥasidim* with Joseph Hahn's *Yosef 'Omeṣ* furnishes a good example.[2] The former, reflecting conditions obtaining in the thirteenth century, contains many provisions for dealing with proselytes; the latter, a typical seventeenth-century counterpart, ignores this subject entirely.

But there is more significant evidence of the lack of interest in

[1] See *infra* and my *Tradition and Crisis*, chap. 3, n. 9.

[2] *Yosef 'Omeṣ* was written in 1630, but appeared in 1723 only. A new edition was published at Frankfort on the Main, 1928, and this is the one quoted below. On the author, see M. Horowitz, *Frankfurter Rabbinen*, 1883, pp. 6–18.

conversion than the *argumentum e silentio*. One section of Isaiah Horowitz's comprehensive book, *Sheney Luḥoth Ha-Berith* (completed in 1623), was arranged in encyclopaedic form, its subjects being listed alphabetically. Thus a long list of terms here serves as the subject for commentary from various religious points of view. When writing about the word *ger* (*proselyte*) the author makes no mention of the specific problems of the proselyte, but treats of the word in the biblical sense of *stranger* (or rather *sojourner*); he uses it symbolically, in the neo-platonic manner, to describe the soul in its temporary sojourn on earth.[1] Similarly, Samuel Edels, commenting on the talmudic passage, 'God exiled Israel among the Gentiles with no other object than that converts should be added unto them' (B.T., *Pesaḥim*, 87b), was reluctant to interpret it literally. He explained it as merely implying the mission of the Jewish people to spread their belief in God among the nations of the world.[2] Such deviations from the true traditional meaning of words reveal the altered approach to conversion in the seventeenth century.

The strongest stand against proselytization was that taken by Rabbi Solomon Luria, about the middle of the sixteenth century. As will be recalled, the *Tosafoth* quoted in Chapter VI mitigated the severity of the talmudic passage, *Yevamoth*, 47b, which pronounces a curse upon those who accept proselytes into the Jewish faith. The *Tosafoth* interpreted the passage as referring to those persons only who took the initiative in inducing Gentiles to become Jews. The Jewish courts, however, were obliged to accept the proselyte if he expressed the wish to be converted and persisted in his wish even after he had been duly warned of the religious obligations involved. Rabbi Luria made the following comments about the *Tosafoth*:

It would seem, nevertheless, that all this was said regarding the time when Israel was settled in its own country, even after the Destruction. For although they had become enslaved to the Roman emperor . . . they

[1] The section is called *sha'arey ha-'othiyyoth* in the Warsaw edn., i, pp. 42b–79b. The term *ger* appears on p. 45b. The application of the word *ger* to the soul is to be found, for example, in Baḥya ibn Paquda's *Ḥovoth Ha-Levavoth, sha'ar ha-biṭṭaḥon*, chap. 4, ed. Zifroni, Tel Aviv, 1949, p. 319.

[2] *Ḥiddushey 'Aggadoth, Pesaḥim*, 87b.

possessed the authority to accept anyone who came to them in the land in order to become a proselyte. But now that we are in a country not our own, like slaves beneath the hands of their owners, should one of Israel accept him [sc. a proselyte], he is a rebel, and is responsible for his own death. . . . Hence I hereby give warning that anyone who is a participant in such acceptance today, when the Gentile kingdom is stringent in its attitude, let his blood be on his own head, whether he himself engages in proselytization, or whether he merely knows of such; so may there be survival and stability for the seed of Israel among the peoples all the days of our Exile, throughout our exalted communities, without aliens joining us. And this is a matter demanding the greatest possible caution.[1]

Rabbi Luria's attitude deserves careful analysis. It may have been the result of his own personal observation of the sufferings endured by the Jewish community because of the charge that they had been active in proselytization. In 1539–40 the Jews of Cracow and other Polish towns were accused of having persuaded Christians to become Jews, and of having sent them to Turkey after circumcision in order to remove the evidence of Jewish guilt.[2] Reading between the lines, one gets the impression that Rabbi Luria suspected some of his co-religionists of having indulged in proselytizing Gentiles.

However, we cannot assume that Rabbi Luria's opposition to proselytizing was due merely to his having witnessed the grave consequences to the Jewish community which it entailed. First of all, the prohibition of proselytization was not new; it had existed since Roman times, and ever since then it had been dangerous to be in any way associated with such activities.[3] Nevertheless, in the Middle Ages it was regarded as a virtue to help a Gentile to become a Jew, and the virtue was considered to be all the greater because of the danger involved.[4] At that time, the Jewish community would certainly not have disavowed anyone who assisted

[1] *Yam Shel Shelomoh*, *Yevamoth*, 4. 49.

[2] See E. Zivier, 'Jüdische Bekehrungsversuche im 16. Jahrhundert', *Festschrift zum siebzigsten Geburtstag Martin Philippsons*, pp. 91 ff.; S. Ettinger, 'The Legal and Social Status of Jews in the Ukraine from the 15th to the 17th Centuries' (Hebrew), *Zion*, xx, 1955, pp. 131–2.

[3] G. Allon, *Toledoth Ha-Yehudim be-'Ereṣ Yisra'el bi-Thequfath Ha-Mishnah weha-Talmud*, i, pp. 73–76; G. Kisch, *Germany*, pp. 197–8.

[4] See Chap. VI.

in conversion, or have abandoned him to his fate.[1] But such disavowal was precisely what Rabbi Luria would seem to advocate, when he states that Jews involved in proselytizing were not entitled to such protection from the Jewish community as was extended in the case of unjust persecution. It was understood that Jews who transgressed those general laws which the Jewish community accepted as just would not be protected from punishment. Rabbi Luria evidently regarded the law against proselytizing as falling into this category. His attitude is made clear in his last sentence, cited above, where he writes that the most that the Jewish community can hope for during the Exile is to retain its own followers.

Furthermore, the view that it was undesirable to absorb outsiders into the Jewish nation was in conformity with the belief in the intrinsic difference between Jew and non-Jew, described in our last chapter. The transition from one world to another became a kind of *salto mortale*, a transmutation of essence, not a change of faith or conviction only. It is no wonder that the holders of this belief found themselves in a dilemma: the divinely revealed *Torah* seemed to be inconsistent in that it permitted a non-Jew to become a Jew, while at the same time regarding the Jewish people as being innately different from all others. Those who held similar theories in the past had also been puzzled by this inconsistency. For instance, Judah Ha-Levi (1086–1167) and the qabbalists were embarrassed by the legal possibility of conversion to Judaism; if the Jew was of a distinct, intrinsic nature, how could a non-Jew acquire that nature by an act of will? Judah Ha-Levi concluded that by joining the Jewish people the proselyte drew nearer to God, but that he could not thereby reach the highest level of religious attainment, i.e. he could not become a prophet.[2] Facing the same dilemma, the *Zohar* (thirteenth century) evolved the theory that, when a proselyte became a Jew, a new soul descended upon him from heaven; how-

[1] The *responsa* of R. Ḥayyim, *'Or Zarua'*, 142 *fin.*, imply no more than that if a man was accused of having circumcised a proselyte, but knew that it had been done by another Jew, he was allowed to tell the truth. It is conceded that the act was a meritorious one.

[2] See his *Kuzari*, I. 115; see J. Guttmann, *Die Philosophie des Judentums*, 1933, p. 146.

ever, it was not of the same high spiritual calibre as the souls of those born as Jews.[1] Since qabbalistic concepts became ever more widespread in the period we are studying, namely in the sixteenth to eighteenth centuries, it is not surprising to encounter similar theories. Although conversions became rare, their possibility remained, and they at least required a theoretical explanation. Rabbi Mordecai Jaffe (1530–1612) prefaced the section on proselytes in his halakhic compendium with the words: 'Our scholars have said that it may be assumed that in the case of the proselyte who, on becoming a Jew, has accepted the yoke of the *Torah* and the commandments and the yoke of the Kingdom of Heaven, there is planted in him a holy spirit and a new soul from on high, and he becomes another man; and that it was as if he was created and born anew on that day, as if his entire former life had never been.'[2] The halakhic statement in the Talmud (B.T., *Yevamoth*, 22a) that 'the stranger who becomes a Jew is like a new-born infant' is here paraphrased, and elaborated into a theological or metaphysical theory. The terms used are clearly reminiscent of their qabbalistic origin; this is easily understood, as the author was a master of both Halakhah and *Qabbalah*.[3] In the same way, Rabbi Isaiah Horowitz used the language of the *Zohar* and the later qabbalists in defining the position of the convert.[4]

Maharal was naturally much occupied with the problem of the proselyte. Believing as he did that the difference between Jew and Gentile was one of innate essence, and not the result of any decision to accept or reject the Divine Law, he felt that the dividing line between them should be impassable. Moreover, Maharal attributed inborn racial qualities to every nation, and denied the possibility that a member of one nation could become part of another.[5] It ought to be all the less possible for an outsider to join the Jewish people. Maharal returned time and again to this disturbing question in his writings, but the solutions that he

[1] *Zohar, Beshallaḥ*, 168a; cf. also *Mishpaṭim*, 95b. A slight apprehension of the problem of the proselyte is indicated in B.T., *Shabbath*, 146a.

[2] *Levush, 'Aṭereth Zahav*, 269. 1.

[3] See S. A. Horodetzky, *Le-Qoroth Ha-Rabbanuth*, Warsaw, 1910, pp. 145–74.

[4] *Shelah, Massekheth Shevu'oth*, Warsaw edn., i, pp. 40b–41a.

[5] *Gevuroth Ha-Shem*, chap. 42, Lublin edn. (1875), p. 98. The nationalistic theory of Maharal is analysed by M. Buber; see preceding chapter, p. 138, n. 4.

proposed were not entirely consistent. On one occasion he seems to assume that the soul of the proselyte had always contained some Jewish quality, which miraculously asserts itself when he becomes a Jew.[1] A more comprehensive theory of his was that, whereas the qualities of other nations could be acquired by birth only, the intrinsic Jewish essence, precisely because of its greater holiness, could be acquired by act of conversion.[2] This is a clear contradiction of his basic theory about the predetermined and innately different characters of Jew and Gentile respectively. He himself seems to have been aware of this, for, on other occasions, he states that the proselyte is an incongruous addition to the Jewish people. The talmudic dictum that 'proselytes are as bad for Israel as a scab' which, as we have seen,[3] had troubled those who favoured conversion could be accepted by Maharal in its original, negative sense, although he explained away its derogatory aspect. The offensive expression *sappaḥath* (*scab*) was taken by him to mean simply *accretion*. The undesirability of the proselyte does not spring from his inherent qualities, as is suggested by the expression *scab*, but from the circumstance of his addition to a body which is perfect and complete in itself.[4]

The same conviction, that an impassable gulf existed between the Jewish people and all others, was reflected in the attitude towards apostasy and apostates. Apostasy did, of course, continue to occur. With the beginning of the era of rationalism in the eighteenth century there was an increase in the number of apostates, particularly in Western countries.[5] In the literature of this period, we find the same halakhic problems as are encountered in the Middle Ages. The attitude is now, however, very different. These jurists appear to have no knowledge of apostates who have left the

[1] *Tif'ereth Yisra'el*, chap. 1 *fin.*

[2] *Gevuroth Ha-Shem*, p. 98; similarly in *Derekh Ḥayyim* on Mishnah, *'Avoth*, 5. 22; Warsaw edn., 1933, p. 138a.

[3] See Chap. VI.

[4] Introduction to *Derush 'al Ha-Torah*, Lodz edn., p. 6; *Neṣaḥ Yisra'el*, Warsaw edn., 1873, p. 104.

[5] Regarding Germany in the first half of the eighteenth century many notes have been collected by A. Shoḥeṭ, *Beginnings of the Haskalah among German Jewry* (Hebrew), Jerusalem, 1960, pp. 174–97. Within the above period fall most of the instances noted by H. Schnee, *Die Hoffinanz und der moderne Staat*, Berlin, 1953–5, 3 vols., especially iii, pp. 216–20.

Jewish faith from conviction: their sole motive was assumed to have been material interest. Rabbi Joel Sirkes (died 1640) wrote: 'Thus it is now common knowledge that most apostates are converted solely out of their lust to permit themselves robbery, promiscuity, and the eating of prohibited foods in public without suffering the rebuke of a Jewish court.'[1]

Rabbi Sirkes thus described the apostate in halakhic terms as an unscrupulous hypocrite. It is difficult to know whether or not this was an exaggeration. Even he allows that a minority may exist who are uninfluenced by material motives. There must also have been some cases of genuine conversion in this period, but they were not a matter of much concern to Jewish society. Even unprincipled converts attracted incidental and casual attention only. The convert was considered as remaining a Jew according to halakhic ruling, with all the logical consequences for his family. Legal devices were occasionally resorted to in order to evade some of these consequences. As will be recalled from Chapter VI, a childless widow whose late husband had a brother was not permitted to remarry even if the latter was an apostate, unless he consented to perform the ceremony of *ḥaliṣah*. In the fifteenth century, in order to circumvent this law—for without *ḥaliṣah* the childless widow could never remarry for the rest of her life—a new practice was introduced when a man with an apostate brother wished to marry. The provision was incorporated into the marriage contract that, should the husband die childless, the marriage was to be considered as having been annulled, thus obviating the necessity of performing the *ḥaliṣah* ceremony with the brother. No prominent halakhic authority appears to have initiated this practice, but once it had gained a foothold it was condoned, and even encouraged.[2]

Two factors may be discerned which gave rise to the above practice. Firstly, it was now difficult—perhaps more difficult than it had been in the Middle Ages, when the gulf between Jewish and

[1] In his *Bayith Ḥadash* on *Ṭur*, *Yoreh De'ah*, 268 *fin.*

[2] Israel Isserlein (died 1460) in his *Terumoth Ha-Deshen*, 223, and Israel Bruna (died 1480) were, according to Moses Isserles and Joel Sirkes on *Ṭur*, *'Even 'Ezer*, 157, the first to mention this usage and to acknowledge its permissibility in certain conditions. A. H. Freimann (*Seder Qiddushin we-Nissu'in*, Jerusalem, 1945, p. 386) seems to assume that the device was originated by Israel Bruna, but this assumption is not borne out by the sources.

Christian society was not so wide—to find the apostate and induce him to perform a Jewish rite. Secondly, Rashi's dictum, once a Jew always a Jew, was now universally accepted. Thus legal measures based on the assumption that an apostate was no longer a Jew, and that therefore a *ḥaliṣah* ceremony with him was not necessary, could not be applied.[1] Precisely because of the greater cleavage between the two societies, the original intention of Rashi's ruling—to make the apostate realize that he could not escape from his Jewishness and that the road back to Judaism was always open to him—no longer operated. Cases of apostates remaining attached to Judaism, which are implied in the recommendations of *Sefer Ḥasidim* in the thirteenth century, certainly did not exist during our period. By now the apostate was, to all intents and purposes, regarded as lost to Judaism.

The attitude towards the apostate was a combination of fear and contempt—fear lest he turn informer against the Jewish community, and contempt because of the base motives ascribed to his conversion.[2] There is a conspicuous absence of any indication that efforts were made to influence him to return to the Jewish fold; indeed, we sometimes hear that Jewish authorities explicitly renounced him. Rabbi Ezekiel Landau (died 1793) declared that the renegade had crossed the dividing line into the world of the unholy, and was beyond hope of rescue and salvation. The religious obligation of admonition, based on the mutual responsibility of members of the Jewish community for each other, no longer applied to him.[3]

The attraction towards Christianity which had agitated Jewish communities in the Middle Ages ceased to arouse conflict within the Jews of these later generations. This does not mean that they were spared the test of loyalty to their own religion. Christianity continued to regard Jews as the stiff-necked people who unreason-

[1] The connexion between the acceptance of Rashi's dictum and the new advice is indicated by Isserlein, *Terumoth Ha-Deshen*, 223.

[2] A recurrent dilemma faced the Jewish authorities—how far could they go in their disciplinary measures, or would harshness lead to the apostasy of the culprit, causing harm to the Jewish community? Cf. Isserlein, *Pesaqim*, 138; Solomon Luria, *Yam Shel Shelomoh*, *Yevamoth*, 10. 20; David Ha-Levi, *Ṭurey Zahav* on *Y.D.*, 334.

[3] *Derushey Ha-Ṣelaḥ*, Warsaw, 1897, p. 37a.

ably persisted in refusing to recognize the truth. Christian forbearance towards Judaism was not the equivalent of any admission of the justification for its existence. Not even the humanists of the sixteenth century rose to that height. Reuchlin, it is true, went out of his way to protect Jewish religious literature from attack and destruction, but one of his arguments was that kindness was the best way to convert Jews to Christianity.[1] The Jewish religion continued to be allowed to exist on sufferance, rather than tolerated in the full sense of the word. That is why Jews became the victims of violence, or were compelled to choose between conversion and death, whenever a crisis arose and the equilibrium of society was upset.

This was demonstrated, on a striking and unparalleled scale, by the Cossack massacres in the Ukraine and Poland in 1648–9. In this uprising of the Ukrainians against Polish domination, the Jews were the first and foremost victims. Tens of thousands of them perished at the hands of the Cossacks along with their protectors, the Polish gentry in whose service they had settled and with whom they were identified politically and economically.[2] The social and political roots of the disaster were so obvious that they could not be overlooked. The chief chronicler of the events, Nathan Neta Hannover,[3] clearly discerned the political causes of the revolt of the Cossacks, as well as the motive of revenge.[4] Politically, it was an attempt by the Cossacks to throw off Polish domination; socially, it was the revolt of the oppressed and despised native population against the new colonists. The latter, whether Polish or Jewish, being of different nationality and religion, became the targets of envy, hatred, and—when opportunity arose—of cruelty. The circumstance that the sufferers were not only Jews, but also Poles, would appear to exclude the conception that these events

[1] Graetz, *Geschichte der Juden*, 3rd edn., ix, pp. 87 ff.

[2] For the detailed description of the events see S. M. Dubnow, *History of the Jews in Russia and Poland*, 1916, i, pp. 144–53.

[3] His booklet *Yewen Meṣulah* appeared in Venice in 1653; it has since gone through many editions, and has been translated into many languages. English translation by A. Mesch, New York, 1950. A monograph about Hannover appeared in Yiddish by I. Shatzky and I. Israelssohn, *Gezeroth Taḥ*, Vilna, 1938. Subsequent quotations from *Yewen Meṣulah* are from the Cracow edn., 1896.

[4] See especially the introductory passages of Hannover, pp. 5–13.

constituted an instance of Jewish fate and martyrdom. But the truth is that specifically Jewish features were present. Even prior to the catastrophe, the Jews themselves felt it to be an anomaly that they, the most despised of all nations, should be forcibly imposed upon another people. Far-sighted leaders had grasped the subtleties and dangers of the situation, and had warned individual Jews to be circumspect in the exercise of their political and economic power.[1] We may safely assume that not all of the Jews exploited to the full the authority vested in them by their Polish protectors. However, such self-restraint on their part could not change the objective situation. Although strained relations existed between both Ukrainians and Jews and Ukrainians and Poles, their character was different. The peculiar nature of the Ukrainian-Jewish tension became apparent at the time of crisis, when the Jews were convinced that the wrath of the insurgents was directed against them with special ferocity. Physical destruction was accompanied by religious outrages, and by the demand that Jews abandon their faith. The invaders of the Jewish quarters broke into the synagogues, tore up the Scrolls of the *Torah*, and desecrated other holy objects—acts reminiscent of the violence encountered in the Middle Ages.[2] The Jews' feeling that their religion was a decisive factor in the attack upon them was strengthened by the fact that Jews were often forced to choose between adopting Christianity and instant death.[3] Thus the old situation of Jewish martyrdom recurred, although the cause of the rebellion was mainly political. Although Poles and Jews were both targets of attack, the latter could not always rely on their Polish protectors to defend them. In one case, at least, in Tulczyn, the Cossacks who were attacking the fortified city and the Poles, who were defending it jointly with the Jews, made common cause; the Poles secured their own safety by

[1] Jewish authorities in Poland tried to deter Jews from tax-farming and Rabbi Joel Sirkes gave the reason—lest people should say that Jews wanted to rule over them (*Responsa*, 61). Cf. I. Halperin, *Pinqas Wa'ad 'Arba' 'Araṣoth*, pp. 1–2. This is exactly the complaint uttered by Chmielnicki himself, as related by Hannover, p. 12.

[2] Hannover, p. 16; similarly the other chronicles: see my Hebrew article, 'Beyn Tatnu le-Taḥ–Taṭ', to appear in the Jubilee Volume in honour of Prof. F. Y. Baer.

[3] See Hannover, pp. 22, 25, and my article quoted in previous note.

sacrificing the Jews.[1] Such occurrences poignantly demonstrated the vulnerable position of the Jews.

All this is sufficient to account for the fact that, although Jewish contemporaries were not lacking in insight into the real, initially political causes of the catastrophe, the martyrological conception of the events superimposed itself on their minds as time elapsed. This shift from a realistic analysis to a religious explanation and evaluation is apparent even in Hannover's report of the events. He begins with an inquiry into the political and social causes of the upheaval, but his main interest is soon diverted to the tragic fate of the faithful, who died *'al Qiddush ha-Shem*, 'for the Sanctification of the Name', although they had the choice of saving themselves by submitting to baptism. The stress on martyrdom was even more apparent in the narrative of Shabbethai Kohen. The importance of his version does not lie in any objective description—as a resident of Vilna, he was not an eye-witness of the massacres—but in his being a recognized religious authority and an official spokesman for Judaism. The direct influence of medieval martyrological literature may be clearly discerned in his version of the story. The idea of martyrdom dominated the memorial prayers and religious poetry composed for synagogue services on the fast day ordained in memory of the victims of the massacres.[2] The poets naturally dwelt on the religious heroism of the martyrs, rather than on the objective causes of their martyrdom. There was a deliberate, conscious, and complete identification of them with the martyrs of old. Rabbi Yom-Ṭov Heller, one of the greatest Jewish personalities of the time, at first refused to compose new elegies for the recent events, asserting that they were but a repetition of former horrors and affliction. He considered the dirges composed on former occasions an adequate expression of contemporary anguish and grief.[3]

[1] Hannover, pp. 21–25; see also my article quoted on p. 152, n. 2.

[2] On the enacting of the fast day see Halperin, op. cit., pp. 77–79. The poems dedicated to the event are collected in Gurland, *Le-Qoroth Ha-Gezeroth*. A special bibliography of them was compiled by Naḥum Wolmann, *Meqoroth le-Tholedoth Gezeroth Taḥ we-Taṭ*, Jerusalem, 1949.

[3] According to the publisher of the *Seliḥoth* which he ultimately consented to write, reprinted by A. M. Habermann in *Li-Khevod Yom-Ṭov*, ed. J. L. Maimon, Jerusalem, 1956, p. 126.

The association and identification of contemporary events with ancient instances of martyrdom were inevitable. The Jewish community was powerless to take practical steps to improve its position in the world, in order to prevent a further tragedy.[1] It could react in the spiritual sphere only, by inner searchings, by an intensification of the messianic yearning, and by an attempt to discover some redeeming feature in its agony. The moralists found all manner of sin in their fellow Jews which, they believed, might have provoked the wrath of God.[2] They also conceived Jewish suffering to be a preparation for imminent divine redemption.[3] In their general conception of what had occurred they understandably stressed individual instances of martyrdom to the exclusion of the objective causes of the catastrophe, and this led them in the course of time to see the events in their religious significance only, as one more link in the long chain of Jewish martyrdom.

Admittedly, the majority of Polish Jewry in our period were prepared to face death rather than submit to conversion.[4] The nature of their readiness was, however, somewhat different from that of the Ashkenazi community in the Middle Ages. As will be recalled, the medieval martyrs when about to die made disparaging and insulting attacks upon the religion which their opponents had failed to force upon them.[5] There is no record of such vocal disparagement among the victims in the Ukraine. They died with the traditional Jewish declaration of faith, the *Shema'*, on their lips. To them the adoption of Christianity was inconceivable, but their rejection was not accompanied by an attack upon it. As we know,

[1] There is a single source, from a hundred years later, with records of an alleged ban supposedly imposed upon every Jew who agreed to resettle in the Ukraine after the massacres; see Halperin, op. cit., pp. 79–80. This tradition is, however, scarcely trustworthy. In fact, Jews returned to their former places of residence unless prevented from doing so by political agreement between Poland and Russia. See Dubnow, *History of the Jews in Russia and Poland*, 1916, i, pp. 158, 167.

[2] See my article quoted on p. 152, n. 2.

[3] The messianic upheaval of Shabbethai Ṣevi in the year 1666 did not fail to be connected with the events of 1648–9, although this connexion has, in the past, been overrated. See Gershom Scholem, *Shabbethai Ṣevi* (Hebrew), 1957, pp. 1–2, 73–74, 233, 377, 464, 493; also my *Tradition and Crisis*, pp. 252–3.

[4] Many forced conversions occurred during the years 1648–9, as the chronicles state. See my article mentioned *supra*.

[5] See Chap. VII.

Jews in the Middle Ages had experienced a real inner struggle with regard to the acceptance of Christianity; in our period Christianity had never presented a temptation. Consequently, in the hour of martyrdom and death there was no violent outcry against it. The choice on this occasion was not felt to be between the true faith and the false, but between a martyr's death and physical existence at the cost of spiritual integrity. In contrast to the Middle Ages, when the martyrs vividly envisaged the celestial reward awaiting them, the records of the seventeenth century report no such specific anticipations. Although instructed in the beliefs of Judaism, seventeenth-century Jews were not visionaries in the sense that they held clear conceptions of life after death. These two motivations of medieval Jewry—hatred of the rival religion, and the longing for a clearly defined heavenly reward obtainable through martyrdom only—were absent. Here, the principal motives for *Qiddush ha-Shem* (a martyr's death) were attachment to the Jewish world and all it stood for, and repugnance of the alien world of the persecutors.[1] This is concisely illustrated in the *'El Male' Raḥamim*—the memorial prayer—composed by Rabbi Shabbethai Horowitz: 'Nor did they spare their own lives, or save themselves by idolatry.'[2]

The estrangement of Jewry from the non-Jewish world, encountered so often in the period under review, becomes strikingly apparent in the choice of martyrdom in preference to the betrayal of Judaism.

[1] I have attempted to substantiate this theory in my article (see p. 152, n. 2).

[2] Gurland, *Le-Qoroth Ha-Gezeroth*, iii, p. 25.

XIII

THE DEVELOPMENT OF COMMON GROUND

THE relationship between Jews and non-Jews between the sixteenth and the eighteenth centuries differed from that prevalent in the Middle Ages; this change extended to the field of business, and likewise made itself felt in ethical standards. In this period there was increased and varied contact between Jews and Gentiles. The earlier type of relationship, as between merchant and customer, or lender and borrower, was superseded by more complex associations. The scope of economic life, being by now based on the investment of capital, was broadened. This afforded Jews an opportunity of employing their money in various undertakings, and of proffering their services in many new ways. The consequent change in Jewish occupational structure will be mentioned here in so far only as it illustrates the socio-ethical relationship between Jews and non-Jews.[1]

The peddling trade developed extensively. As a result, the consumer was approached in his own home, by an agent of the producer; this may be regarded as a symptom of the new and dynamic character of business. Many Jews in middle and eastern Europe became pedlars, as a direct result of their numerical increase and their inability to earn a livelihood in any other way. Peddling could be practised with but little capital, the amount required being often obtained as a charity, as a business-loan, or through the extension of credit. The fact that Jews were able to move about as pedlars implied the provision of at least a modicum of security by the authorities. This new occupation is of special interest to us, because it brought Jews into close contact with non-Jews in such a way as to afford an opportunity for ethically dubious practices.

The selling of goods at fairs and markets was in many ways similar to peddling. Here Jews offered their wares to prospective

[1] For a more detailed description, cf. my *Tradition and Crisis*.

buyers who were otherwise unknown to them. In view of the prevalence of double moral standards as between the individual Jew and members of Jewish and Gentile society respectively, the temptation to indulge in unsavoury practices must have been great—increasingly so, in proportion to the measure of anonymity. The tax-farmer, permanently stationed at his customs house—and there were many such among the Jews of our period in Poland and Moravia—or the tradesman at a fixed location, were less prone to dishonest dealings, despite the fact that their customers were casual passers-by. It was only when permanent business relations existed between Jews and non-Jews, such as became common between Jewish bailiffs and stewards and the Polish aristocrats whose estates they farmed, or between 'Court Jews' and their royal patrons, that self-interest demanded absolute honesty and the inspiring of confidence. The degree of honesty was thus apt to depend upon the permanence of the relationship between the parties concerned, and their knowledge of each other.

The Court Jew enables us to understand one aspect of Jewish-Gentile relations. From the middle of the seventeenth century he was an ubiquitous figure in the German principalities and courts, and served his patron as money-lender, agent, emissary, and in various other capacities.[1] The tendency of the petty potentates to employ Jews is partly explained by their preference for an outsider who had no political and social standing or ambitions. The association was impersonal, based on purely business considerations. But in the course of working together, intimate relationships sometimes developed. There is evidence of cases of deep attachment to their royal masters by Court Jews,[2] who were sometimes raised to power in the face of political opposition. Nevertheless, the principal motive for loyalty must necessarily have been the hazardous position of the Court Jew, who was utterly dependent upon his patron for his career and even for his life. Although Court Jews earned handsome profits in the handling of their masters' affairs, they were certainly careful in practice to remain within the bounds

[1] See S. Stern, *The Court Jew*, Philadelphia, 1950; H. Schnee, *Die Hoffinanz und der moderne Staat*, Berlin, 1953–5, 3 vols.

[2] See my *Tradition and Crisis*, p. 289.

of the accepted standards of business honesty; their dependence on their employers' favour amply ensured this.[1]

The anonymity of a Jewish tradesman was a personal anonymity only in so far as he was unknown in any given place. But his Jewish nationality could not be concealed, nor indeed did he care to hide it; his physical appearance and attire, his detachment from the common way of life, and his dietary habits marked him out as a Jew. Any questionable act on his part was likely to be laid at the door of the Jewish community as a whole, even if he could not be held personally answerable. This had been the case ever since Jews had been living as a minority among Gentiles; indeed, it is a general sociological rule that all minority groups are held collectively responsible for the actions of their individual members. The measure of this collective responsibility varies with the extent to which the minority is distinguishable in appearance, and with the degree of its group-isolation from the general community. As the distinguishability and isolation of the Jewish community were, in our period, more marked than ever, collective Jewish responsibility was correspondingly increased. Indeed, this general rule sometimes received legal expression, and the Jewish community was occasionally held accountable before the law for transgressions of individual Jews. It had, for instance, to pay damages for thefts, and similar crimes.[2]

Jewish detachment and collective responsibility were the two factors determining morality as taught between the sixteenth and eighteenth centuries, as far as external ethics were concerned. The earlier view, viz. that a Jew ought to be honest in order to attract others to his faith, was motivated by a missionary objective and played no part in our period. Even the notion implied in the terms *Qiddush ha-Shem* ('Sanctification of the Name') and *Ḥillul ha-Shem* ('Desecration of the Name')—that a Jew should be honest

[1] H. Schnee certainly does no justice to the Court Jew. He would saddle him with the responsibilities of a public servant, who is under an obligation to curb his master's extravagances. But the position of the Court Jew was very far from imposing upon him the duties of a servant of the public.

[2] This was the case, for instance, in Prussia down to the Emancipation; cf. I. Freund, *Die Emanzipation der Juden in Preußen*, 1912, i, p. 29; for the practical application of the rule, see L. Moses, *Die Juden in Niederösterreich*, p. 185. See also Menaḥem M. Krochmal, *Responsa*, 36.

because he is thereby evincing to the non-Jew the high moral standards of his religion, and, if he were not, would be implying the reverse—was absent. These terms, especially *Ḥillul ha-Shem*, continued to be used, albeit not so much as in the Middle Ages;[1] but it seldom implied any consideration for the opinion of non-Jews. Instead, the meaning of *Ḥillul ha-Shem* came to be that a Jew should not wrong a Christian because of the consequent danger to the Jewish community,[1] or because so doing constituted in itself an act of rebellion against God, as did all transgressions of His *Torah*.[2] Jews were taught to deal honestly with non-Jews, either because of the fear of being considered untrustworthy, or because of objective religious considerations of right and wrong. Some thinkers attempted to give a more comprehensive explanation for the prohibition of wronging Gentiles. For instance, Rabbi Solomon Luria and Rabbi Ṣevi Ashkenazi wrote:

> Robbery of a Gentile is forbidden even apart from *Ḥillul ha-Shem*, because a man should keep aloof from ugly deeds and the like, and should eat and drink his own food, not accustoming himself to theft and robbery.[3]

> We are commanded not to perform ugly acts . . . nor to accustom ourselves to steal . . . and are also commanded to take account of the suffering of dumb animals . . . not to butcher an animal and its offspring on the same day, and to observe the commandment of freeing the mother in the nest. . . . The commandment also relates to plants, forbidding us to destroy a tree, and all this is not for the sake of the object of the act, but for ourselves, who do these things; that we may acquire with our minds true notions and honest virtues, that will be to our merit and benefit.[4]

With the same object in mind, preachers warned their congregations that people who acquire wealth by dishonest means—whether from Jews or non-Jews—never prosper in the end.[5] This

[1] Some instances may be noted: M. Balaban, 'Die Krakauer Judengemeinde-Ordnung von 1595 und ihre Nachträge', *JJLG*, x, 1912, p. 328; S. Dubnow, *Pinqas Ha-Medinah*, Berlin, 1925, 605; I. Halperin, *Taqqanoth Medinath Mehrin*, Jerusalem, 1952, 254, 265, 648.

[2] The former is the common connotation. For the latter, see Judah Loeb Pochowitzer, *Diverey Ḥakhamim*, 24b.

[3] Luria, *Yam Shel Shelomoh*, *Bava Qamma*, 10. 20.

[4] Ashkenazi, *Responsa*, 26.

[5] R. Samuel Edels, *Ḥiddushey 'Aggadoth*, *Kethubboth*, 67a; Moses Rivkes, *Be'er Ha-Golah*, *Ḥ.M.*, 348.

was a well-known theme from the thirteenth-century work *Sefer Ḥasidim*, which asserted a belief in the divine justice and a condemnation of a double moral standard.[1] But the preachers were basing their warning on the lessons of their own personal experience, and were not merely repeating old precepts.

Yet, as a rule, the appeal of the Jewish authorities to their people to deal honestly with non-Jews was based on fear of the consequences to the organized community. There was a clear shift in ethical orientation from the individual in the Middle Ages to the group in the period under review. In earlier times, the Jew still had some hope of being judged on his own merits as an individual; now, he was certain that the Jewish community as a whole would be held responsible for his actions. This awareness of the danger to the community might also have acted as a deterrent to dishonesty in the Middle Ages. But in our period the individual's consideration for the community was not left entirely to his own choice. Jewish authorities tried to control the behaviour of the members of their communities. They were able to do so, because they had achieved a high degree of communal organization and had established close ties with all other Jewish communities in the same country—in both cases with the consent of the rulers, who bestowed far-reaching legal powers upon them.[2] Severe punishment was meted out to those who defrauded Gentiles—fines, imprisonment, and excommunication; in extreme cases the offender was even handed over to the non-Jewish authorities for punishment.[3] The collective responsibility which knitted the Jewish community together thus led to the control of the individual by the organized group.

The severe threats and denunciations, as well as the stern penalties imposed upon the transgressor against non-Jews, appear to have been motivated by an additional factor. Jewish society became in our period more diversified than before. In addition to the well-to-do, permanently established residents, who enjoyed

[1] *Sefer Ḥasidim*, 133, 1426; see Chap. VIII.

[2] See my *Tradition and Crisis*, chaps. 9–13.

[3] Balaban, *JJLG*, x, 1912, pp. 328–9; S. Dubnow, *Pinqas Ha-Medinah*, 26, 163, 637, 665, 830; I. Halperin, *Pinqas*, p. 124; idem, *Taqqanoth*, 260, 263, 264; Moses Rivkes, *Be'er Ha-Golah*, *Ḥ.M.*, 388; B. D. Weinryb, *Texts and Studies in the Communal History of Polish Jewry*, New York, 1950 (Hebrew part), p. 14.

commercial privileges and social prestige, there was a large number of persons who had no right of permanent residence, no social standing, and were economically insecure.[1] This element, having little to lose, tended to take advantage of every opportunity to eke out a living. Ethics in general, in particular towards the non-Jew, were of little consideration to such people. The Jewish community tried to protect Gentiles from them, thus, in turn, protecting the community itself. The following extract from the *Taqqanoth* (*Regulations*) of the Council of Jews of Moravia in 1649 will illustrate our point:

With regard to all those vagabonds, worthless people, robbers, and cut-throats who endanger the entire Jewish community, profaning the Name of God in public on market-days at Kremecz, Linz, and similar places, permission is given to every man to disavow them and all responsibility for their property, and to hand them over to the [civil] authorities. This being so, *a fortiori* it is hereby declared permissible to thrust them out and expel them from the community in which they have taken up residence, by use of force and violence, and despite the absence of the unanimous will or consent of the members of the community. And if any such ungovernable man, the source of all evil, comports himself so iniquitously as to attempt himself to influence the authorities (may their majesty be held in high respect) then permission is given to all members of the community concerned to issue forth against him with all vigour, to deprive him utterly of his capital and his home.[2]

The above *Taqqanah* refers to persons who did not possess the right of permanent residence, and were thus handicapped in earning a livelihood. Severe measures could be adopted against them, even to the point of banishment, unless they succeeded in finding a non-Jewish protector. Such outside interference was, of course, inconsistent with the right of the Jewish community to decide who was permitted to reside among themselves. The *Taqqanah* quoted implies that such intervention could occur, and reveals the precariousness of the Jewish community's power.[3] Moral appeals alone could not suffice in such a situation. Indeed,

[1] See my *Tradition and Crisis*, chaps. 7, 19.

[2] I. Halperin, *Taqqanoth*, 265.

[3] See *supra*, Chap. XII, p. 150, n. 2.

the term *sakkanath ha-ṣibbur* ('danger to the community') recurs more frequently than *Ḥillul ha-Shem*; and it was intended less as an appeal to the potential transgressor, than as a justification for the severe penalties threatened.[1]

Attempts to eliminate double ethical standards and to establish common, objective standards for Jew and non-Jew alike could not succeed with the public at large. The deep social and religious cleavage which we have encountered in the Middle Ages still existed. In order to overcome this obstacle, even only in theory, it was necessary to find a common religious basis for the adherents of the two faiths. Such a development could hardly be expected, in view of the absence of any contact between Judaism and Christianity, even in the form of the intellectual disputations described in our previous chapter. But, paradoxically enough, this very estrangement paved the way to common ground within the ethical field.

As explained in the early chapters of this book, Christianity in the Middle Ages was still considered to be *'avodah zarah* ('idol worship'): for certain practical purposes, however, it was not regarded as such.[2] For instance, the talmudic law forbidding certain business dealings with idolaters was not applied to Christians, on the assumption that they were not heathen. Practical considerations required the dissociation of Christianity from idolatry, and this was rationalized by means of halakhic casuistry. But this rationalization cannot be assumed to imply that, from a theological point of view, Christianity was no longer regarded as a 'pagan' religion.

Between the sixteenth and eighteenth centuries certain developments took place. The disassociation of Christianity from idolatry became more widely applied. Restrictions on business which were based on the segregative laws were now dropped. Trade in Gentile wine became a source of living for many pious Jews.[3] This may be attributed mainly to the growing need for Jews to

[1] See the sources noted on p. 160, n. 3.

[2] See Chaps. III–IV.

[3] Moses Isserles gave permission to trade in rosaries, *Shulḥan 'Arukh, Y.D.*, 151; I have described in *Tradition and Crisis*, chap. 3, the stages of development in respect of Gentile wine.

adapt their laws to an ever-increasing economic association with Christians. However, if we examine the reasoning advanced to justify this lenient attitude towards Christianity, we shall find that it was no longer motivated entirely by considerations of expediency, but that a new evaluation of Christianity, as a non-idolatrous religion, was evincing itself. It will be recalled (see p. 34) that one of the tosaphists permitted the acceptance of an oath by Christians, on the ground that they did not swear by idols. The possible objection that Jesus was referred to in Christian oaths was countered by the argument that Gentiles were exempt from the prohibition of associating (*shittuf*) any other name with that of God. The word *shittuf* was used here in the same sense as in B.T., *Sanhedrin*, 63a, where it appears as a verb, not as a noun, and refers merely to the specific command not to equate the name of God with any other by mentioning both in one sentence. However, as a result of Arabic influence, the word *shittuf* acquired a broader connotation in medieval philosophical literature—unknown, of course, to the tosaphists—and came to mean the opposite of monotheism, i.e. duality of the Godhead.[1] When seventeenth- and eighteenth-century scholars studied the *Tosafoth*, they read this specific meaning, with which they were familiar, into the tosaphists' use of the word *shittuf*.[2] They were thus misled into believing that the tosaphists had stated that it was not obligatory upon Gentiles to reject a dual Godhead. The Christian Trinity was therefore not assumed to be, in all circumstances, objectionable, as a non-Jewish belief. This constituted a convenient theory, permitting Jewish tolerance of Christianity as the faith of others, but retaining

[1] D. Kaufmann, *Geschichte der Attributenlehre*, Gotha, 1877, p. 460, n. 148.

[2] From the parallel sources *Tosafoth*, *Sanhedrin*, 63b; Rosh, *Sanhedrin*, 7, 3; R. Yeruḥam, *Sefer 'Adam we-Ḥawwah*, 17, 5; only the last-cited has the full statement: 'The sons of Noah are not commanded as to the *shittuf*.' The other two sources read '*'al kakh*' (concerning this). The word *shittuf* appears in *Tosafoth*, *Bekhoroth*, 2b, in another connexion. The version of R. Yeruḥam (from fourteenth-century Spain) may be an unwitting emendation after the term *shittuf* had gained currency. In any case, it was thanks to this version alone that it could become a standing quotation. The change in meaning of this dictum was first pointed out by R. Ephraim Kohen, *Responsa*, 24; see also R. Jonah Landsofer, *Responsa*, 22, and R. Samuel Landau in *Noda' Biyhudah* (2nd edn.), *Y.D.*, 148. It is interesting that it was a modern Gentile scholar, G. Dalman, who (independently of the halakhists, it seems) noticed this point. See G. Marx (pseudonym), *Jüdisches Fremdenrecht*, 1886, p. 50, n. 1.

absolute monotheism as obligatory upon Jews. There is ample evidence that this view was prevalent among seventeenth- and eighteenth-century Jews.[1]

A second line of argument led to similar conclusions. Medieval halakhists excluded Christians from the category of idolaters on the additional ground that contemporary Gentiles were not versed in the forms of idol worship. As explained in Chapter X, Rabbi Menaḥem Ha-Me'iri was the only scholar, until the fifteenth century, to elaborate this view into a comprehensive philosophy and to draw the logical conclusions. He did this by adding the positive to the negative, i.e. by attributing virtues to Christians in addition to stating that they were not idolaters. Ha-Me'iri's writings remained largely unknown, and therefore of little influence. But independently of him, a similar line of reasoning was followed by certain seventeenth-century scholars, among them Moses Rivkes, a Lithuanian halakhist who had left Vilna for the West after the upheavals of 1648–9. He wrote a gloss to the *Shulḥan 'Arukh*, with the principal purpose of noting the main sources. Occasionally, he added remarks on the rulings themselves, limiting or defining their applicability. When dealing with the section on the status of Gentiles, he made some remarkable comments. Let us consider the most lengthy of these, concerning the chapter on the right of self-defence. Self-defence was permitted by the *Shulḥan 'Arukh*, as it had been by the talmudic authorities, not only against those who, by specific actions, endangered the life of the individual or the community, but also against informers or renegades who constituted a potential danger. There were other categories of persons—for instance shepherds, who for some reason were held in bad repute in talmudic times—who were not to be assisted when in danger, although Jews were not allowed to kill them.[2] *'Akkum*, i.e. idol worshippers, were included in this

[1] The dictum gained currency through its having been quoted by Moses Isserles on *Shulḥan 'Arukh*, *'O.Ḥ.*, 156. There is some indication that he himself interpreted it in the wider sense. See *Pithḥey Teshuvah*, *Y.D.*, 147. This interpretation was explicitly adopted by Samuel b. Joseph, *'Olath Tamid*, 1681, *'O.Ḥ.*, 156. That the dictum was much quoted is testified by the authors (cited in the preceding note) who contested it. Jacob Emden quotes the dictum as if it was of talmudic origin (*'ameru rabbothenu zikhronam liverakhah*), *Responsa*, 1. 41, *'Eṣ 'Avoth*, 41b.

[2] *Shulḥan 'Arukh*, *Ḥ.M.*, 525, 5.

category. As the term *'Akkum* was sometimes used synonymously with 'Gentile', Rabbi Rivkes felt prompted to disabuse his readers of any possible error, and wrote as follows:

> The Rabbis said this in relation to the pagans of their own times only, who worshipped stars and the constellations and did not believe in the Exodus or in *creatio ex nihilo*. But the peoples in whose shade we, the people of Israel, are exiled and amongst whom we are dispersed do in fact believe in *creatio ex nihilo* and in the Exodus and in the main principles of religion, and their whole aim and intent is to the Maker of heaven and earth, as the codifiers have written. . . . So far, then, from our not being forbidden to save them, we are on the contrary obliged to pray for their welfare, and as Rabbi Eliezer Ashkenazi wrote at length on the Passover *Haggadah*, concerning the sentence *Pour out Thy wrath upon the peoples who have not known Thee* (Ps. lxxix. 6), it was King David, peace be upon him, who prayed to God to pour out His wrath on the heathen who did not believe in *creatio ex nihilo* and in the signs and wonders which God, Blessed be He, performed for us in Egypt, and at the giving of the *Torah*. But the Gentiles, in whose shadow we live and under whose wings we shelter, believe in all these things, as I have written; hence we stand on guard to pray continually for the welfare and success of the kingdom and the ministers, for all the States and places over which they rule; and indeed Maimonides ruled, in concurrence with Rabbi Joshua (B.T., *Sanhedrin*, 105a), that the pious of the Gentile nations too have a portion in the world to come.[1]

Rabbi Rivkes drew the conclusion that, regarding the obligation to save life, no discrimination should be made between Jew and Christian; the same degree of merit was attached to saving either. He based his statement on a comprehensive evaluation of Christianity, and for that reason it deserves our special attention.

Rivkes's outlook comprised basic views which we have already encountered, viz. that Christians were not idolaters in that they, like Jews, worshipped the Creator of heaven and earth, and that the inferior political status of the Jews obliged them to be grateful and loyal to their benefactors. But he added a personal contribution, namely, the opinion that Christians shared the Jewish belief in prophecy and revelation and in the truth of the Bible, i.e. that they had a common tradition. In support of his view, Rivkes referred to

[1] *Be'er Ha-Golah*, on the reference in the preceding note.

a passage in the writings of an earlier authority, Rabbi Eliezer Ashkenazi, a prolific homilist who lived in the middle of the sixteenth century. Ashkenazi's commentary, *Ma'aseh Ha-Shem*, on the *Haggadah* for *Pesaḥ* (i.e. the domestic liturgy for the *Seder* nights, the first two nights of Passover), deals with the passage in which some verses from the Bible that beseech revenge upon *the nations that knew Thee not* (i.e. Ps. lxxix. 6–7, &c.) are recited. The exact connotation of such biblical passages was normally a matter of little concern for participants in the *Seder*. Doubtless they were originally included in the *Haggadah* as prayers for the speedy coming of the Messiah, to be preceded by the Day of Judgement and the doom of non-believers, who, for the average sixteenth-century worshipper, would have included Christians. But Rabbi Ashkenazi, influenced probably by the Italian scholar Solomon Ibn Verga of the humanist era,[1] shrank from such an interpretation. He thought that the literal meaning of the prayer was intended, i.e. that, as in the actual words of the biblical verses, it applied only to heathens who rejected the notion of revelation.

As Rabbi Ashkenazi's views had been expressed in homiletic form, they possessed no more than theoretical significance. They acquired a legal force through their inclusion by Rivkes in his gloss to the *Shulḥan 'Arukh*. As they shared the Jewish belief in Revelation, Christians were legally defined as a specific group of Gentiles; what the Talmud said about idolaters, therefore, did not apply to Christians. Rivkes's comments were quoted, or hinted at, whenever the relationship between Judaism and Christianity was discussed, as happened very often during the eighteenth century, especially in western European countries. It was there that the first signs of tolerance towards Jews appeared, and gave rise to corresponding attitudes on the part of Jews to Christians. The influence of this development on enlightened Jews (the *Maskilim*) will be described in the next chapter. Here we shall concern ourselves with the exponents of traditional Judaism only, who were no more impervious than the *Maskilim* themselves to the effects of surrounding non-Jewish religious tolerance. Rabbi Ya'ir Ḥayyim

[1] See his *Shevet Yehudah*, Jerusalem edn., 1947, p. 29. Christians are there characterized as subscribing to the belief in *creatio ex nihilo*.

Bacharach (1638–1702) and Rabbi Jacob Emden (1697–1776) were the outstanding Jewish personalities of their times.[1] They and their circles reacted to their environment by stressing the common religious heritage of Judaism and Christianity, as expounded by their predecessors, Rivkes and Ashkenazi.[2] Rabbi Emden, in minimizing the difference between the two faiths, even went so far as to state that Jesus had never intended to abrogate the *Torah* so far as Jews were concerned, but had wished merely to spread Jewish tenets and the Seven Noachide Commandments among non-Jews. The ultimate clash between Judaism and Christianity, as well as the Christian persecution of Jews, stemmed from a fatal misunderstanding.[3] The above Rabbis represented the mental attitudes of the old school of Jewish tradition. Emden lived to see the beginnings of the *Haskalah* movement, and became its vehement opponent. Nevertheless, he and his like were influenced, despite themselves, by the same stimulus which had given rise to that movement. For instance, they acquired a certain degree of secular knowledge; Bacharach and Emden even attained a critical attitude towards tradition and its sources.[4] They had no difficulty in reconciling their new knowledge and attitudes with the traditionalism in which they were steeped, and their tolerance towards Christianity was one of the indications of this lack of conflict.

The highest measure of tolerance towards Christianity which it was possible for traditional Judaism to adopt was reflected in the views of the leading halakhists. Some of their statements seem, indeed, to be very far-reaching. They must be understood, however,

[1] Ya'ir Bacharach, *Responsa,* I (fol. 5b). See D. Kaufmann, *R. Yair Chajim Bachrach und seine Ahnen*, Trier, 1894; M. J. Cohen, *Jacob Emden, A Man of Controversy*, Philadelphia, 1937.

[2] A. Shoḥeṭ, 'The German Jews' Integration within their non-Jewish Environment in the First Half of the 18th Century' (Hebrew), *Zion*, xxi, 1956, pp. 229–34, listed the sources reflecting the Jewish attitude towards Christianity in the period. Some others may be added, e.g. Jacob Joshua, *Peney Yehoshua'*, Frankfort on the Main edn., 1756, on the last page; Ezekiel Landau, *Responsa*, Prague edn., 1776, on the first page.

[3] Emden was the first to question the authenticity of the *Zohar*; see Y. Tishbi, *Mishnath Ha-Zohar*, Jerusalem, 1949, pp. 52–56.

[4] The fact that Landau and Emden were strong opponents of the Sabbatian movement and also opposed Hasidism does not affect the fact that they were, themselves, imbued by the spirit of *Qabbalah*, as an examination of their writings incontrovertibly shows.

against the background of their times and of the prevailing mental attitudes. The halakhic exponents of these tolerant views were imbued with qabbalistic ideas which ascribed a unique, innate essence and depth to Jews and Judaism.[1] It may well be that their very immersion in traditional Jewish life and thought made their relative tolerance of Christianity possible. Their views, however, remained for them but abstract theories. They did not proceed to draw the logical and practical conclusions, nor did they intend to diminish social segregation of Jews from Christians or to minimize their ritual differences. When they stated that both religions had a common heritage, they did not mean that the boundaries between them should be effaced, but wished merely to promote friendly and tolerant relations on the occasions when contact between the members of the two faiths was necessary. They required from the Jews correct behaviour in neighbourly and business associations.[2] But that did not imply an abandonment of the Jewish birthright in matters spiritual, or of the separately organized Jewish way of life. Even in the field of dogma, they confined themselves to a more or less arbitrary interpretation of Christianity without proceeding to a critical examination of their own doctrines. They evaluated Christianity as a religion for Gentiles only, and did not for a moment conceive that it might face Jews with the temptation to become converted themselves. They certainly did not realize that their line of thought, if followed consistently and applied to changing conditions, might lead to grave consequences for traditional Judaism. But that was exactly what happened in the case of the *Haskalah* movement.

[1] Both Jacob Joshua and Landau, in the passages quoted on p. 167, n. 2, state that they preached to their congregants on the duty of being fair to non-Jews. This is the only conclusion they drew from their premisses.

[2] Thus especially R. Jacob Emden in the addition to *Seder 'Olam Rabba* edited by him, Hamburg, 1797, 33a–35b, reprinted in his *Sefer Shimmush*, pp. 15–17.

XIV

ENLIGHTENMENT AND TOLERATION

It is beyond the scope of this book to describe the great social changes which paved the way for the emergence of the new type of Jew—the 'Enlightened' Jew, or *Maskil*—whose relationship to Christianity is the subject of this chapter.[1] We must here limit ourselves to stating that the tolerant attitudes which developed and spread in both Christian and Jewish society during the second half of the eighteenth century found expression in a new kind of association between the members of each group. Jews and non-Jews alike discovered that they could meet on common human ground, such a relationship involving no attempt to deny or obscure their different religious affiliations.

The best-known and most characteristic example of this new type of relationship was that which existed between Lessing and Mendelssohn in the 1750's.[2] Their first meeting, which is said to have taken place over a game of chess,[3] was the beginning of a lifelong friendship, based on common literary, philosophical, and even theological interests. Although Lessing cannot be said to have been a Christian in the orthodox sense of the word, he was certainly immersed in Christian ways of thought, having been born and brought up in a strictly Christian home as the son of a minister. Mendelssohn, on the other hand, was an observant Jew who adhered to the beliefs of Judaism as he understood them. He differed from his Jewish contemporaries in that he regarded non-Jewish

[1] I have dealt with the social implications of the problem in my *Tradition and Crisis*, chaps. 21, 23, 24, and in my dissertation (Frankfort on the Main, 1935), *Die Entstehung der Judenassimilation in Deutschland und deren Ideologie*.

[2] The classical biography of Mendelssohn is still M. Kayserling's *Moses Mendelssohn*, 1862, but countless minor studies have added to the understanding and evaluation of his life and work. The various introductions to the Jubilee edition of his writings (Berlin, 1929–32, 6 vols. only published) are the best point of orientation. Mendelssohn's writings are here quoted, unless otherwise stated, according to the Leipzig edn., 1843 (*Moses Mendelssohn's gesammelte Schriften*).

[3] M. Kayserling, op. cit., p. 33.

cultural fields of activity as being not only useful, but worth while cultivating for their own sake also. He studied all branches of philosophy—epistemology, ethics, aesthetics—read German and other European literature, and interested himself in mathematics, the theory of music, &c.; in some of these fields, especially philosophy, he became a prolific writer. All this involved contact with non-Jews, very few Jews being then interested in such subjects.

It was natural for Mendelssohn to conclude that cultural fields existed which had common human values for Jew and non-Jew alike. He felt an affinity with Christian friends, as well as with all who were active in fields of work similar to his own. This is clearly revealed in his correspondence with Herder and Lavater, two writers with whom he was but merely acquainted. In a letter to the former, he wrote: 'Moses, the human being (*Mensch*), is writing to Herder, the human being, and not the Jew to the Christian preacher (*Superintendent*).'[1] The significance of this remark can be understood only if we recall the change in meaning which the word *Mensch* was undergoing at that time. From the simple definition of the human species, it became one of the central concepts of Rationalism—*Aufklärung*—which assumed the existence of inherent human values capable of development without religious stimulus or reinforcement.[2]

Mendelssohn's use of the word *Mensch* to denote the common humanity of Jew and Christian illustrated the new relationship which Rationalism could be expected to establish between the followers of the respective faiths. At the same time, Mendelssohn's attitude implied that, in some respects at least, Jews and Christians were in point of fact different. The exact nature of this difference, and at what point it superseded and became even more important than their common humanity, were questions which could not have failed to suggest themselves to a thinker of Mendelssohn's acumen and integrity. Moreover, external circumstances compelled him to come to grips with such problems. Mendelssohn represented a

[1] Kayserling, *Moses Mendelssohn*, p. 546. Similar terms in Mendelssohn's letter to Lavater, *Schriften*, iii, p. 88.

[2] See my *Judenassimilation*, pp. 47–50.

new type of Jew, and as such he aroused notice and curiosity. Jews and Christians alike asked: Is he a Jew? If so, why doesn't he confine himself to Jewish society and interests? Has he become estranged from Judaism? If so, why doesn't he become a Christian? As long as such questions were whispered behind his back, Mendelssohn pretended not to hear them.[1] But when they were put to him directly and publicly by Lavater, who was a well-known Christian theologian, he could not evade his obligation to reply.[2] He attempted to meet the challenge without permitting himself to be drawn into an open controversy with Christianity, and expressed his conviction of the truth of Judaism, whose foundations were based on Divine Revelation.

Mendelssohn's statement, so far as the practice of Judaism was concerned, implied that no part of the *Torah* could be abrogated except by a new act of revelation.[3] Hence his conservatism with regard to religious observance. He regarded the fundamental concepts and teachings of Judaism as divinely revealed truth, but he conceded that rational thinking would lead to the recognition of the same truths.[4] He could therefore maintain both that Judaism was a revealed religion and that it did not teach dogmas which were irrational. In his opinion, the principal superiority of Judaism over Christianity lay in its rationality.

During his controversy with Lavater, in 1769–70, Mendelssohn was reluctant to state his objections to Christianity explicitly. He had not yet become aware of the change that was imminent in the status of the Jew in European countries, and felt that Jews must content themselves with remaining a minority of inferior political status, whom it would ill become to criticize the religion of the ruling majority.[5] It is, however, not difficult to prove that Mendelssohn's

[1] That Mendelssohn was repeatedly approached in private by would-be missionaries is clearly stated in his *Schriften*, iii, p. 47.

[2] The course of this controversy is clearly described by S. Rawidowicz in the introduction to the Jubilee edition of Mendelssohn's works, vol. vii.

[3] *Schriften*, iii, pp. 42–43. More explicitly in *Jerusalem* (1783), *Schriften*, iii, pp. 356–7.

[4] For Mendelssohn's conception of Judaism see J. Guttmann, *Die Philosophie des Judentums*, 1933, pp. 303–17; M. Wiener, *Jüdische Religion im Zeitalter der Emanzipation*, 1933, pp. 34–40. I. Heinemann, 'Ha-'Aḥduth ba-Philosophia Ha-Dathith shel Mosheh Mendelssohn', *Meṣudah*, 1944, pp. 197–219.

[5] *Schriften*, iii, pp. 46–47; see my *Judenassimilation*, pp. 72–73.

restraint had deeper roots than considerations of propriety or mere expediency. In the conversations with Lavater which preceded the latter's public challenge, Mendelssohn appears to have mentioned the Jewish objection to the divinity of Jesus.[1] In his public reply to Lavater, he alluded to the conviction—clearly and fully stated in his later writings—that many Christian beliefs were incompatible with reason.[2] Basically, Mendelssohn did not depart from the stand taken by the traditionalists in their polemics. Like them, he took for granted the truth of his own religion and the consequent untruth of his opponent's. He differed from his predecessors in this only, that the conviction of the truth of his own faith did not impel him to prove his belief, or to convince others of its correctness; it merely obviated any possible temptation to change his religion. Furthermore, Mendelssohn believed that such self-restraint was in keeping with the teachings of Judaism, and not merely the expression of his own personality and his tolerant attitude towards others.

Paradoxically enough, from Mendelssohn's controversy with Lavater one almost receives the impression that what Mendelssohn valued above all in Judaism was not its objective truth, but its desire to keep that truth to itself. He stated that religious tolerance was one of the basic characteristics of Judaism, and that this constituted its moral superiority over Christianity. As proof of his contention that Judaism was not interested in converting others, Mendelssohn pointed to the halakhic procedure that must be followed before a proselyte is accepted into Judaism—the warning that the latter would, with his conversion, assume the responsibility of observing the *Torah* and that great hardships were involved in joining a politically and socially inferior community.[3] Mendelssohn paraphrased the admonition to proselytes, and, in doing so, perhaps unintentionally—but nonetheless significantly—inserted a statement not contained in the halakhic

[1] *Schriften*, iii, p. 42.

[2] Ibid., pp. 45–47; Mendelssohn's objection to the Christian dogmas are stated in his 'Betrachtungen über Bonet's Palingenesie', ibid., pp. 160–76; cf. J. Guttmann, op. cit., pp. 307–8.

[3] The sources referred to by Mendelssohn are B.T., *Yevamoth*, 47a–b, Maimonides, *Hilkhoth 'Issurey Bi'ah*, 13. 14, 14. 1–5.

formulation of the procedure to the effect that, even without becoming a Jew, a Gentile was assured of salvation by observing the Seven Commandments of Noah.[1] This belief, although shared by good Jewish authorities, did not constitute part of the warning to would-be proselytes. And the admonition certainly did not imply that a Gentile had no greater prospect of religious salvation after becoming converted to Judaism than he had had before. On the contrary—and this Mendelssohn seems to have overlooked—the proselyte who persisted in his resolve to adopt the Jewish faith despite all discouragement was later informed that he had joined the ranks of those destined to inherit the world to come.[2]

Historically, too, Mendelssohn was wrong in stating that the Rabbis had never been zealous in bringing influence to bear on Gentiles to become Jews. He read into Jewish sources, as well as into Jewish history, the prevailing attitudes of his own and preceding generations. As we know, attempts to convert Gentiles to Judaism diminished at the end of the Middle Ages.[3] Mendelssohn could reasonably state, with the support of the rabbinical authorities of his own time, that Judaism was a religion with no missionary tendencies. He enunciated this view with obvious satisfaction, as it was in complete harmony with the teachings of the philosophy of *Aufklärung*, and in this he scored a significant point over his Christian opponents. Without coming into conflict with the Church the latter could hardly repudiate the Christian view that missionary activity was an incontestable duty and virtue. Let us quote Mendelssohn on this point:

I have the good fortune to count among my friends quite a number of fine (*vortrefflich*) men who are not of my faith. We have a genuine affection for each other, although we take it for granted that in matters of religion we have very different beliefs. I enjoy their company and benefit from it. Never has it occurred to me to sigh, 'Alas for that

[1] 'Wir sollen ihm zu bedenken geben, daß er sich durch diesen Schritt, ohne Noth, einer sehr beschwerlichen Last unterziehe, daß er sich in seinem jetzigen Zustande nur die Pflichten der Noachiden zu beobachten habe, um selig zu werden.' *Schriften*, iii, pp. 43–44.

[2] See the authorities quoted on p. 172, n. 3.

[3] See Chap. XII.

beautiful soul!' One who believes that there is no salvation outside his own Church has perforce only too often to heave such a sigh.[1]

It could indeed be stated, and on good authority, that Judaism did not exclude non-Jews from the hope of salvation. In talmudic times, it is true, this attitude had still been contested; in the first century of the common era, one of the sages denied the contention.[2] But once the more liberal view had been accepted by Maimonides (in the twelfth century), the contrary opinion ceased to be expressed.[3] Maimonides' succinct wording, 'The righteous of all peoples have a part in the world to come',[4] became proverbial, and was regarded as the official Jewish view. The word *righteous* (*ḥasid*) was clearly defined by Maimonides; he related it to the Seven Commandments of the Sons of Noah, which the Talmud held to be binding upon all mankind.[5] As the Seven Commandments had sometimes been regarded as identical with Natural Law,[6] the term 'righteous' could be applied to all civilized peoples, and it had indeed been so applied by early Jewish thinkers. And it could certainly be applied by Mendelssohn to his own generation of 'Enlightenment'.

Mendelssohn set forth his view in detail and felt himself to be in agreement with past and present Jewish authorities, one of whom, his contemporary Rabbi Jacob Emden, he mentioned by name.[7] In actual fact, he went much farther than even the most progressive Rabbis of his time. As we shall presently see, Mendelssohn consulted Emden on one point. The latter, whose view assured salvation to worthy non-Jews, undoubtedly had Christians in mind, in line with the familiar reasoning that Gentiles who

[1] *Schriften*, iii, p. 47.

[2] See B.T., *Sanhedrin*, 105a; cf. G. F. Moore, *Judaism*, 1946, ii, p. 386.

[3] See my article 'Sheloshah Mishpaṭim 'Apologeṭi'im', *Zion*, xxiii–xxiv, 1958–9, pp. 174–93.

[4] Maimonides, *Hilkhoth Melakhim*, 8. 11; *Hilkhoth Teshuvah*, 3. 5; *Hilkhoth 'Eduth*, 11. 10; and the commentary on the Mishnah, *Sanhedrin*, 10. 12. The dictum occurs also in Maimonides' correspondence, *Teshuvoth Ha-Rambam ve-'Iggerothav*, Leipzig, 1859, part 2, p. 23b.

[5] Maimonides, *Hilkhoth Melakhim*, 8. 11.

[6] F. Y. Baer, *Galuth*, Berlin, 1936, p. 53, attributes this identification to Isaac Abravanel. See, however, B. Netanyahu, *Don Isaac Abravanel*, Philadelphia, 1953, pp. 154–7.

[7] *Schriften*, iii, p. 43, n. 4. For the identification of Rabbi Jacob Hirschel with Jacob Emden, see Jubilee edn., vii, p. 456.

shared the Jewish faith in revelation and the Bible could not be excluded from salvation.[1] This attitude was not intended to do more than express the feasibility of mutual toleration as between the Jewish and Christian religions. Mendelssohn, however, based his tolerance not on a common belief in revelation, but on the common humanity of all those led by reason to live in accordance with the Law of Nature which, the philosophy of Rationalism taught, was both good in essence and innate in every human being. It is no accident that, when giving examples of possible friends whom he would not have cared to see converted to Judaism, Mendelssohn mentioned two figures far removed from the Jewish-Christian world, namely, Confucius and Solon.[2] Did he believe them to be saved? He writes: 'He who inspires others to be virtuous in this world will certainly not be damned in the next.'[3]

Unfortunately, Mendelssohn's broad-minded view was not that of Maimonides, the principal authority on whom he relied concerning the fate of the world's righteous men. Maimonides defined the term 'the righteous of the world' as those who observed the Seven Commandments of the Sons of Noah because they were divinely revealed. Others who came to practise them through their own process of reasoning were merely the 'sages of the world'.[4] In this distinction Maimonides was following earlier authorities, who refused to accord salvation to those living outside the orbit of revealed religion.[5] This subject was much discussed in Christian theology and found its counterpart in Jewish thinking.[6] Although Maimonides accepted the distinction between 'the righteous' and 'the wise', he did not deny the virtue of the latter. There was a corruption in the editions of Maimonides' text available to Mendelssohn, due to the changing of one letter—the first (*'alef*)—in the word *'ella'* (*but*), which appeared as *we-lo'* (*and not*). Consequently, Mendelssohn, like many earlier scholars, including Spinoza,[7]

[1] For the attitude of Emden, see previous chapter, pp. 167, 168.

[2] *Schriften*, iii, p. 44.

[3] Ibid., pp. 44–45.

[4] Maimonides, *Hilkhoth Melakhim*, 8. 11.

[5] The actual authority on which Maimonides relied has become known in our own generation only. It is found in *Mishnath Rabbi 'Eli'ezer*, ed. H. Enelow, New York, 1934, p. 121.

[6] Maimonides' letter, quoted on p. 174, n. 4, also deals with this problem.

[7] *Tractatus Theologico-Politicus*, chap. 5, 47.

believed Maimonides to have stated that no virtue attached to good deeds—such as the Seven Commandments of the Sons of Noah—performed merely because man's reasoning led him to them. This assertion must have embarrassed Mendelssohn considerably. It may well be, as the late Professor Julius Guttmann suggested,[1] that Mendelssohn's attention was drawn to this passage in particular because Spinoza quoted it in his *Tractatus Theologico-Politicus* as proof that Judaism attributed no value to good deeds and true conceptions if they were prompted by natural intelligence alone. On the other hand, Maimonides' supposed view must have constituted a challenge to Mendelssohn, since it seriously affected the prevailing tolerant attitudes of himself and the other rationalists. They extended their tolerance not only to the deists—and sometimes even to the free-thinkers[2]—in their own communities, but also, in theory, to peoples who, according to report, were to be found living virtuous lives in far-off countries without acknowledging Divine Revelation. Mendelssohn himself referred to the people of Greenland, who were said to have 'lived in accordance with the Law of Nature'.[3] If Maimonides' formulation were valid, they could not be included in the category of the 'righteous of the world', since they did not share the Jewish-Christian tradition.

According to the accepted rules of halakhic hermeneutics, Mendelssohn could reject Maimonides' alleged view if Maimonides could be shown not to have based it on uncontested talmudic authority. Rabbi Joseph Caro, to whom Maimonides' sources were likewise unknown, stated in his Commentary on Maimonides that the granting of salvation to those only who followed the Divine commandments represented Maimonides' own personal—and, in Caro's opinion, correct—view.[4] This did not satisfy Mendelssohn,

[1] J. Guttmann, 'Mendelssohn's Jerusalem und Spinoza's Theologisch-politisches Traktat', *Beilage zum Jahresbericht der Hochschule für die Wissenschaft des Judentums*, 1931, p. 42.

[2] Mendelssohn seems to have hesitated as to whether full tolerance should be extended to atheists and epicureans, since according to his view these would undermine the welfare of society; see *Jerusalem*, *Schriften*, iii, p. 287. Cf. p. 55 of Guttmann's article referred to in the previous note.

[3] *Schriften*, iii, p. 44.

[4] *Kesef Mishneh* on *Hilkhoth Melakhim*, 8. 11.

and he turned to Rabbi Jacob Emden to ask whether any known talmudic authority served as the basis of Maimonides' statement.[1] Emden, too, failed to find direct authority for Maimonides' view, but he suggested the process of deduction which might have led to the conclusion.[2] Mendelssohn must certainly have been reluctant to accept such a doubtful line of argument. In the course of his own presentation, Mendelssohn revealed the real motive for his rejection of Maimonides' alleged formulation: 'For shall not the inhabitants of the earth, from the rising of the sun unto the going down thereof, except ourselves, descend into the pit and become an object of abhorrence to all flesh, if they do not believe in the *Torah* which has been given as an inheritance to the congregation of Jacob only?'[3]

This passage is enlightening. It clearly demonstrates that Mendelssohn was completely true to himself in displaying a tolerant attitude during the controversy with Lavater. Here, in an exchange of views with a quasi-official authority of his own faith—for Emden was a self-appointed defender of the purity of the Jewish religion—he continued to insist upon tolerance towards all non-Jews. From the passages quoted we learn the whole reason for his philosophy of tolerance; it was neither religious indifference, nor the view that Judaism and Christianity had the same roots, but his deep belief in the common humanity of all men. The tolerance which Mendelssohn practised, and which he advocated for the entire Jewish community, was put to the test in contacts with Christians only. But the fact they were Christians was but incidental —not the reason for his tolerance. Thus Mendelssohn went farther than Emden and the others whose philosophy of tolerance was limited to Christians, and was based upon the relative affinity of Christianity to Judaism.

In the realm of thought the philosophy of tolerance, preached on the Jewish side by Mendelssohn, was linked with the emergence

[1] Hebrew letter dated 26 Oct. 1773. Jubilee edn., xvi, p. 178. But he mentions an earlier appeal to Emden in the same matter, and this probably occurred at the time of his controversy with Lavater, as Guttmann (op. cit., n. 30) surmised.

[2] Jubilee edn. of Mendelssohn's *Schriften*, xvi, pp. 179–83.

[3] Ibid., p. 178.

of Rationalism, starting with Bayle and Locke.[1] In the sphere of reality it was related to the transition which was taking place from a society that imposed severe restrictions upon its members, who were divided into classes and groups and unable to move freely from one class to another, into a society in which individuals were free as far as social objectives were concerned. The process of class disintegration reached the Jewish ghetto during the last third of the eighteenth century. From then onwards, the Jew, too, was freed from compulsory attachment to his group. Objectively, he began to be regarded as a human being, quite apart from his historical and religious background. Subjectively, he was able to establish contacts with the outer world, without reference to his own Jewishness.

This new type of association between Jew and non-Jew, as well as between men of all classes, was a great human experience and inspired a new vision of the future. Lessing and Mendelssohn, as we have explained, were its principal exponents as far as the relations of Jews and non-Jews were concerned. In his play *Nathan der Weise* Lessing depicted a Jewish character who was morally superior to the Christian and Moslem characters and was also more tolerant towards others. It was not Lessing's intention to imply that the Jewish religion was itself superior, but that a person's own ethical standards were quite distinct from his faith. As Dilthey said of the characters in *Nathan der Weise*: 'The value of their personality is independent of the value of the historical religion to which they formally belong.'[2] The conclusion which Lessing obviously wished his audience to draw was that religious differences were unimportant, and that there was every reason for the adherents of the various religions to be tolerant towards each other. Mendelssohn, whether justifiably so or not, was the original on whom Lessing based his character-portrait of Nathan the Wise.[3] To Mendelssohn, the appearance of such a character on the German stage was proof that the philosophy of Rationalism—of a

[1] On the indebtedness of Mendelssohn to Locke, see Guttmann, op. cit., pp. 54–55; on the differences between the two, see *infra*, p. 179, n. 4.

[2] W. Dilthey, *Das Erlebnis und die Dichtung*, 1910, p. 137.

[3] This seems to be the consensus of opinion among biographers of both Lessing and Mendelssohn; see Kayserling, *Moses Mendelssohn*, pp. 330–2.

common humanity—had finally become a real social force.[1] This, together with certain other events of the 1780's—such as the Edict of Toleration issued by the Austrian Emperor Joseph II in 1780—convinced Mendelssohn that the Jewish community of Europe was on the verge of major changes of status.[2] Ten years earlier he would not have ventured to predict such a radical development.[3]

Mendelssohn felt impelled to describe his vision of the Jewish future in the Gentile world, and he did so twice—in his Introduction to Menasseh ben Israel's *apologia*, *The Vindication of the Jews*, translated into German in 1782 at Mendelssohn's suggestion, and a year later in his own major treatise, *Jerusalem*. The world that he pictured might be termed Utopian. It was the product of the first flush of his enthusiasm at the new horizons which were opening before his eyes. Mendelssohn based his predictions upon the assumption that there would come about a complete severance between the Church and State, i.e. between the institutions of religion and of government. The latter, he thought, should concern itself with man's actions, and the former with his motives and spiritual life. Political institutions should not concern themselves with a man's religion, and religious institutions were to be restricted to the spiritual affairs of mankind. In such a society, a man's racial origin or religious affiliations would play no part in any sphere of life except that of religion, and the mutual relations of Jews and Christians would be unaffected by their faith. Mendelssohn wished to divest the Church, as then organized, of all coercive powers, including the right of ecclesiastical discipline and exclusion.[4] As the Jewish community had, up to this time, been governed by its own institutions, the secular and religious powers of which were

[1] Cf. the Introduction to Menasseh ben Israel's *Vindiciae Judaeorum* (1782), *Schriften*, iii, p. 180.

[2] Ibid.

[3] The tone of resignation in which he speaks of the status of the Jews at the time of the controversy with Lavater (1769) is in telling contrast to the optimism of the eighties. See my *Judenassimilation*, p. 72.

[4] See *Schriften*, iii, pp. 194–202, 293–8. In this point Mendelssohn went beyond the position of Locke, as a comparison with the latter's *Letter Concerning Toleration* proves. See the edn. by J. W. Gough, Oxford, 1946, pp. 131–2. Cf. Guttmann, op. cit., p. 55.

almost identical, what Mendelssohn advocated would have brought about the dissolution of the whole fabric of organized Jewish society.[1] All that would have remained was a synagogue, where people of the same faith met, of their own free will, in order to worship together. Ethical values would be instilled by common religious worship and thus religion would, indirectly, fulfil a wholesome function in society. This whole conception was almost tantamount to revolution, as a moment's comparison with the part played by organized religion in Mendelssohn's time, particularly in Jewish society, will show.

Mendelssohn doubtless projected into his vision of the future his own experience of tolerant mutual relationships with friends and co-workers of different faiths. He saw no reason why the harmonious atmosphere which existed among men of good will in a small circle should not be possible in society at large. In actual fact, the kind of relationship which Mendelssohn enjoyed with friends of a different faith existed among a limited circle of intellectuals only. Even for them it was but a brief social episode; less than a generation after Mendelssohn's death in 1786, there was once again a social cleavage to be found between Jews and Christians, even in Berlin. By and large, they ceased to meet socially. When occasionally they did come together, both were acutely aware of their different status as ruling majority and inferior minority, and intercourse was no longer free or easy.[2]

Mendelssohn's vision must be discarded as illusory. It was based on the philosophy of Rationalism, which was itself the victim of a misconception of the nature both of religion and of human society. The actual course of events was very different from what the rationalists had envisaged. Nevertheless, Mendelssohn's Utopia, which was conceived at a time of great social change and inspired by pure, humanistic motives, was not entirely without influence. His vision served for generations to come as an ideal towards which

[1] In his Introduction, Mendelssohn still accepted the possibility of Jewish jurisdiction where voluntarily opted for by Jewish litigants: *Schriften*, iii, p. 193. In his *Jerusalem* he dropped even this feature. See my *Tradition and Crisis*, chap. 24, n. 7.

[2] See Graetz, *Geschichte der Juden*, 2nd edn., ii, chap. 7. For a revealing description of the change of atmosphere in Berlin, see H. Arendt, *Rahel von Varnhagen*, London, 1956, pp. 98–102.

to strive. Despite its failure to materialize, the fact that it had been exemplified in the lives of Mendelssohn and Lessing made it a goal of possible attainment. Mendelssohn's noble dream thus fulfilled a worthy function, and even our own disillusioned generation cannot, with propriety, treat it with disdain.

XV

THE POLITICAL APPLICATION OF TOLERANCE

THE new era ushered in by the French Revolution, only three years after the death of Mendelssohn, did not bring in its wake the free society envisaged by the rationalists in which religion was restricted to personal conviction and private worship. Instead, the modern national State arose and came to terms with the Church, there being a more or less tacit agreement ensuring reciprocal support between government and organized religion. Reluctantly, and after much delay, the State finally granted equal political rights to Jews and recognized Judaism as one of the religions with which it was expedient to establish a *modus vivendi.*[1] Jewish emancipation implied the revocation of civic and political disabilities affecting the individual. It also led to the establishment of communal and supra-communal Jewish organizations, either with the active support of the State or under its benevolent tutelage.[2]

Many factors were responsible for the radical change in the status of the Jew and Judaism. For instance, the new era of legal equality made it impossible to perpetuate the former state of affairs, in which an organized Jewish community existed on the fringe of society as a whole, and was governed by different laws and restrictions. The ideal of religious toleration was also an essential factor; indeed, without it Jewish emancipation would have been inconceivable. True, many of its Christian advocates hoped that it would ultimately lead to the acceptance of Chris-

[1] For general reference, see S. M. Dubnow, *Die neueste Geschichte des jüdischen Volkes*, 3 vols., Berlin, 1920–3. For a short survey, see M. L. Margolis and A. Marx, *A History of the Jewish People*, Philadelphia, 1945, chaps. 80–81, 85, 88.

[2] A comprehensive study of the Jewish organizations in the various countries exists in Hungarian only—L. Venetianer, *A zsidók szervezete az európai államokban*, Budapest, 1901. There are several monographs on different countries: A. E. Halphen, *Recueil des lois concernant les Israélites*, Paris, 1854; L. Auerbach, *Das Judentum und seine Bekenner in Preußen und in den anderen deutschen Bundesstaaten*, Berlin, 1890.

tianity by the Jewish minority.[1] But legislation could not take cognizance of such expectations; and the granting of civil rights to Jews itself implied that they were entitled to retain their own religion.

In the nature of things, tolerance could not remain a one-sided affair. Even if Gentiles had not asked questions—as they certainly did—about the sentiments of Jews towards others, the integration of Jews as equal citizens into State and society would have compelled them to clarify their attitude towards their country and fellow citizens.

The Jewish attitude towards a Gentile State and Gentile society had been discussed in detail ever since the possible emancipation of the Jews—then referred to as 'civic betterment' (*bürgerliche Verbesserung*, or *régénération*)—was first broached in Mendelssohn's time. Philosophers, statesmen, and government officials concerned themselves with the problem.[2] Finally, a quasi-official Jewish body, the Assembly of Notables, was constituted in Paris in July 1806, by Napoleon I, and he submitted a series of written questions to it. Later, in 1807, a superior Jewish authority, the 'Sanhedrin', was convened by the Emperor and charged with the task of formally endorsing the Assembly's replies to the Imperial questions. Many notables in the Assembly became members of the Sanhedrin.[3]

Historians have often regarded the Sanhedrin's answers as evasive and not truly representative of contemporary Jewish

[1] This was the attitude of Wilhelm Humboldt, for instance; see his memorandum on the question of emancipation in 1804, I. Freund, *Die Emanzipation der Juden in Preußen*, Berlin, 1912, ii, p. 276. What the general Christian public expected from the emancipated Jew is well summed up by H. D. Schmidt, 'The terms of Emancipation', *Year Book of the Leo Baeck Institute*, 1956, pp. 28–47.

[2] The most extensive treatment of the Jewish problem at this time is Ch. W. Dohm, *Über die bürgerliche Verbesserung der Juden*, 1781. Countless pamphlets and articles on the subject appeared in various countries.

[3] The records of the proceedings of the Sanhedrin were published by D. Tama, *Collection des procès-verbaux et décisions du Grand-Sanhédrin*, Paris, 1807; idem, *Collection des actes de l'assemblée des Israélites de France et du royaume d'Italie, convoquée à Paris*, Paris, 1807. Both books appeared in English in one volume: *Transactions of the Parisian Sanhedrin*, London, 1807. The latter is the edition quoted below, unless otherwise stated. For facts concerning the two conventions see Graetz, *Geschichte der Juden*, 2nd edn., ii, chap. 6, and R. Anchel, *Napoléon et les Juifs*, Paris, 1928, pp. 128–225.

opinion, since it was obviously dangerous to express views displeasing to the Emperor.[1] Careful analysis will show that the seeming inconsistencies are rather the result of internal Jewish problems, and of the clash of opinions arising from them.

The Sanhedrin, like the Assembly of Notables before it, was composed of representatives of various French, Italian, and German groups. In addition to enlightened Jews of the Mendelssohn school, these bodies included outright reformers holding deistic beliefs who, though they did not disavow the Bible, certainly did not accept Jewish tradition. At the other extreme, there were a number of old-type German Rabbis who were unaffected by the movement of Enlightenment. In the centre stood the tolerant traditionalists, outstanding among them being Rabbi David Sinzheim of Strasbourg and Rabbi Jacob Israele Carmi of Reggio, Italy. The former was elected President of the Sanhedrin. There was naturally a clash of ideas, both in the debates of the working Commission and in the plenary session of the entire Assembly. The final answers to Napoleon's questions were largely a compromise; their wording reveals the reconciliation of opposite views.[2] For this very reason they offer us admirable source-material from which it is possible to ascertain the conflicting contemporary attitudes to some of the burning questions of the day.

Six of the twelve questions put to the Assembly of Notables by the Emperor's Commissars dealt directly with Jewish-Gentile relations. We shall now deal with those answers that concern our subject, not in the order debated by the Assembly, but in the order of their importance for the Jewish authorities. Questions 4, 5, and 6 were as follows:

4. In the eyes of Jews, are Frenchmen considered as their brethren? Or are they considered as strangers?
5. In either case, what line of conduct does their law prescribe towards Frenchmen not of their religion?

[1] See, for instance, Dubnow, op. cit., pp. 145–8; even more so R. Mahler, *History of the Jewish People in Modern Times* (Hebrew, Merḥaviah), 1952, i, pp. 188–97. The best evaluation is that of Graetz, loc. cit.

[2] Graetz's assertion that Sinzheim was commissioned to formulate the answers (op. cit., pp. 260–1) is unfounded.

6. Do Jews born in France, and treated by the laws as French citizens, consider France as their country? Are they bound to defend it? Are they bound to obey the laws and to conform to the dispositions of the civil courts?

These questions do not appear to have aroused controversy. The answers were unanimous from the outset. The extensive quotations from the Bible were probably due to the influence of the representatives of the 'Enlightened' school of thought: (1) Deut. xxiv. 19; Exod. xxii. 20; Lev. xxv. 35; Deut. x. 18—injunctions to Israel, when living in their own country, to deal kindly and justly with strangers and to extend loving-kindness to them; (2) Lev. xix. 18 (*Thou shalt love thy neighbour as thyself*), and Ps. cxlv. 9 (*The Lord is good to all . . .*), giving expression to man's duty to love his fellow man, and God's love for all mankind. The *Torah* clearly imposed an obligation to love every human being. The inference regarding French Jews was: 'A religion whose fundamental maxims are such . . . must surely require that its followers should consider their fellow-citizens as brethren. . . . This sentiment was at first aroused in us by the mere grant of toleration. It has been increased, these eighteen years, by the Government's new favours to such a degree that now our fate is irrevocably united with the common fate of all Frenchmen.'[1]

The practice of the *Maskilim* (men of Enlightenment) using biblical quotations in support of their ideology is one of the signs of a significant turning-point in Jewish thinking. Enlightened Jews, living with Gentiles in an atmosphere permeated with the awareness of their common humanity, had rediscovered the emphasis of the Bible on the equality of all mankind. They stressed the scriptural teachings in new translations and biblical commentaries which they introduced into their educational institutions.[2] They were thus consistent in representing Judaism—as,

[1] Tama, *Transactions*, pp. 179–80.

[2] Mendelssohn's German translation of the Pentateuch and his colleagues' Hebrew commentaries to it became, as is well known, an instrument of education. See P. Sandler, *Ha-Be'ur la-Torah*, Jerusalem, 1941, pp. 11–16. M. Eliav, *Jewish Education in Germany in the Period of Enlightenment and Emancipation* (Hebrew), Jerusalem, 1960. The hope of moral betterment through the new approach to the Bible was voiced by Mendelssohn, see Eliav, op. cit., pp. 32–33, and by N. H. Wessely, *Diverey Shalom we-'Emeth*, Berlin, 1782, chap. 5.

in the present instance, they did to the Emperor—as a broad-minded and tolerant religion, in order to justify the Jewish claim to full citizenship.

The traditionalists were confronted with a different problem. They could hardly confine their argumentation to the Bible alone. For them the final authority was the Talmud—or, rather, the halakhic decisions based upon it. The Rabbis were, of course, accustomed to interpret the Bible according to their own lights. But in their ingenious homiletics they generally read into biblical passages the interpretations that they had absorbed from later Jewish sources. There was no controversy between them and the Enlightened Jews with reference to the general problem of relations with non-Jews. Passages from the Talmud could be quoted in support of a tolerant attitude towards Gentiles. The famous story of Hillel was cited in the answer to the Emperor's fourth question. When Hillel was consulted by a pagan who wished to be told in a few words what constituted the Jewish religion, Hillel replied: 'Do not do unto others what you do not wish to be done unto yourself. That is the entire *Torah*. The rest is commentary.'[1]

The Rabbis could not leave it to each individual to draw from such general principles his own conclusions concerning his daily conduct, but had to insist upon the acceptance of the Halakhah as laid down by the Jewish authorities. Accordingly, in the replies to the Emperor's questions, they included the following specific and familiar halakhic rulings governing relations with non-Jews: 'We are bound', says a talmudist, 'to love as our brethren all those who observe the Noachite commandments, whatever their religious opinions may otherwise be. We are bound to visit their sick, to bury their dead, to assist their poor',[2] &c. This was followed by a citation of the Seven Commandments of Noah, the inference being that contemporary Frenchmen observed those laws, and that '. . . therefore all the principles of our religion make it our duty to love Frenchmen as our brethren'.[3]

The above passage, probably written by David Sinzheim, reflects an approach similar to that of the eighteenth-century

[1] Tama, *Transactions*, p. 179; B.T., *Shabbath*, 31a.
[2] Tama, *Transactions*, p. 178.
[3] Ibid., p. 179.

Enlightened conservatives—Rabbi Jacob Emden, for example. According to their principles, directives could not be drawn from the Bible without due consideration of talmudic exegesis. The Talmud had ruled that the biblical injunction to love the stranger applied only to the *ger toshav*, a half-citizen who had abandoned idolatry and even, as Maimonides put it, observed the Seven Commandments of Noah.[1] On the assumption, therefore, that Frenchmen did likewise, Jews were commanded to love them. The writer in all likelihood accepted the tenet that Gentiles are not obliged to believe in the absolute unity of God; his words, 'whatever their religious opinions may otherwise be', seem to support this assumption.[2] In the involved argumentation included in the reply to the Emperor, the Rabbis were certainly addressing not Napoleon—who could neither appreciate nor even understand their complicated reasoning—but their learned Jewish contemporaries.

Sinzheim and his colleagues continued to think along pre-Mendelssohnian lines, that is to say, they approached all problems of human relationships in terms of 'Jew' and 'Christian'. They extended brotherhood to Frenchmen—on the assumption that they were Christians—an approach not quite in keeping with the views of the Emperor himself who, to judge by the questions put to the Jews in his name, regarded French citizenship and nationality as the binding ties. Religious differences were to be superseded by common citizenship, and thus common religious principles were of no consequence. Apparently these conservative Rabbis did not realize that a profound change had occurred in the alignment of Jews in the Gentile world. Instead of being faced, as before, with Christianity as such, Judaism was now confronted with the secular State, which had absorbed Christianity into its framework as a complementary factor and was similarly prepared to absorb Judaism, provided it adapted its teachings and precepts to the interests of the State.

From the reply to the fourth question, that Jews regarded Frenchmen as brothers, the answer to the fifth question followed as a matter of course: '. . . it is impossible that a Jew should treat a

[1] Maimonides, *Hilkhoth Melakhim*, 8. 11, 10. 12.
[2] For the controversy on this point, see *supra*, Chap. XIII.

Frenchman, not of his religion, in any other manner than he would treat one of his Israelitish brethren'.[1] The answer included the statement that '. . . Jews no longer constitute a separate nation and they regard their incorporation into the Great Nation as a privilege and as political redemption'.[2] Taken literally, this might seem to constitute an appeal to Jews to become assimilated with the French nation and to give up their own nationality and the expectation of national restoration in their ancient homeland. Indeed, that was doubtless the intention of the more radical reform elements. On the other hand, Rabbis like David Sinzheim would certainly have rejected such an implication. The word *redemption* was probably qualified by the adjective *political* because they wished the inference to be drawn that their faith in the ultimate Jewish national redemption remained unaffected by their reply to the Emperor. Here, again, we have a formulation which satisfied both camps, the Enlightened and the traditionalists.

In their answer to the sixth question, which concerned the loyalty of Jews to their country of residence, the notables merely followed time-honoured precedents. They cited Jer. xxix. 5–7 (*Build ye houses, and dwell in them; and plant gardens, and eat the fruit of them. . . . And seek the peace of the city whither I have caused you to be carried away captives, and pray unto the Lord for it*), a passage which had long been used to illustrate Jewish loyalty to the countries in which they lived.[3] Since the French Revolution, a broader Jewish loyalty had been required, including active participation in public life and military service. Whether or not the obligation of military service had been welcome—the traditionalists must certainly have had serious misgivings because of the difficulty of observing Jewish law in the army—it had been regarded as the price that must be paid for the full citizenship which all desired. In their reply, the notables recalled that 'To such a pitch is this sentiment [love of country] carried among them, that, during the last war, French Jews have been seen fighting des-

[1] Tama, *Transactions*, pp. 180–1.

[2] Ibid. In this instance I have not followed the English translation. In the French edition the sentence occurs on p. 173.

[3] The passage was quoted in this connexion as early as the twelfth century—see *Maḥzor Vitry*, p. 505. Cf. *supra*, Chap. V, p. 51, n. 1.

perately against other Jews, the subjects of countries then at war with France.'[1]

The Assembly was at great pains to reply correctly to Questions 11 and 12, which concerned the Jewish law about interest on money, because they knew their answer would have serious practical implications. Napoleon's attention was first drawn to the Jewish-French problem by the complaints which reached him that Alsatian Jews were actively practising usury.[2] This led to the convening of the Sanhedrin, which was expected to give him satisfaction on this point. It is clear that usury was one of the main points on which Napoleon wished to hear the Sanhedrin's views, because he included in the decree convening the Assembly the provision that all Alsatian debtors to Jews were released from the obligation to repay loans for one year.[3] There was acute apprehension, especially among the Italian members of the Assembly, that similar regulations would be proclaimed in Italy, with the resultant ruin of the Jewish community there,[4] which earned its livelihood mainly by lending money. Whoever drafted Questions 11 and 12 apparently assumed that Jewish law permitted usury *vis-à-vis* Gentiles but not from Jews, the word *usury*, not *interest*, being used. The Assembly felt constrained to make every effort to correct the prevailing misconception.

The fundamental issue can be briefly stated: In the Middle Ages the task of lending money to Gentiles was assigned by society to Jews, a maximum rate being sometimes set. Jews saw nothing wrong in fulfilling this function.[5] But there was no abrogation of the Jewish law, which forbade borrowing from and lending money to fellow Jews on interest, thus fostering the practice of giving free loans to the needy as a kind of charity. In order to meet the requirements of formal Jewish business transactions, various circumventions were introduced (similar to the development in Canon Law), culminating, in the seventeenth century, in the *hetter ʿisqa.*

[1] Tama, *Transactions*, p. 182.
[2] Anchel, *Napoléon et les Juifs*, pp. 62–75.
[3] Tama, *Transactions*, p. 106; Anchel, op. cit., pp. 102–6.
[4] The correspondence of Rabbi J. I. Carmi, *All'Assemblea ed al Sinedrio di Parigi*, Reggio Nell'Emilia, 1905, reflects the situation most clearly.
[5] See *supra*, Chap. V.

This was a formula stating that the interest due should be regarded as a share in the business profits earned. Under cover of the *hetter ʿisqa* any rate of interest could be regarded as legal among Jews, unless a maximum was fixed officially by the Jewish community.[1]

This was the historic background against which the Assembly of Notables framed their reply. As Frenchmen, they willingly submitted to the law of the land in civic matters, in compliance with the ancient Jewish directive that 'the law of the State is the law'. The rate of interest was legally fixed in France, and thus applied to money-lending between Jews as well as between Jews and Gentiles. The only difference was that, when both parties concerned were Jews, religious law demanded resort to the fiction of the *hetter ʿisqa*. The Jewish notables could have simply stated that, with reference to lending money, there was no real difference in the Jewish law as between Jews and non-Jews. It remains a matter of conjecture why they did not do so. Perhaps it would have been too difficult to explain to non-Jews the obvious contradiction between the biblical injunction and its halakhic circumvention; besides, the Enlightened Jews probably hesitated to draw attention to a tortuous aspect of Jewish law which they would have found it hard to defend. The Assembly resorted to an *apologia*, a presentation not previously used by the traditional authorities.[2] First, it rejected the word *usury* as a correct translation of the Hebrew *neshekh* and *tarbith*, which mean *interest*, and claimed that it was wrong to say that the Scriptures expressly sanctioned usury. It pointed out that the Hebrew words contained no reference to the rate of interest concerned, the implication being that reasonable rates only were expected from a non-Jew; and it was forbidden to take any interest at all from a Jew.[3] The Assembly was, however, not content with this explanation, and maintained, secondly, that even with reference to Gentiles it was permissible to charge interest in commercial transactions alone.[4] It hoped in this way to

[1] See my *Tradition and Crisis*, chap. 8.

[2] For the traditional Jewish view see S. Stein, 'The Development of the Jewish Law of Interest, &c.', *Historia Judaica*, xiii, 1955, pp. 3–40; idem, 'Interest taken by Jews from Gentiles', *Journal of Semitic Studies*, i, 1956, pp. 141–64. De Pomi's view (see Stein, ibid., pp. 159–61), which has some resemblance to that of the Assembly, can be disregarded as an *apologia*.

[3] Tama, *Transactions*, pp. 197–8.

[4] Ibid., pp. 200–7.

ameliorate the impression made by the translations of biblical law. Whatever the merits of this interpretation of the real intention of the Bible may be, it was certainly a projection of the contemporary attitude towards money-lending on to the original scriptural meaning.

Question 3, which led to an open clash between the two camps, read as follows: 'Can a Jewess marry a Christian, and a Jew a Christian woman? Or does the law allow the Jews to intermarry only among themselves?'[1] Two different answers to this question were submitted to the Assembly, one by its specially appointed Commission and the other by some of the Rabbis.[2] It was only after a heated debate that the compromise was reached that both be combined in the official answer.[3] The Commission stated that the Bible forbade Jews to marry idolaters only, and that 'The Talmud declares formally that modern nations are not to be considered as such, since they worship, like us, the God of heaven and earth.'[4] One cannot but wonder how the Talmud, edited *c.* 500 C.E., could have commented on the character of 'modern' nations. The writers doubtless had in mind the repeated assertions of later talmudists that Christians were not to be included in the category of idolaters because of their monotheistic beliefs.[5] But the purpose of the talmudists had been to ensure fair dealing by Jews with Christians, and to make certain Jewish-Christian business relationships possible. They certainly never anticipated that their ruling would be interpreted to permit the abrogation of any ritual law, least of all the marriage laws.[6] This is precisely what now occurred, the *Maskilim* confronting the conservative Rabbis in the Assembly with the logical inference to be drawn from their predecessors' teachings.

One of the *Maskilim* threw the traditionalists' inconsistency in their teeth with the challenge, 'You all acknowledge that they [the Christians] are no idolaters, that they worship, as you do, the

[1] Ibid., p. 154.

[2] Ibid., pp. 141–2. As the Commission comprised Rabbis also, the opening proposal must have been the work of some of the more radical among them.

[3] Ibid., p. 147.

[4] Ibid., p. 155.

[5] See *supra*, Chaps. III, XIII.

[6] R. Menaḥem Ha-Me'iri protested against such an inference. See Chap. X, p. 127, n. 1.

Creator of heaven and earth. . . . What more is necessary to make marriages lawful between Jews and Christians?'[1] The conflict was clearly not one of logic, but of religion and politics. The Rabbis were prepared to accept the idea of tolerance and mutual respect as far as civic and public relations were concerned. But they were not willing to countenance the breaking down of all barriers between Jews and people of other faiths. The Enlightened, on the other hand—or rather, the extremists among them—were only too ready to compromise, even to the point of intermarriage, as was clearly indicated by their spokesman: 'Great stress has been laid on the domestic inconvenience which would result from such marriages; but has a word been said of the great political advantages they would produce? If both should be thrown in to the scale, could the superiority of the last be doubted?'[2] Thus the *Maskilim*, too, were influenced not only by logic, but also by their willingness to go to any lengths in order to achieve political equality.

Neither side, of course, could impose its views on the other, and compromise was unavoidable in the reply to the Emperor. The Rabbis acceded to the wishes of the *Maskilim* to the extent of stating that 'The law does not say that a Jewess cannot marry a Christian, nor a Jew a Christian woman; nor does it state that the Jews can only intermarry among themselves. The only marriages expressly forbidden by the law are those with the seven Canaanite nations, with Ammon and Moab, and with the Egyptians.'[3] But they insisted upon adding that '. . . although the religion of Moses has not forbidden the Jews from intermarrying with nations not of their religion, yet, as marriage, according to the Talmud, requires religious ceremonies called *Qiddushim*, with the benediction used in such cases, no marriage can be *religiously* valid unless these ceremonies have been performed. This could not be solemnized for persons both of whom did not regard these ceremonies as sacred; . . . they would then be considered as married *civilly* but not *religiously*.'[4] They went on to say that no Rabbi would officiate at the marriage of a Jew with a Christian. Their formulation was tantamount to stating that the Jewish religion did not permit

[1] Tama, *Transactions*, p. 146.
[2] Ibid.
[3] Ibid., p. 154.
[4] Ibid., p. 155.

mixed marriages. But the Rabbis conceded—reluctantly, one may imagine—that '. . . a Jew, who marries a Christian woman, does not cease on that account to be considered as a Jew by his brethren, any more than if he had married a Jewess *civilly* and not religiously'.[1] In this concession the Rabbis were supported by halakhic principles, as a Jew remains a Jew whether or not he observes religious law.[2] But it was significant that they were compelled to admit the fact explicitly. The idea of tolerance had begun to play an important part in the relations between various groups of Jews holding different views on basic issues.

Our analysis reveals the sharp contrasts in views and attitudes within the Jewish community at the opening of the era of emancipation. These differences concerned more than the mere question of tolerance towards non-Jews. The opponents of intermarriage were not necessarily intolerant towards adherents of other faiths. But they realized that intermarriage would lead to the complete absorption of the Jewish minority into the larger community. The idea of tolerance faced those who strove for the preservation of Jewry and Judaism with the problem of how the *raison d'être* of Judaism could be maintained and, at the same time, friendly tolerance be practised towards another religion, with whose adherents Jews strove to attain common ties of citizenship. It would be necessary to trace the entire history of Jewish thought in the nineteenth century in order to give a detailed account of how this dilemma was solved. Here, we can but indicate the direction in which the solution was sought.

The orthodox groups, who clung to a belief in the fundamental superiority of Judaism as the revealed religion, followed the teachings of the tolerant among traditionalists of the seventeenth and eighteenth centuries. They emphasized that the righteous of other nations have a share in the world to come and that Gentiles (the sons of Noah) are not commanded to believe in absolute monotheism. These themes were constantly restated and re-elaborated.[3] Reform Jews likewise referred to these earlier Jewish

[1] Ibid., p. 156.

[2] See *supra*, Chap. VI.

[3] See Wolf Boskowitz, *Seder Mishnah*, 1820, on Maimonides, *Yesod Ha-Torah*, 1. 7; Jakob Mecklenburg, *Ha-Kethav weha-Qabbalah*, 1839, on Deut. iii. 19; Ṣevi H. Chayyoth (Chajes), *Darekhey Mosheh*, 1841, ff. 21b–22a.

teachings,[1] but not so much in order to explain their own position as to prove that earlier Judaism was not intolerant. They, for their part, accepted the verdict of modern history and regarded Judaism as but one creed among others.[2] Thus they found less difficulty in achieving tolerance towards Christians than in justifying their adherence to Judaism. They allied themselves with the prevailing German conceptions of the philosophy of history, and defined the past and present position of Judaism on that basis;[3] they sometimes even predicted the ultimate triumph of a purified Judaism.[4] For the time being, complete tolerance was taken for granted and Jews refrained from attempting to convert others.[5]

The first generations of Jews to emerge from the ghetto were not so much occupied with theoretical questions as with the practical need to adjust themselves to full citizenship, to perform civic duties, and to educate their children to meet others as equals on common ground. Their problems stemmed from the long estrangement between Jews and non-Jews, which reached its pitch in the two or three centuries before the emancipation. Such difficulties could not be overcome in a day. There were by now much stronger motives for finding ways to live in harmony with non-Jews than there had been in the ghetto period, when the Jewish leaders had first tried to find a *modus vivendi* with Christians. A positive attitude towards non-Jews, based on the ideology which had emerged in Mendelssohn's time, was advocated by nineteenth-century Jewish leaders. The Paris Sanhedrin, whose decisions became widely known, was one of the first Jewish public bodies to advocate and propagate this attitude.

[1] The prohibition in Lev. xviii. 3 (*neither shall ye walk in their ordinances*), on account of which the traditionalists objected to the introduction of an organ into the synagogue, was said by the promoters of this innovation to be invalid in regard to Christian customs. (D. Caro), *Berith 'Emeth*, 1820, p. 36. Cf. A. Chorin, *Davar be-'Itto*, pp. 6–19.

[2] See N. Rottenstreich, *Ha-Maḥashavah Ha-Yehudith be-'Eth Ha-Ḥadashah*, 1945, i, pp. 9–17.

[3] The different schools of thought are analysed by Rottenstreich, op. cit.; so, earlier, by M. Wiener, *Jüdische Religion im Zeitalter der Emanzipation*, Berlin, 1933.

[4] Salomon Formstecher, Salomon Hirsch, and others held such a belief. See J. Guttmann, *Die Philosophie des Judentums*, pp. 326, 337; Wiener, op. cit., pp. 171–4.

[5] The mutual tolerance of Judaism and Christianity is postulated by S. Hirsch, *Die Religionsphilosophie der Juden*, Leipzig, 1842, p. vii.

The idea of a common humanity, with the consequent need to abolish all double standards between Jews and non-Jews, was both well known and accepted among the Jewish well-to-do classes and the men of Enlightenment who had acquired secular European knowledge. They felt that it was important to disseminate their views among the larger groups of Jews who were still under the influence of their former estrangement from non-Jews, and whose poverty might incline them to resort to dubious practices in connexion with Gentiles. During earlier periods the upper strata of Jewish society, including its rabbinical and lay leadership, had been able to bring influence to bear upon their fellow Jews to obey the orders of the authorities concerning relations with non-Jews. In the nineteenth century, with the growing independence of the individual, Rabbis and communal leaders no longer had any way of influencing behaviour except through education and persuasion.

Although Jewish communities were no longer distinct and closely organized groups, Jewish society at large continued to be held responsible for the shortcomings and inadequacies of each individual Jew. Great efforts were therefore made to raise all Jews to the moral and cultural standards of the highest strata. Associations were established for teaching handicrafts and other useful occupations to the Jewish poor, in the belief that their moral inadequacy was due to their being pedlars and petty tradesmen.[1] The *Haskalah* movement envisaged the penetration of Jews into every field of activity and their consequent detachment from commerce and finance.[2] The general trend towards urbanization in the nineteenth century frustrated this hope, and training in crafts, agriculture, &c., had but little influence on Jewish occupational structure.[3] The dissemination of progressive and humanitarian ideas was more successful. The doctrine of human equality became a basic educational tenet and was preached by all public agencies—the press, the pulpit, the school, &c.[4] The study of those ancient

[1] A. Kober, 'Emancipation's Impact on the Education and Vocational Training of German Jewry', *Jewish Social Studies*, xvi. 1, 1954, pp. 3–32; 11, 1955, pp. 151–76.

[3] See my *Tradition and Crisis*, chap. 24.

[3] See A. Ruppin, *The Jews in the Modern World*, London, 1934, pp. 130–43.

[4] It will be sufficient to note here that the first two collections of sermons in German deal in the first place with the problem of tolerance and universal

Jewish authorities whose teachings had led, in the past, to the practice of a double standard ceased. People familiar with early writings interpreted them, more or less unconsciously, in the light of modern practices.

By the time full civic emancipation was granted to Jews in all the Western countries, i.e. between the 1860's and the 1870's, the re-education of Jewish society in Western countries was an accomplished fact. Even learned Jews sincerely maintained that Judaism had always taught universalistic ethics only.[1] When the 'scientific' antisemites of the 1880's discovered and published the extracts from ancient Jewish authorities on which earlier antisemitism had been based, the general Jewish public was not only outraged but genuinely astonished. Even after the inaccuracies in the quotations were eliminated, they were still far from what Jews themselves had believed to be the early teachings of Judaism. Jewish leaders and scholars reconciled the contemporary views with the ancient authorities by resorting to apologetics.[2] It was only after many years had passed that Jews were less inclined to take equal standards as between members of diverse groups for granted, and less afraid to face the different attitudes of previous periods. It remained for a later generation—our own—to lay aside the notions of static doctrine and teachings, and courageously to trace the true development of ideas and practices down the centuries.

brotherhood. J. Wolff, *Sechs deutsche Reden*, Dessau, 1812; J. L. Auerbach, *Die wichtigsten Angelegenheiten Israels*, Leipzig, 1818. For the tendency of Jewish schools, see Eliav, op. cit., p. 143.

[1] See the two most influential compendia of Jewish religion and ethics: S. R. Hirsch, *Choreb, Versuche über Jissroels Pflichten*, 1921, pp. 194–202 (1st edn., 1837); H. B. Fassel, 'Die mosaisch-rabbinische Tugend- und Rechtslehre', Gross-Kanizsa, 1862, pp. 100–5. See Zunz, *Gesammelte Schriften*, ii, pp. 167–9.

[2] The most learned of the many publications of this period is D. Hoffmann, *Der Schulchan Aruch und die Rabbinen über das Verhältnis der Juden zu Andersgläubigen*, 1st edn., 1885.

BIBLIOGRAPHY

AGUS, J. A. *Teshuvoth Baʿaley Ha-Tosafoth*, New York, 1954.

ARONIUS, J. *Regesten zur Geschichte der Juden im fränkischen und deutschen Reiche bis zum Jahre 1273*, Berlin, 1902.

BERGMANN, J. *Jüdische Apologetik im neutestamentlichen Zeitalter*, Berlin, 1908.

BRESSOLES, A. *Saint Agobard, évêque de Lyon*, Paris, 1949.

CARO, G. *Sozial- und Wirtschaftsgeschichte der Juden*, 2 vols., 1908, 1920.

EIDELBERG, S. *Teshuvoth Rabbenu Gershom Me'or Ha-Golah*, New York, 1955.

FINKELSTEIN, L. *Jewish Self-Government in the Middle Ages*, New York, 1924.

GRAETZ, H. *Geschichte der Juden*, 11 vols. (3rd edn., 1891, unless otherwise stated).

GRAYZEL, S. *The Church and the Jews in the XIIIth Century*, Philadelphia, 1933.

GUTTMANN, M. *Das Judentum und seine Umwelt*, Berlin, 1927.

HABERMANN, A. M. *Sefer Gezeroth 'Ashkenaz we-Ṣarefath*, Jerusalem, 1946.

HALPERIN, J. *Taqqanoth Medinath Mehrin*, Jerusalem, 1952.

HOFFMANN, D. *Der Schulchan Aruch und die Rabbinen über das Verhältnis der Juden zu Andersgläubigen*, Berlin, 1885.

HOFFMANN, M. *Der Geldhandel der deutschen Juden während des Mittelalters bis zum Jahre 1350*, Leipzig, 1910.

KISCH, G. *The Jews in Medieval Germany*, Chicago, 1949.

PARKES, J. *The Conflict of the Church and the Synagogue*, London, 1934.

—— *The Jew in the Medieval Community*, London, 1938.

SCHERER, J. E. *Die Rechtsverhältnisse der Juden in den deutsch-österreichischen Ländern*, Leipzig, 1901.

SCHNEE, H. *Die Hoffinanz und der moderne Staat*, 3 vols., Berlin, 1953–5.

SCHOLEM, GERSHOM G. *Major Trends in Jewish Mysticism*, New York, 1954.

STOBBE, O. *Die Juden in Deutschland während des Mittelalters*, Berlin, 1923.

TAMA, M. D. *Transactions of the Parisian Sanhedrin*, London, 1807.

URBACH, E. E. *Baʿaley Ha-Tosafoth—Toledotheyhem, Ḥibbureyhem we-Shiṭṭatham*, Jerusalem, 1955.

WEINRYB, B. D. 'Texts and Studies in the Communal History of Polish Jewry', *Proceedings of the American Academy for Jewish Research*, New York, 1950.

ZIMMELS, H. J. *Beiträge zur Geschichte der Juden in Deutschland im 13. Jahrhundert, insbesondere auf Grund der Gutachten des R. Meir Rothenburg*, Vienna, 1926.

ZUNZ, L. *Die synagogale Poesie des Mittelalters*, Frankfort on the Main, 1920.

—— *Literaturgeschichte der synagogalen Poesie*, Frankfort on the Main, 1865.

INDEX